CONSPIRACIES IN THE EGYPTIAN PALACE

CONSPIRACIES IN THE EGYPTIAN PALACE

Unis to Pepy I

Naguib Kanawati

LONDON AND NEW YORK

First published 2003
by Routledge
11 New Fetter Lane, London EC4P 4EE

Simultaneously published in the USA and Canada
by Routledge
29 West 35th Street, New York, NY 10001

Routledge is an imprint of the Taylor & Francis Group

Typeset in Garamond by Florence Production Ltd
Printed and bound in Great Britain by
St Edmundsbury Press, Bury St Edmunds, Suffolk

British Library Cataloguing in Publication Data
A catalogue record for this book is available from the British Library

Library of Congress Cataloging in Publication Data
A catalog record for this book has been requested

ISBN 0–415–27107–X

CONTENTS

FIGURES

PREFACE

During the last two decades I have had the privilege of working in the Unis and Teti Cemeteries in archaeological excavations and/or recording and publishing previously uncovered tombs. The work was conducted as a joint project between the Australian Centre for Egyptology and the Egyptian Supreme Council of Antiquities and more recently in conjunction with the University of Suez Canal. From the outset it became clear that not only do these two cemeteries contain some of the most beautifully decorated tombs from the Old Kingdom, but also conceal evidence for the study of one of the most intriguing periods in Egyptian history. It should, however, be emphasized that the aim of this book is not to study the history of this period but some specific events which occurred within the period. With the progress of the fieldwork intriguing secrets continued to unfold, fitting together like a jigsaw puzzle, giving the picture of an unusually troubled time, full of turmoil and conspiracies. The exact interpretation of these events is neither simple nor certain, as the Egyptian himself presumably did not wish to overly publicize them. The task was challenging, and still is, for the reader may explain the same evidence differently, or look at it from another angle. New discoveries in other cemeteries may confirm, modify, or drastically change the present interpretation; yet one should not shy away from offering an opinion lest it be criticized by some or proven wrong by future finds. Such is the nature of historical investigations and it is only through the wide exchange of opinions that problems are better understood. With this in mind, the reader is here presented with the data and a possible interpretation – but perhaps not the only one!

I was helped on site and in the preparation of this book by many individuals, too many to be able to list here, but to them all goes my deepest appreciation for their contribution to the project. Special thanks, however, are due to the regular team, Ann McFarlane, Sameh Shafik, Elizabeth Thompson and Naguib Victor, for their dedication and hard work, and to Kim Wilson who ably edited the manuscript, and Joan Beck and Joan Pollett who carefully proof-read it. With the exception of Figure 2.2, all photographs published here are from the expedition's records, while line drawings not originating from our own publications have been redrawn from the acknowledged originals by Elizabeth Thompson. A complete survey of the Teti cemetery is in progress, but a sketch plan was prepared by Naguib Victor (Figure 2.24) in order to familiarize the reader with the location of the tombs discussed.

During the years, our sites were visited by many individuals and groups, with whom I had the pleasure of discussing the ideas expressed in this book. Such discussions not only helped me in my analysis of the various aspects of the subject but also emphasized its fascination and popular interest. For this reason, the present book was written in such a way as to take readers on a quick visit to the sites, present them with the data as well as a possible interpretation and only the necessary references, and invite them to join in the debate. It is hoped that both the scholar and the layperson will find the book stimulating.

Naguib Kanawati
Macquarie University
Sydney, Australia

INTRODUCTION

To the Egyptians the king was not an ordinary mortal for he combined human and divine entities and as such was the link between mankind and the world of the gods, both in life and the hereafter. The king owned everything and was the source of all powers; he was the centre of all existence. Change of dynasty, struggles for the throne, collapse of regimes, calamities such as famines and plagues, foreign occupations, etc., no doubt changed the image of the monarchy, but the basic nature of kingship persisted. To achieve this and to maintain a façade of stability and continuity in the face of all changes the king had to remain secluded, surrounded by a small elite of family members and trusted officials, and the palace was shrouded with secrecy as may be inferred from some of the titles of officials employed in the personal service of the king. These included the titles of 'privy to the secrets of the king in his every place', 'privy to the secrets of all the king's repasts', 'privy to the secrets of the god's treasures', 'privy to the secrets of the god's words', 'privy to the secrets of the king in every secret command', 'privy to the secrets of the fields of offering', 'privy to the secrets of what one sees', etc.

With such emphasis on secrecy and the need to project an image of normality, the Egyptian monarchic system gives the impression of being very steadfast during most of its long history, perhaps unrealistically so, and the truth might have been completely different. The king's multiple marriages and frequently large numbers of children were bound to produce many aspirants to the throne, supported by different wives in the harem and perhaps by various branches of the extended royal family. With no standing army in the Old Kingdom the king was able to rule only through his personnel, and his strength was almost certainly based on theirs; yet paradoxically the more powerful these got the more dangerous they theoretically became. Even the king's divinity had to be bolstered by the priesthood, and the loyalty of these priests could not always be relied upon. The multiplicity of gods, temples and priests must have created a complex and expensive problem for the government. The presence of at least two strong cults, those of Re and Ptah, in the vicinity of the capital, Memphis, for example, must have given rise to rivalry, even if hidden. Such circumstances were bound to create a very fertile ground for intrigues, with those aspiring to the throne enlisting the support of one powerful group against the others, or perhaps these groups themselves sometimes plotting to crown an 'heir' of their choice, all behind a curtain of secrecy.

A survey of Old Kingdom history suggests that the succession to the throne at certain times might not have been entirely smooth. Both the beginning and end of the Third Dynasty, for example, are not clear. Although Nebka was probably the first king of this dynasty, the archaeological evidence, the king lists and the later traditions suggest that Djoser was the founder of it. And while Huni is generally regarded as the last king of the dynasty, the place of Neferka, who built a pyramid at Zawiyet el-Aryan, and his relationship to Huni are not understood. The beginning of the Fourth Dynasty is also problematic. Snefru, whose mother, Meresankh, was not of royal blood, perhaps only a concubine of Huni, married his half-sister, Hetepheres I, to legitimize his accession. Whether this move went unchallenged we are not told; but we know that the king curiously moved his cemetery southwards, to Maidum and Dahshur, at a distance from his own capital, Memphis. One of the dangers of such a method of succession, however, was that it widened the scope of the aspirants to the throne. Accordingly, following Khufu, son of Snefru, a struggle over succession appears to have occurred between rival branches of the royal family. The first winner was Djedefre who came to the throne by marrying Hetepheres II, his half-sister and widow of his half-brother, Khufu's crown prince Kawab. Djedefre's reign is curious in that he again moved his cemetery away from Giza, where his father built his pyramid, this time to Abu Rawash, 10 kilometres to the north, a site which may have had links to the sun cult. He also introduced the title 'son of Re' for the first time. How Khafre, Djedefre's half-brother, succeeded in taking over the throne is not clear, but he legitimized it by marrying Meresankh III, daughter of Khufu's crown prince, Kawab, and Hetepheres II (before she married Djedefre). Khafre returned to the Giza necropolis, where the pyramid of his father and the mastaba of his father-in-law were found and where his son Menkaure later constructed his pyramid. Shepseskaf, son of Menkaure and the last king of the Fourth Dynasty, married Khentkaues, the daughter of Djedefhor, another son of Khufu, and again moved the site of his tomb back to Saqqara and built it in the form of a sarcophagus, rather than a pyramid, which may be interpreted as a move away from the Heliopolitan traditions.

The struggle between the different branches of Khufu's successors does not seem to have ended with the change of dynasty. Although the Westcar Papyrus, a popular piece of propaganda literature justifying the accession of the Fifth Dynasty kings, suggests that Userkaf, Sahure and Neferirkare were triplets born to Re of Sakhebu, by Rewedjedet, the wife of a priest of Re, it is very much disputed whether the first three, or only two, kings of the Fifth Dynasty were actually brothers. Rewedjedet was perhaps a pseudonym for Khentkaues I, who was buried at Giza and was described as 'mother of the two kings of Upper and Lower Egypt'; but Neferirkare is now believed to be the son of Khentkaues II, who was buried at Abusir. It has even been suggested that Userkaf was not the son of Khentkaues I, but that of Neferhetepes and accordingly the grandson of Djedefre and Hetepheres II. Userkaf's father is not known. Perhaps he was the priest of Re mentioned in the Westcar Papyrus, for Userkaf built a pyramid to the north-east of that of Djoser at Saqqara and a sun temple, the first to be constructed at Abusir, presumably the town referred to as Sakhebu in the Westcar Papyrus. The problem is far from being settled.

Little is known about the genealogy and the achievements of the Fifth Dynasty kings. However, from Sahure to Niuserre, they seem to have followed one policy, they all have Re as an element in their names, and each built a pyramid and a sun temple, both located at Abusir. In the latter part of the dynasty problems might have erupted once more. Neither the sun temple nor the pyramid of Menkauhor was found. The former is known only by name from inscriptions and his pyramid is suggested to be at north Saqqara near Teti's; also the king did not form his name using that of Re as an element. While his successor, Djedkare, again acknowledged the supremacy of Re, as evident in his name 'the ka of Re is stable', he abandoned the tradition of building sun temples and moved his burial place to south Saqqara, away from Abusir and north Saqqara and closer to his capital Memphis. The last king of the Fifth Dynasty, Unis, might have been the son of Djedkare. He did not have Re in his name, did not build a sun temple, and constructed his pyramid immediately to the south-west of that of Djoser and for the first time inscribed his burial chamber with the so-called pyramid texts, a set of spells aimed at helping and protecting the king in the afterlife. The reason for the introduction of these texts by Unis and their possible significance for his relationship with the priesthood are unclear, but the pyramid texts became a tradition followed by the Memphite kings and some queens until the Eighth Dynasty and the fall of the Old Kingdom.

Like most transitions between dynasties, the transition from the Fifth to the Sixth leaves some unanswered questions. Who was Teti, founder of the new dynasty? There is no evidence that he was related to Unis, and in fact he appears to have acceded to the throne by marrying the latter's daughter, Iput, who bore him a son, Pepy I. But did Unis have any male descendant to challenge such a succession? Who was the king's son Unisankh, owner of the large mastaba opposite that of Unis' queen, Nebet? Was Unisankh alive when King Unis died? We are not told. It is also uncertain whether the transition to Teti's reign was peaceful, as his Horus name Seheteptawy, 'He who pacifies the Two Lands', might well hint at dealing with some difficulties. Yet no evidence, literary or archaeological, has been brought forward in support of, or against, such a possibility. Like Djoser, Userkaf, Menkauhor and Unis, Teti did not include Re in his name, and built his pyramid to the north-east of that of Userkaf and on one axis with the whole group, although the location of Menkauhor's pyramid to the north-east of that of Teti is still unconfirmed as the site needs systematic excavation. Whether these kings had common political and/or religious policies needs to be studied.

Manetho wrote in the third century BC that Teti was assassinated by his bodyguards. No contemporary written evidence supports this claim, but what of the archaeological evidence found in the tombs of contemporary officials? The recent excavations in the Teti cemetery have uncovered related data that needs to be considered. The very short reign, perhaps only one year, of Teti's successor, Userkare, is curious and the explanation that he acted as a kind of regent during the minority of Pepy I is unconvincing. The period is too short to be valid and a regent does not hold full royal titulary. Interestingly, his name, Userkare, 'the ka of Re is powerful', has the resonances of the Fifth Dynasty. Does he represent a return to the supremacy of the sun cult? His relationship to Teti is also unclear; but even if he was connected by blood to Teti, as some argue, he took over the throne instead of the legitimate heir Pepy I, son of the main queen and daughter of Unis, Iput, who carried the royal blood into the Sixth Dynasty.

Pepy I, however, regained the throne, most probably at a very young age – perhaps not much more than ten years. We do not know who supported him, but the fact that early in his reign he changed his coronation name from Nefersahor to Meryre might suggest that he was backed by those loyal to his father, but that he later reached a compromise with his opponents, thus changing his name to Meryre ('Beloved of Re'). Such a change might have been linked to a conspiracy in the royal harem, in which the queen was brought to trial as recorded in a well-known biography of an official named Weni. As a result, the king successively married two sisters, both named Ankhenesmeryre, each producing a successor to the throne, Merenre and Neferkare (Pepy II). But the remaining part of Pepy I's reign was not without problems, and it is believed that in the twenty-first count a vizier named Rawer was probably implicated in another plot. Yet Pepy I's reign continued, at least until the thirty-second count/year, the highest currently known for him.

Following the relatively short reign of Merenre, his half-brother, Neferkare/Pepy II had a long reign. Traditionally he is credited with ninety-four years, but most probably it was much shorter, with the highest count known for him being the thirty-third. His long reign and many marriages and children, as well as an increasing dissatisfaction among the bureaucracy, resulted in an inefficient administration incapable of dealing with the apparently growing internal and external problems, and in a succession crisis which led to dynastic confusion and plunged Egypt into the so-called First Intermediate Period.

This brief survey of the periods of political difficulties in the Old Kingdom suggests that these were somewhat linked to the succession to the throne. The system itself had some flaws. If the king had no male heir – that is the eldest living son of the official queen – the son of any other wife or concubine, or indeed any other man, could theoretically reach the throne by marrying the eldest daughter of the king and queen who carried on the royal blood. Such political marriages must have been open to manipulation and pressure by powerful men and groups, and their results could have delighted some and displeased others. A vivid example of such a marriage, albeit from a much later period, is the case of Tutankhamun's widow, Ankhesenamun, who, refusing to yield to pressure from the strong man of the time, Ay, wrote to the Hittite king Suppiluliumas begging him to send her one of his sons to marry her and become king of Egypt. The letter reads: 'My husband died and a son I have not. But to you, they say, the sons are many. If you would give me one son of yours, he would become my husband. Never shall I pick out a servant of mine and make him my husband . . . I am afraid!' (Some scholars argue that the Egyptian queen was Nefertiti herself.) Suppiluliumas sent his son, prince Zennanza, who mysteriously died before reaching Egypt. Ay presumably married Ankhesenamun, officiated on the Opening of the Mouth to Tutankhamun's mummy, a rite performed by a son/successor, and became Pharaoh of Egypt.

Kings who succeeded to the throne by the above-mentioned method presumably risked creating a dynastic feud after their death, or perhaps even during their lifetime. As they were probably the most powerful men in the country, they were likely to have already been of age, married and have children, or sons in particular. Whether these sons, and their mothers, would have always accepted the throne to pass on to a younger half-brother, the result of the political marriage to a princess, is questionable.

In their struggle for office, Egyptian kings and aspirants to the throne in the Old Kingdom had to rely on the support of the top officials and priests. They probably had to frequently play one power against another, possibly extending to them unusual favours and material benefits. It might not be a mere chance that the most troubled periods for the monarchy coincided with the time when the wealth of officials, as demonstrated in their tombs, reached its peak. The above-mentioned survey shows that the latter part of the Fifth Dynasty and the earlier part of the Sixth – to be exact, from the reign of Menkauhor to that of Pepy I – were not free from dynastic problems, and it is this period in particular which produced the most lavish tombs of officials. It is sufficient to examine some of the tombs of the viziers in this period, such as those of the Ptahhetep and Akhethetep group, Seshemnefer III, the Sendjemib group, Ihy, Mehu, Kagemni, Mereruka, Ankhmahor and Khentika, to realize the amazing wealth which must have been available to them, and which appears not just in the mere size of their mastabas but in the multiplicity of rooms in their chapels and the amount of intricate scenes and inscriptions, all rendered in coloured relief.

While the king was projected as supreme and powerful, in reality he was probably very vulnerable and needed the support of his officials and priests.

The loyalty of these could not always be guaranteed and there are indications that all parties frequently changed sides.

This book and its contents

The archaeological fieldwork undertaken in the last three decades or so in the Unis and Teti cemeteries at Saqqara by various institutions, and particularly by the Australian Centre for Egyptology, has substantially increased the body of evidence suggesting possible intrigues during the troubled period of the end of the Fifth Dynasty and the earlier part of the Sixth. Although further excavations and examination of tombs in the other cemeteries might produce additional data for the study of the events of this period, the evidence now available from the two almost fully excavated main cemeteries of Unis and Teti adequately documents these events to allow us to draw preliminary conclusions, even if these were later to be refined somewhat through new discoveries in other sites. It therefore appears timely to undertake an investigation of the possible difficulties and intrigues in this period, but not of those of the Third and Fourth Dynasties, which at present lack sufficient evidence and require further excavations and more meticulous recording.

Our starting point for this study is a statement made by the Egyptian historian/priest of the third century BC, Manetho, who mentioned that King Teti was assassinated by his bodyguards. Chapter 1, 'Assassination claim', therefore deals with two problems: the first, 'Manetho's validity', discusses this historian's sources and the level of trust which should be placed in his writings; the second, 'The palace guards', requires a detailed and rather technical analysis, for no Egyptian title is currently understood to be that of a guard, yet the identification of this title is essential for the present study.

Chapter 2, 'The suspects: case studies', introduces the reader to the evidence, all drawn from the tombs of individuals who played a role in the events. The tombs are divided into two groups according to their location in the Unis or the Teti cemeteries, with only two other individuals buried outside these two cemeteries and listed under North Saqqara. In each case the tombs are arranged in alphabetical order according to the owner's name. The tombs discussed in Chapter 2 are given consecutive numbers written in square brackets [ ] for ease of reference when discussing the same tomb/tomb owner in Chapter 3. The purpose of Chapter 2 is to make the book less dependent on the numerous excavation reports describing individual tombs. By providing the reader with a brief description of each tomb and photographs of the relevant evidence to be discussed in Chapter 3, the book is hopefully self-contained, although the reader may wish to consult some individual tomb reports for more details. Some readers may opt to familiarize themselves with the evidence presented in Chapter 2 before reading the analysis of the events in Chapter 3. Others may prefer to use Chapter 2 to check the evidence as presented in Chapter 3.

Chapter 3, 'The investigation', presents the main arguments, relying primarily on the examination of the mostly archaeological evidence. I am well aware of the possibility that different readers may reach somewhat different interpretations of the same evidence, or take the analysis a step further than that in this book. However, I hope that by presenting the evidence in a concise and accessible manner, and by offering my personal interpretation, I have opened the discussion on an important and fascinating topic of Old Kingdom history.

1

ASSASSINATION CLAIM

Manetho's validity

Of King Teti (Othoês), founder of the Sixth Dynasty, Manetho wrote that he reigned for 30 years and that 'he was murdered by his bodyguards'.[1] Both claims are open to question. The length of Teti's reign is partly damaged in the Turin Papyrus, with only the figures [. . . years], 6 months, 21 days preserved,[2] thus no years of reign to correlate with Manetho's, and the highest animal count/census known from his reign was the year after the sixth count.[3] As this operation during the Old Kingdom was believed to have taken place every two years, or less on occasion, Teti was assigned a reign of anything between 12 and 30 years by different scholars. With regard to the assassination claim some treat it with more scepticism than others. Gardiner, for example, says that 'it is impossible to know whether there is any truth in Manetho's report that he was murdered by his bodyguards',[4] while Grimal seems more prepared to entertain this possibility.[5]

Before any examination of the evidence from the Teti cemetery itself, it is appropriate to evaluate the validity of Manetho and his writings. This historian lived during the third century BC and wrote his history of Egypt in Greek probably under Ptolemy II Philadelphus, to whom he presumably sent a letter describing himself as 'high-priest and scribe of the sacred shrines of Egypt, born at Sebennytus (Samannûd in the Delta) and dwelling at Heliopolis'. It is unfortunate that Manetho's book on Egyptian history has survived only in extracts by Jewish historians, particularly Josephus, who were interested in his work because of the connection with the Egypt of their ancestors – Abraham, Joseph, Moses – and the Exodus. A summary of Manetho's history had also been made – perhaps not by Manetho himself – and this consisted of lists of dynasties and kings, with short notes on unusual events. Parts of this are preserved by Christian chronographers, especially Africanus and Eusebius, with the former being probably the most faithful to the original. It is clear therefore that the transmission of Manetho's history is not without problems, and it is almost impossible to be certain whether any part is a genuine or a corrupt quotation from Manetho. This is particularly so when dealing with the Hyksos period and the New Kingdom, where both Egyptian and Jewish historians have reasons to distort facts to their advantage or to condemn the other. However, when dealing with the earlier Old and Middle Kingdoms, such motives apparently did not exist and one would expect quotations to be more true to the original.

As an Egyptian high priest during the Ptolemaic period, Manetho was educated in both the Egyptian and Greek languages. He no doubt had access to, and the ability to read, all sorts of records – temple archives, monumental inscriptions and numerous king lists, such as the Palermo Stone, the List of Abydos, the List of Karnak, the List of Saqqara and the Turin Papyrus. His Greek education enabled him to read the works of earlier Greek historians who wrote on Egyptian history and from whom he probably learned the methodical use of the abundant material at his disposal. However, unlike Herodotus, whom Manetho criticized and contradicted, and Hecataeus, who did not write a history of Egypt but rather a philosophical romance, Manetho was capable of consulting the original sources and was not dependent only on Egyptian informers to whom Herodotus, for instance, frequently refers. Egyptians, on the other hand, although very interested in their past, had not developed an analytical sense of history, and Manetho was no exception. His *Aegyptiaca* was not a critical history of the country, but mainly annals and dynastic framework, which remains until today the accepted scheme of Egyptian chronology.

Manetho's aim in writing the *Aegyptiaca* was to inform foreigners about the history of his country and to correct the errors of Greek historians, especially Herodotus. However, Manetho's own work no doubt has many errors. The lengths of reigns of many kings are highly unlikely, and the names and sequence of some kings are not in agreement with monumental evidence. Perhaps Manetho was to a certain extent influenced by already corrupted dynastic lists – such as the Turin Papyrus – and if so, his history should not be considered more trustworthy than his own sources. Furthermore, certain periods in Egyptian history, as in that of any other nation, suffer from the paucity of evidence which naturally results in an uncertain or even a confused reconstruction of their chronology and events. From Manetho's summary of the Sixth Dynasty, this period does not fall into this category.[6]

Another very important source of information which must have been available to Manetho, and most probably formed the origin of some of the unusual events mentioned under certain kings, was popular tradition, whether written or orally transmitted. The accuracy of such traditions may well be questioned where the lengths of individual reigns or dynasties are concerned, although it is possible for a particularly long reign to be remembered from one generation to the other. Pepy II of the Sixth Dynasty presumably had such a long reign, even if he did not rule for close to a hundred years as reported by both Manetho and the Turin Papyrus. One would expect important and memorable events, such as the murder of a king, to leave permanent impressions on these traditions. The assassinations of presidents Kennedy and Sadat, for example, will, one would expect, remain in the popular legends of their respective countries and are unlikely to fade or be forgotten.

That popular traditions survived for such a long time in ancient Egypt may be proven by the examination of the image and character of King Snefru and King Khufu of the Fourth Dynasty as described in the fifth century BC, some two millennia after their reigns, by Herodotus and after him by Africanus and Eusebius.[7] In *The Histories*, Book Two, Herodotus wrote:

> Up to the time of Rhampsinitus (Snefru), Egypt was excellently governed and very prosperous; but his successor Cheops (Khufu) (to continue the account which the priests gave me) brought the country into all sorts of misery. He closed all the temples, then, not content with excluding his subjects from the practice of their religion, compelled them without exception to labour as slaves for his own advantage.[8]

Many scholars have rejected and tried to demolish the reputation of slave-driver and a cruel tyrant attributed to the builder of the Great Pyramid, Khufu, suggesting that Egyptian sources provide no evidence at all to support these stories. They argue that the Greeks' more moderate sense of dimension and public interest would have been shocked by these gigantic monuments built especially for the glory of one particular man, hence the idea of a tyrannical king.

A study of Egyptian literature, however, shows that the images of King Snefru and King Khufu as described by Herodotus have their origin in Egyptian popular lore.[9] The Westcar Papyrus,[10] which from the simplicity of its style may be ascribed to a storyteller, consists of four individual stories which supposedly took place under different kings, with one each under Snefru and Khufu. For entertainment, a magician was brought to each of these kings; while Khufu addressed his by his name, 'Djedi', Snefru called his 'Djadja-em-ankh, my brother'. Moreover, the story which occurred under Snefru demonstrated the caring and fun-loving character of the king. Suggested by the magician, and approved by the king, a boat picnic was organized on the palace lake, with twenty young women dressed only in nets rowing for the king. When one of these girls dropped her turquoise pendant into the water and stopped rowing, the king took a personal interest in her and offered to replace it, but she insisted on hers. The king concurred and brought the magician, who performed his magic and recovered the pendant.[11]

The story of King Khufu presents him in a completely different light. His magician claimed to be able to reattach a severed head, and Khufu asked him to perform his experiment on a prisoner. The magician refused, saying 'But not to a human being, O king, my lord! Surely, it is not permitted to do such a thing to the noble cattle!' The experiment then took place on a goose, a waterfowl and an ox. However, it is important that Khufu showed himself unconcerned with the human dignity of his people and that he received a moral lesson from a commoner. The magician Djedi was also able to foresee the future and he told Khufu that a woman was pregnant by Re with triplets who would succeed to the Egyptian throne, driving out Khufu's line. Thus the Sun-god declared himself against Khufu and caused the dethronement of his family. When the time of delivery came, Re sent all the deities related to childbirth to deliver the three children and assured the deities that, when kings, these children 'will build your temples. They will supply your altars. They will furnish your libations. They will increase your offerings.' This seems like indirect criticism of Khufu and his line for neglecting the temples, a picture close to that described by Herodotus.

We are uncertain whether the characters of Snefru and Khufu as described in the literature corresponded to reality, or whether the kings of the Fifth Dynasty, most probably the instigators of the story (although the copy we have comes from a later period), wanted to justify their succession by casting doubt on the best-known king of the previous dynasty and the builder of the largest monument in the country. The important fact is that the image of these kings, presumably at the beginning of the Fifth Dynasty in the twenty-fifth century BC, remained unchanged for twenty centuries when it was related to Herodotus. The assassination of a divine king, if it happened, should have been even more shocking to the Egyptians than the memory of an arrogant and tyrannical king, even if it were true that he closed all the temples and deprived his subjects from the practice of their religion. Such an assassination, one would expect, would have its permanent place in popular traditions.

The validity of Manetho's claim that King Teti 'was murdered by his bodyguards' could be assessed in view of the frequency of similar claims in his book. If too many kings are reported to have been assassinated, with a consistent lack of contemporary archaeological or written evidence to document the events, his reports would naturally have to be very seriously questioned. But apart from Teti, only one other king is stated by Manetho to have been murdered, this time 'by his own eunuchs'. This is King Amenemhat (Ammanemês) II.[12] It is likely that Manetho confused Amenemhat I, against whom we know a conspiracy took place in the palace, with Amenemhat II; that is, the successor of Senusert I rather than his predecessor. Although it is not impossible that Amenemhat II was murdered as Manetho claims, such an error could have easily occurred due to the frequent recurrence of the same names during this period and the fact that Manetho placed Amenemhat I as the last king of the Eleventh Dynasty rather than the first of the Twelfth; and it was in the latter dynasty that the plot against Amenemhat I happened. Nevertheless, whether Manetho's sources were accurate on this murder, or were somehow confused, the contemporary evidence suggests great troubles in the palace at that time.

In a literary piece usually called the 'Instruction of King Amenemhat I for his son Senusert I', the old king says:

> Beware of subjects who are nobodies, of whose plotting one is not aware. Trust not a brother, know not a friend, make no intimates, it is worthless . . . He whom I gave my trust used it to plot . . . It was after supper, night had come. I was taking an hour of rest, lying on my bed, for I was weary. As my heart began to follow sleep, weapons for my protection were turned against me, while I was like a snake of the desert. I awoke at the fighting, alert, and found it was a combat of the guard. Had I quickly seized weapons in my hand, I would have made the cowards retreat in haste. But no one is strong at night; no one can fight alone; no success is achieved without a helper.
>
> Thus bloodshed occurred while I was without you; before the courtiers had heard I would hand over to you, before I had sat with you so as to advise you. For I had not prepared for it, had not expected it, had not foreseen the failing of the servants.[13]

This text is quoted at length because of its relevance to the assassination of Amenemhat, the only assassination other than that of Teti which is reported by Manetho. It was first thought to be written by King Amenemhat I after escaping an attempt on his life. However, most scholars now believe that the king was actually murdered in a conspiracy in the royal harem and that the text was composed on the request of the young king to convey the message that his father intended to hand over the reins of power to him. Amenemhat I is thought to be speaking from the tomb in a revelation. But this is the only piece of the genre, probably because it directly conflicted with the dogma of the divine kingship. Possibly for this reason also the actual assassination of the king is not stated, although sufficiently alluded to.[14] That the death of Amenemhat I was surrounded by mysterious circumstances may also be seen in the well-known Story of Sinuhe.[15] This harem official was in the company of Senusert during his campaign in Libya when he overheard the news of the death/assassination of the old king, Amenemhat I. For reasons which are not told, Sinuhe panicked and fled to Syria. The story follows his adventures until he was pardoned and returned to Egypt.

Whether Manetho had access to copies of such literary pieces as the Instruction of King Amenemhat I for his son Senusert I and the Story of Sinuhe is uncertain, but hundreds of copies of these compositions, discussing the themes of loyalty and ingratitude, have survived and obviously many more have been lost. Furthermore, some of the copies we have of these texts can be dated to much later periods than those of the events they describe, indicating their continuing popularity. With such an interest in their contents it is also very likely that both texts were equally appreciated in oral traditions.

No text mentioning the assassination of King Teti is known to us, yet the lack of evidence should not automatically mean that a text never existed, and one should not argue from silence. Whether such evidence was once available to Manetho is uncertain, but it should be borne in mind that this historian is placed halfway between the reign of Teti and the present time; Manetho is some 2,000 years after this reign and we are some 2,000 years after him. The chances that he had access to information which is now lost, written or oral, should not be dismissed. This, however, excludes any data found in tombs which have been uncovered in the present, or the relatively recent excavations in the Teti cemetery itself. These excavations have demonstrated that the tombs from Teti's reign were buried not long after his time and the upper strata used for later burials of modest individuals from the First Intermediate Period to the New Kingdom. In fact, at the end of the Eighteenth Dynasty and early Nineteenth, the upper stratum of the cemetery was then covered with a layer of compact rubble, upon which new mastabas were built. As most of these modest burials were undisturbed when discovered, there is no possibility that Manetho, in the third century, could have had access to information found in the Old Kingdom tombs at the bottom stratum.

The palace guards

The main aim of this chapter is to identify the title of 'guard', and it deals with this in some detail. While the chapter may seem an interruption to the flow it is essential for an understanding of the book's argument.

Despite the multitude of titles known from the Old Kingdom, none of these has been translated or interpreted to mean 'guard', in the sense of a person whose duty was to provide protection for a person or a place. Yet it is inconceivable that no such individuals existed in order to protect the king, the royal family, the top administrators, the palaces, the rich temples, etc. While the presence of 'guards' would have been important in all periods, it should have been particularly so during the Old Kingdom, when the country did not have a standing army or police force to maintain public order. During periods of trouble or potential trouble, such as a change of dynasty or a dispute over succession, for example, the presence and loyalty of the guards would no doubt have been essential. An examination of the Old Kingdom titles suggests [hieroglyphs] as the most likely to mean 'guard'. Yet this translation is certainly unorthodox and therefore needs to be discussed in some detail.

Holders of the office of [hieroglyphs] (usually pronounced as *ḫntj-š* khenty-she) appeared suddenly and in relatively large numbers in tombs dated to the late Fifth Dynasty. Baer dates the earliest of these tombs to the reign of Unis, the last king of the dynasty, but remarks that the mention of holders of the title in the temple records known as the Abusir papyri suggests that the office was introduced before the death of Djedkare.[16] Roth argues for an earlier date, perhaps between the reigns of Niuserre and Menkauhor,[17] and Posener-Kriéger thinks that it started at least under Neferirkare and perhaps as early as Snefru. She bases her argument on the fact that holders of this title are mentioned in the decree of Pepy I in favour of Snefru's pyramids at Dahshur. She assumes that Pepy I was confirming a situation which had already existed since the construction of Snefru's pyramid.[18] Such an assumption is hazardous, for Pepy I may well have been describing in his decree the situation in his own time and not necessarily that when Snefru's pyramids were built. Whenever a position was created to deal with existing circumstances, its holders were surely appointed to all establishments, old and new. However, the earliest attested examples of such officials are in the funerary temple of King Sahure where they accompany him in a hunting expedition.[19] But their regular and increasing appearance from the end of the Fifth Dynasty onwards, and their ownership of private tombs, may well represent a rise, perhaps a considerable rise, in their importance and, presumably, numbers.

To evaluate the significance of the office one needs to examine its responsibilities and the role its holders played in the administration. The title *ḫntj-š* has traditionally been translated as 'tenant' or 'tenant landholder'[20] – that is, a person somewhat involved in agriculture and in the 'provisioning' of the palace or of a temple. Such a translation was presumably reached because holders of this title had the right to cultivate the land of Snefru's funerary estate, as mentioned in the decree by Pepy I. By examining the duties performed by these officials Fischer concluded that they were not only preoccupied with farmlands but also executed the king's orders, protected funerary property, and in general had a wide range of other responsibilities and were closely connected with the court.[21] The analysis of the temple records in the Abusir papyri by Posener-Kriéger also demonstrated the wide involvement of these officials in various daily rituals, and accordingly she opted for a more general translation of the office as 'employee'.[22] More recently Roth has also rejected the translation of the title as tenant landholders, and noted the rare inclusion of agricultural scenes in tombs of holders of this title, which one would expect to be a common representation if cultivation was their main occupation. Instead, Roth proposed the term 'attendant', 'because it suggests the relationship of personal service to the king that seems to be the distinguishing feature of the office'. She reasonably suggests that these 'attendants' attached to royal mortuary temples performed services for the deceased king, such as dressing and feeding his cult statues, similar to those provided for the living king in the palace by officials with the same title.[23]

It has been suggested that the 𓈙 *š* in the title 𓍃𓈙 was presumably identical with the 𓈙 referred to in other titles, such as 'overseer of the 𓈙 (or of the two 𓈙𓈙) of the palace', and variously interpreted as 'quarry work', 'weaving rooms', 'pools', etc.[24] Posener-Kriéger regards the *š* as representing terrain or a locality where certain activities, probably of production, take place. Accordingly, some of these officials were attached to the central administration, others to a pyramid, a funerary temple or the palace. However, she believes that a person attached to these localities needs not be a cultivator himself, but more likely was involved in the organization of the work, perhaps to assure the production and transportation of offerings from these domains.[25] Goedicke, on the other hand, defines the (the *š* of the palace) as the district in which the palace existed,[26] and Posener-Kriéger draws attention to the incident of Neferirkare inadvertently striking the foot of the official Rawer with his staff. A 'verbal process' was made in front of the king himself in the '*š* of the palace'.[27] If the was a locality or a district where the palace was located, it could equally apply to a district where a pyramid or a funerary temple existed.

The in the title *ḫntj-š* is usually followed by the sign *ḫꜣst*-for desert or foreign land, although this sign is not infrequently omitted.[28] Whether should be considered as determinative or as a separate word, 'desert' or 'foreign land', is uncertain, but in favour of considering it as a separate word is the fact that the palace was not located in the desert nor in a foreign land. The title therefore seems to combine responsibilities in the *š* and the *ḫꜣst*, and when the latter was missing the title may have more limited scope. When this was added the office should perhaps be read as *ḫntj-š ḫꜣst*. *ḫntjw* almost certainly refers to people, holders of these responsibilities, and probably describes their duties. *ḫntj* is literally 'one who is in front of', perhaps a 'watcher', an 'escort', or a 'guard', and it is exactly in these terms that the official Weni describes the tasks entrusted to him when he was promoted to the office of 'overseer of the *ḫntjw-š* of the palace' under Pepy I (Figure 1.1). He says 'I did that which His Majesty would praise, in providing protection, in preparing the king's way and in preparing the daises. I did all that His Majesty would praise me for more than anything.'[29] Later in his career, as a sandal-bearer under Merenre, Weni mentions that 'His Majesty praised me for my vigilance and for the protection which I provided on the dais.'[30] Moreover, in his study of wall scenes in funerary temples of the Fifth Dynasty kings, Schott shows that the *ḫntjw-š* acted as escorts to the king in victory celebrations, military reviews and hunting events.[31] A group of *ḫntjw-š* holding long batons is clearly shown accompanying King Sahure in a desert hunting expedition depicted in his funerary temple (Figure 1.2).[32] Occasionally holders of the title were also dispatched by the king with objects or messages to the provinces. Thus Pai of Naga ed-Deir mentions that 'the *ḫntj-š* of the king gave me my coffin'.[33] Djau of Deir el-Gebrawi makes an identical statement,[34] and a holder of the title was sent to Coptos with a royal decree organizing the funerary cult of the vizier Idi.[35] It is almost impossible to reconcile the above-mentioned activities with those of a 'tenant landholder', whose main expertise would be expected to be in the agricultural domain. The *ḫntjw-š* seem to be mainly occupied with transport, escorting and guarding.

Figure 1.1 Found in Weni's tomb at Abydos is one of the longest biographical inscriptions from the Old Kingdom. The almost complete text is inscribed on two limestone slabs, now in the Egyptian Museum, Cairo.

Like most Egyptian officials the *ḫntjw-š* combined this office with many others. Fischer has already noticed that they were not just preoccupied with farmlands; on occasion they had a wide range of other responsibilities, and a close connection existed between them and the court.[36] Roth further examines the close ties that a group of these officials, buried at Giza, had with the palace. She notes that some also bore titles relating to the administration of the palace, such as 'assistant inspector of the palace', 'overseer of tens of the palace', 'overseer of palace messengers', 'overseer of the two *š* (s) of the palace' and 'chief of the household'.[37] Interestingly, she remarks that a striking feature in the decoration of their chapels is the prominence of musicians, which might reflect their involvement in the entertainment aspects of court life. Some *ḫntjw-š* depict members of their families as musicians in banquet scenes, which may suggest that children were trained to succeed their fathers in a position that required a knowledge of music. One *ḫntj-š*

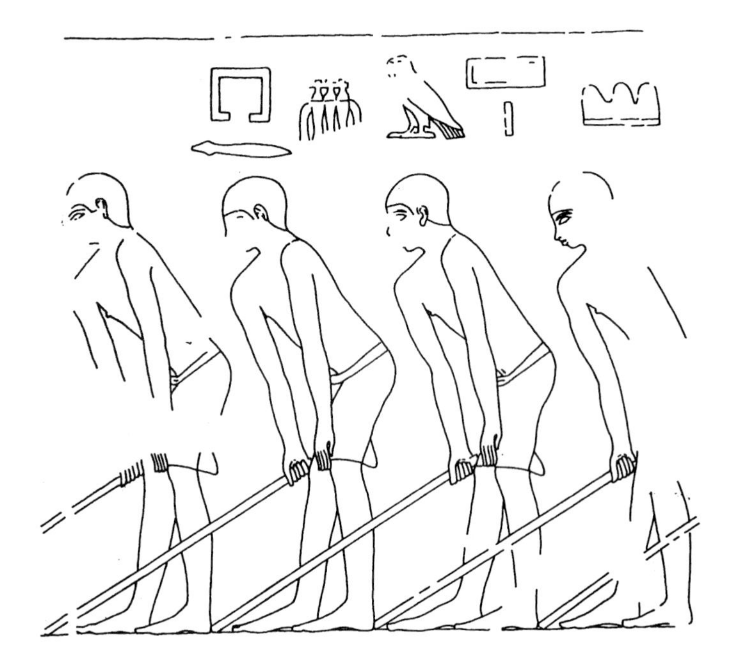

Figure 1.2 Accompanying King Sahure in a desert hunt scene, a number of officials holding batons are clearly designated as *ḫntjw-š*.

held the title of 'flautist' and another that of 'overseer of flautists and of palace singers'. A third overseer of the *ḫntjw-š* says that he was 'privy to the secrets of the king in the secret interior of the palace'.[38]

With the beginning of the Sixth Dynasty, and perhaps due to events which took place in the court, we notice that the *ḫntjw-š* began to hold other diverse positions within the palace, some of which no doubt put them in a close and more 'intimate' relationship with the king. Titles related to feeding, bathing and clothing the king were combined with that of *ḫntj-š*; for example 'overseer of the king's repasts in all his places', 'privy to the secrets of all the king's repasts', 'overseer of the two cool rooms [bathrooms?] of the palace', 'controller of clothing' and 'overseer of the two chambers of the king's adornment'.[39] Even the chief physician Seankhuiptah [37] was 'overseer of *ḫntjw-š* of Teti's pyramid'.[40]

Some viziers also held *ḫntj-š* titles, perhaps at an earlier stage of their careers; thus Mereruka [30] was a *ḫntj-š* of Teti's pyramid,[41] Tjetju [43] was a *ḫntj-š* of Pepy I's pyramid,[42] and Khentika [24] recorded in prominent places in his chapel that he was 'overseer of the *ḫntjw-š* of the palace', and also 'overseer of the two ☰ of the palace' and 'overseer of the two chambers of the king's adornment'.[43] This evidently close connection with the palace led Roth to translate the *ḫntjw-š pr-ʿꜣ* as 'palace attendants', a term which she describes as 'unorthodox' but which suggests their personal service to the king.[44] The term 'attendant' almost certainly describes the office of *ḫntj-š* more accurately than that of 'tenant landholder', and it is a term which the present writer has adopted in recent publications. However, 'attendant' is a very broad term, which may imply that the person it describes was called upon to perform various, unspecific tasks. If this were the case there would have been no need specifically to list the other titles which clearly detail the specialized services of these individuals to the king, the palace or a temple, which would simply amount to a kind of repetition and renders the *ḫntj-š* title, in such cases, meaningless. Thus, in addition to the title of 'overseer of the *ḫntjw-š* of the palace', Semdent [39], in the Teti cemetery, was for example 'overseer of the king's repasts in all his places', Ihyemsaf [16] was 'overseer of the two cool rooms of the palace' and 'controller of clothing',[45] and Mereri [28] was also 'overseer of the two cool rooms of the palace' and 'overseer of the two chambers of the king's adornment'.[46] In all cases *ḫntj-š* appears to be an independent and specific title, the main duty of which seems to be the provision of security and may be better translated as 'guard'. In this respect it is of particular importance that some overseers of the palace guards combined this title with the responsibility for weapons. Thus, in addition to their titles of guards, Nefer-mesdjer-Khufu[47] and Nyhetepptah[48] were overseers of weapons, and Imysetka[49] was overseer of the two houses of weapons. Tjetetu [41], on the other hand, held three titles relating to the 'entry of the deserts/foreign lands'.[50] That these guards had some soldierly training may be understood from Weni's biography, where he states that he led a huge Egyptian army six times against the Asiatics.[51] Although Weni clearly states that his choice was due to the trust the king had in him, which must have been crucial under Pepy I, it remains inconceivable that such a responsibility, particularly the drawing of the plans of attack that he mentions, would be given to someone with no military experience at all. Another contemporary of Weni, Niankhpepy [7], who also held the title of 'overseer of the palace guards', says that he was the greatest of the great in fighting.[52] Although all officials could be called upon during the Old Kingdom to join the army in times of war, as stated by Weni, there must have been some personnel with military expertise who could train these men in the use of arms and who could lead them in battles. The same personnel could serve in other posts during peace time, including the provision of security and related matters. The fact that the guards were also involved in feeding, bathing, clothing, or even entertaining the king, does not negate or contradict their security duties. In fact the protection of the king everywhere, and of royal institutions, must have required a great deal of organization, certainly at some times more than others.

The examination of the various ranks of the guards clearly demonstrates that they belonged to a well-structured department,[53] in many respects similar to other administrative and religious departments. In addition Roth shows that the guards (attendants) were organized in divisions,[54] and an isolated instance of the title 'overseer of six palace guards' is held by Iasen of Giza.[55] The highest title is the 'overseer of the palace guards',[56] followed, perhaps very closely, by the 'overseer of the department of the palace guards',[57] then the 'superintendent of the palace guards',[58] followed by the 'under-supervisor of the palace guards',[59] and finally the ordinary guards. The translation of these ranks is arbitrary and only meant to place them in hierarchical order. We are certain that the 'overseer' is higher than the 'superintendent', who is ahead of the 'under-supervisor', even if the choice of the English equivalents is not particularly appropriate. This order is also supported by Roth's study of the comparative sizes of tombs of the holders of various ranks.[60] It is clear that at any one time there was more than one holder of any rank, including that of the 'overseer'. This is suggested by the number of possible contemporary holders of each title and the clear statement of the overseer of the palace guards, Weni, who says that under Pepy I he replaced/expelled four holders of the same office who were there.[61]

From the analysis of the Abusir papyri Posener-Kriéger concluded that the young *ḫntjw-š*, qualified as 'cadets', were probably responsible for transport, while the older ones served as guards.[62] The evidence suggests that this department was joined at a young age. Weni, for example, says that he was a 'boy' under King Teti and that he held the office of 'superintendent of the palace guard',[63] and Qar of Edfu mentions that he was a child under Teti, brought to the capital by Pepy I to be educated with the children of the provincial governors and rose under the same king to the position of 'overseer of the palace guards'.[64] Roth has already noted that the children and retainers depicted in the tombs of the palace guards (whom she calls 'palace attendants') at Giza bear similar titles to those of the tomb owners.[65] The same observation is also true of individuals buried at Saqqara. For instance, the 'overseer of the palace guards', Niankhpepy [7], had his eldest son described as 'overseer of the department of the palace guards', another son designated as 'superintendent of the palace guards', and a retainer with the last title depicted in his tomb in the Unis cemetery.[66] In the same cemetery Niankhptah [9] represents six sons in a row, presumably in order of age, carrying offerings of meat and fowl to his seated figure. All sons are named, but only the first four bear titles, all relating to the palace guards; the eldest was 'overseer of the department', the following two were 'superintendents' and the fourth was 'under-supervisor'.[67] The same feature is also found in the Teti cemetery; for example, the overseer of the palace guards, Mereri [28], represented in his chapel two sons who followed his career, one at the level of 'superintendent' and the second at 'under-supervisor'.[68] The case of the palace guard Khufuankh of Giza is interesting, for both his father, Iaunesut, and mother, Iupu, held the simple title of 'guard'.[69]

Employment as a guard was by no means restricted to the sons of the guards. Sons of the higher officials, even the viziers, were appointed to these positions, attached to the palace or a pyramid. Thus the vizier Neferseshemre [34] in the Teti cemetery, for example, shows three of his sons holding such titles;[70] his neighbour Ankhmahor [12] has one son and one brother with these titles;[71] Neferseshemptah [33], who was not a vizier but was married to a king's daughter, has one son appointed as guard.[72] Perhaps the most interesting case is that of the vizier Mereruka [30], who was married to the eldest daughter of King Teti, and who had one son and seven brothers employed by this department, the last seven shown accompanying him on a trip where he is carried in a palanquin.[73] The examination of the evidence strongly suggests that the department of guards was rapidly expanding. The above-mentioned case of Niankhptah [9] in the Unis cemetery is interesting, although perhaps not typical, in the number of sons he shows. The six sons are represented in the original decoration of the chapel, which is executed in raised relief and definitely shows no evidence of later additions. It is unfortunate that we have no human remains of the tomb owner in order to estimate his age, but even if these existed they would show the age at death and not at the time the tomb was built and decorated. Generally, we may assume that the Egyptian officials prepared their resting places as soon as they reached the positions destined for them and were allocated places in the cemetery. It is uncertain at what age this took place, but it was probably at a relatively young age by modern standards, considering perhaps the shorter life expectancy in ancient Egypt. Thus, the overseer of Upper Egypt, Nikauisesi [35], who died at the maximum age of forty-five, left a fully built and decorated large stone mastaba in the Teti cemetery. He was married probably more than once, judging by the number of his eldest sons shown in his tomb as already occupying high positions in the administration.[74] When Niankhptah [9] decorated his chapel, presumably at a relatively young age and certainly during his tenure of office, four of his sons were employed by the same department, and at supervisory levels. This could only happen if such appointments took place at a young age. The other two sons bear no titles and one may assume that they were then too young to be appointed, but it is not impossible that this took place later. The expansion in the number of the guards, particularly at the end of the Fifth Dynasty and in the first half of the Sixth, must have been remarkable.

The position of guard was fundamentally a male occupation. However, very rare instances of female guards are known. For example, Raramu at Giza, who held the relatively modest title of under-supervisor of the palace guards, had one son and one daughter, who were at the most basic level of their father's profession, 'guard' and '(female) guard' respectively, the latter bearing the name Tjez-Tjazet.[75] Iupu, mother of the palace guard Khufuankh of Giza, was also a guard,[76] and another woman with the name Merynebty [29], who is buried in the Teti cemetery at Saqqara (see p. 97), also held the simple title of '(female) guard'.[77] We are uncertain about the responsibilities of female guards, but they may have been appointed to perform a special task, perhaps in the most intimate parts of the royal harem. No female guard with supervisory rank is known to me and the rarity of female guards, since the position existed, in comparison with the huge number of their male counterparts, is surprising. It is true that the simple 'guards' did not usually possess independent tombs, but it remains astonishing that simple female guards do not appear more often in the tombs of the higher-ranking officials as wives, daughters or retainers.

During the last part of the Fifth Dynasty tombs of the guards were built at Giza, and Roth has noticed unusual concentrations of holders of this office in a certain part of the cemetery,[78] although isolated cases are also found elsewhere. In the Sixth Dynasty the burial grounds of these officials moved to Saqqara, with the same concentration observed at Giza. The Teti cemetery is a particularly small one, with limited area available for tombs of officials (see p. 138). The cemetery appears to have been well planned, with the king's pyramid to the south and those of his queens to the east. The most important officials were allocated areas for their tombs immediately to the north of Teti's pyramid, or to the west of those of his queens in a street now known as the Rue de tombeaux. Less important or later officials are buried further north from Teti's pyramid, or further west from those of the queens. The north-west section of the cemetery was almost fully occupied by tombs of holders of palace guard titles. This may reflect their relatively modest status, which is also reflected in their comparatively small mastabas, mostly of mud-brick with some stone elements. However, being allocated a piece of land of any size in this unusually small cemetery, and being able to construct a tomb in the cemetery of a reigning king, must have been of great importance; it must also indicate the need Teti, like no other reigning king, felt to be so close to his guards. Another concentration of tombs of guards is found in the Unis cemetery,[79] but these are small tombs either built in the available space or cut underground in the streets of the cemetery. A careful examination of this group of tombs indicates that they belonged to the reign of Pepy I (see pp. 22–47). The placement of Pepy I's guards in the Unis cemetery, considerably away from his pyramid, is curious, but is in agreement with the fact that most of his officials and all of his known viziers are buried outside his cemetery, mostly in the Teti cemetery. Despite the available space around Pepy I's pyramid, it seems that he chose not to have his officials buried close to him, a general attitude of this king which appears very unusual.

The concentration of the guards' tombs in certain sections of the cemeteries, whether at Giza or Saqqara, and the apparent tradition of family succession to such posts suggest that they formed a close-knit class of society and probably a rather privileged profession, though not at the top of the administrative hierarchy.[80] However, the number of tombs owned by guards, although relatively large, is astonishingly smaller than the number of the known holders of the office. What happened for instance to the seven brothers of Mereruka [30], or to the four sons of Niankhptah [9], or to the numerous other guards depicted as sons and retainers in the scenes of known tombs? By examining the Teti and Unis cemeteries at Saqqara we observe that the streets and other open areas are filled, in an organized fashion, with shafts, which occasionally end in small burial chambers but frequently do not. These shafts are usually taken to be of later dates than that of the original cemetery and are mostly referred to as belonging to the First Intermediate Period. Yet they may well be contemporary with the main mastabas of the cemetery and used as burial places for the large numbers of relatives and retainers. Small false-door stelae, sometimes belonging to guards,[81] were found and were probably originally placed at the mouths of these shafts. The rather crude style of art of these false doors, or of other objects found in these shafts, should not automatically indicate a date in the First Intermediate Period, but presumably reflects the rather modest means of their owners. It should be emphasized that the symmetrical layout of these shafts suggests that the streets in which they were excavated were clear and visible at the time, an unlikely condition during the First Intermediate Period. Unlike these shafts, later ones were dug through the accumulated sand and debris, cut through the walls of Old Kingdom mastabas and frequently breaking through the walls of earlier shafts and burial chambers. One must also bear in mind the possible reuse of some shafts in later periods.

The evidence suggests that only a privileged few guards, even among the highest rank, the 'overseers', were granted a place for a tomb in the cemetery; the others were buried in simple shafts. While the size of the tomb reflected the social status of its owner,[82] the allocation of a piece of land in the cemetery does not seem to have been automatic and subject only to promotion to a certain level; it was probably through the special favours of the king. In that respect a quote from an inscription on an architrave above the entrance doorway of the tomb of the overseer of the department of the palace guards, Iri [19], is of particular interest.[83] He says: 'As for this tomb which I made in the necropolis, it was the king who granted its place for me, as one who is honoured before the king, one who does what his lord favours. I made payments to the stonemason. I did it so that he was satisfied about it. I did the work in it with my hands, together with my children and brothers.' In this remarkable and frank declaration Iri tells us that the site was assigned to him by the king, a statement of the obvious which is therefore not made by others, but which may be understood from the traditional funerary formula which is written in every tomb and which begins with 'An offering which the king gives and an offering which Anubis gives, etc.' Perhaps Iri felt the need to make such a statement as he was not even among the highest-ranking guards, for he was not overseer of the palace guards but overseer of the department of the palace guards, a slightly lower ranked post. This might also explain his second unusual declaration that he built the tomb with his own hands, helped by his children and brothers. He probably refers to the mud-brick work of the mastaba, but for the more technical stone work, like that of the architrave, and despite his apparent lack of means, he had to employ a stonemason. The favours of the king are clearly stated by Iri and many other tomb owners, who frequently refer to themselves as 'one who was honoured by the king . . .' or 'one beloved of his lord', etc. Perhaps we should take these often repeated expressions literally and not consider them as simple boasting or stereotypical phrases.

2

THE SUSPECTS

Case studies

THE UNIS CEMETERY

Tomb of Akhethetep/Hemi – reused by Nebkauhor/Idu [1][84]

Original owner

Akhethetep, also called Hemi, was a chief justice and vizier who held many other titles usually associated with this office, such as overseer of Upper Egypt, overseer of the scribes of the king's documents, overseer of the six great courts, overseer of the two treasuries, overseer of the two houses of gold, overseer of the two granaries, etc. Some of his titles also show close service to the king and the palace, such as he who is privy to the secrets of the house of morning, keeper of the head ornaments, confidant of his lord, beloved of his lord, one who is honoured before the king; and he held the ranks of hereditary prince, count and sole companion.

Tomb

The tomb is the last in a series of large mastabas progressing from east to west in the area to the north of Unis' causeway and south of the enclosure wall of the Step Pyramid. It is large, fully constructed of limestone blocks and has a chapel occupying a large section of the mastaba's perimeter and consisting of five rooms, a large pillared hall, a serdab, a series of magazines and apparently a stairway to the roof. The burial chamber is reached through a sloping passage, 7.5 metres long, leading to a horizontal passage, 3.15 metres long. The chamber itself is large, plastered, but not decorated, and contains an inscribed stone sarcophagus. The walls of some rooms in the chapel are decorated in good-quality relief, but the fragmentary condition of the scenes and the incomplete publication of this tomb does not allow an accurate assessment of its contents.

Figure 2.1 To the left is Unis' pyramid with the small tombs of the guards in front of it. In the centre are the two stone-built mastabas of Queen Nebet (left) and Ihy (right) with a narrow passage between them. To the right is the enclosure wall of the Step Pyramid of Djoser.

Date

The location of the mastaba, its magnitude and the fact that the owner was a vizier and priest of Unis' pyramid, leave little doubt that Akhethetep served under this king. The fact that it is the last in a series of tombs may indicate a late date in this reign.

Suggested date: Unis, probably late.[85]

Later treatment

The names Akhethetep and Hemi have been deliberately erased and replaced by those of Nebkauhor, who is also called Idu. As the latter did not alter the other inscriptions of Akhethetep, or add any reference to a later king, the excavator has reasonably deduced that the reuse of the tomb occurred 'not very long after the disappearance of the original builder'.[86]

Reuse of tomb

The mastaba was reused by a man named Nebkauhor, also called Idu, who is designated as eldest king's son of his body. The excavator commented that

Figure 2.2 While the original figure of Akhethetep was left intact in raised relief, the inscriptions of the new owner, Nebkauhor/Idu, were incised after erasing the name and title of the original owner.

this designation and the name of the new owner are sculpted in very low relief, and in inferior style to the remainder of the inscriptions, and he indicated that the reason was that the name of the original owner of the mastaba had been erased at this spot (Figure 2.2).[87] The same also happened to the inscriptions on the sarcophagus,[88] yet in many instances the name of the original owner has survived in full or in part. Whether Nebkauhor/Idu enjoyed all the titles originally held by Akhethetep is impossible to tell without further examination of the reliefs themselves.[89] It is certainly likely that the new owner left titles which he did not hold, in order to avoid spoiling the appearance of the wall decoration. The case of the tomb of Hesi [15], reused by Seshemnefer, in the Teti cemetery, clearly demonstrates this point.

Tomb of Hermeru [2][90]

Owner

Hermeru, also called Merery, was overseer of the guards, overseer of the department of the guards, superintendent of the palace guards, and guard and priest of Unis' pyramid. He also held titles related to the personal service of the king, being chief of clothing and overseer of the king's repasts in all his places. He had the ranks of sole companion and king's nobleman of the palace.

Tomb

Hermeru's rock-cut tomb is situated immediately to the west of the mastaba of Akhethetep [1] (reused by Nebkauhor) and to the north of Unis' causeway. It consists of a stairway descending to an open court, from which a chapel is excavated in the rock below the cemetery's floor level. The façade and entrance were cased with limestone and decorated. The shaft, 10.2 metres deep, leads to a small burial chamber with a burial pit cut into its floor.

Date

The owner is described as one who was honoured before the king of Upper and Lower Egypt, Unis, and there is no mention of a later king in the tomb. It is therefore tempting to date the tomb to the reign of Unis, except that the group of tombs of this particular type, rock-cut below ground level, located in the near vicinity are dated by inscriptional evidence to the reign of Pepy I (Niankhpepy [7], Iy [4] and Tjetu [10]). The owners of these tombs, like Hermeru, mention the fact that they were honoured before Unis, and some held offices related to the service in his pyramid. It seems likely that this group of officials started their careers under Unis and constructed their tombs in this cemetery under Pepy I, when there is strong evidence that his officials built their tombs in various cemeteries, but at a distance from his own pyramid.

Suggested date: early Pepy I.

Later treatment

There is no evidence of any damage to any part of the tomb, but the decoration appears certainly to have come to a sudden halt. While the work on the architrave, usually the first part to receive decoration, is finely completed (Figure 2.3), the rest of the decoration is most certainly unfinished. The northern false door, that of the tomb owner, has the upper part – the upper lintel, the panel and a few signs in the top section of the outer jambs – executed in relief, the rest of the inscriptions being in black paint only (Figure 2.4). The southern false door, belonging to the wife, Wadjkaues, is totally uninscribed on the upper lintel and the left outer jamb. Perhaps they once bore inscriptions in paint (Figure 2.5). A spear-fishing scene on the north entrance thickness is only partly sculpted and below it a net-fishing scene is only in red outline (Figure 2.6).

Tomb of Ihy – reused by Idut [3][91]

Original owner

Ihy was a vizier and held other titles usually associated with the office, such as overseer of all the works of the king, overseer of the scribes of the king's

Figure 2.3 The scenes and inscriptions on the architrave above the entrance to Hermeru's tomb were finished in fine incised relief.

documents, overseer of the two granaries, overseer of the two treasuries, and held the ranks of hereditary prince and count.

Tomb

Fully constructed of limestone blocks, this mastaba lies in the Unis cemetery next to, and presumably built as a single project with, that of Unisankh, a probable son of Unis.[92] The chapel is formed of six rooms, five of which are decorated, a serdab, magazines and stairway to the roof. The shaft is 11.45 metres deep and leads to a very large burial chamber, the walls of which were plastered and beautifully decorated in painting, but are now in a very poor condition. The chamber contains a large inscribed stone sarcophagus and its lid.

Date

The location of the tomb in a series of mastabas opposite the queens' mastabas, progressing eastwards – Iynefert (a vizier of Unis), Unisankh (probably a son of Unis), Ihy, and finally Mehu (who served from Unis to Pepy I)[93] – leaves little doubt that Ihy's tomb was constructed under Unis.[94]

Suggested date: Unis, probably late.

Later treatment

The name and figure of Ihy have been erased from the decoration of the chapel, and it is with some difficulty that the name can now be read in a

Figure 2.4 Following the recording of scenes and inscriptions on Hermeru's false door in black paint, the relief work started but was interrupted, sometimes in the middle of a sentence or word.

number of places. Ihy's name and titles in the inscriptions of the sarcophagus, although chiselled out, remain very clear.

Reuse of the tomb

The tomb was reassigned to a woman named Idut, also called Seshseshet, who bears the title king's daughter of his body. The scenes, originally cut for Ihy, have been adapted to suit a woman, and the figure of the princess replaced that of the vizier everywhere in the chapel. However, her figures were executed in a very shallow and rather mediocre relief, in sharp contrast to the superb relief of the original tomb owner (Figures 2.7, 2.8). It is uncer-

Figure 2.5 While the false door of Hermeru's wife, Wadjkaues, has progressed further than that of her husband, the upper lintel and left outer jamb are now blank, even though they might have been originally decorated in paint.

tain whether Idut was a daughter of Unis or of Teti, the latter having a number of daughters all named Seshseshet, and it is almost certain that she died under this king. One of her attendants, whose name was inserted as part of the alteration of the tomb for her, was called Tetiankh.[95] Idut appears to have died young, which is evident in her hairstyle and the fact that she was shown accompanied by her nurse.[96] It is very curious that the tomb of a vizier was reallocated to a young princess. That she died young before any burial place was prepared for her might explain the haste evident in the quality of her decoration, but for a vizier to lose his tomb after it was fully built and decorated can only represent a severe punishment.

Figure 2.6 A spear-fishing scene on the north entrance thickness of Hermeru's tomb was obviously left unfinished. The facial details of the tomb owner and his wife were never carved and the front part of the small figure mimicking the tomb owner was never sculpted.

Figure 2.7 Original scenes and inscriptions in Ihy's chapel were executed in very fine raised relief. The offering bearers and the accompanying hieroglyphs are exquisite.

Figure 2.8 Ihy's figures were erased and replaced by those of Idut, but, unlike his reliefs, hers are very shallow, with only incised outlines and minimal modelling.

Tomb of Iy {4}[97]

Owner

Iy held the titles overseer of the palace guards, guard of Pepy I's pyramid, priest of Unis' pyramid, royal chamberlain, and was described as nobleman of the king and companion of the house. He may be the son of Niankhpepy {7}, who is designated in the latter's tomb as superintendent of the palace guards.

Tomb

The tomb is situated in the Unis cemetery to the north of the causeway, south of the mastaba of Ihy (reused by Idut) and east of that of Queen Nebet. It is cut in the rock below ground level and formed of a descending stairway, leading to an open court and a small rock-cut chapel (Figure 2.9). The façade and entrance doorway were cased with good limestone blocks and decorated in relief. A limestone false door was placed into the chapel wall, but was left uninscribed. At 7.7 metres deep the shaft opens into a small burial chamber containing a burial pit cut into the floor.

Date

The reference to the owner as one who was honoured before the king of Upper and Lower Egypt, Unis, might suggest that he served under this king, but he was certainly still actively employed under Pepy I in whose pyramid he was a guard. As the tomb remained unfinished it seems less likely that its building started under Unis, thus taking an unusually long time to be completed.

Suggested date: early Pepy I.

Figure 2.9 Like most of the tombs of guards in the Unis cemetery, that of Iy is excavated into the rock slightly below ground level and is reached by a flight of steps leading to a small open court.

Later treatment

There is no evidence of any deliberate damage to the tomb, but the decoration was abandoned at an early stage of completion. The northern false door in the forecourt and the entrance drum were inscribed in paint only; the southern false door does not show any evidence of decoration nor does the one inside the chapel (Figure 2.10). The south entrance thickness is sculpted in good relief (Figure 2.11), while the figures on the opposite north thickness are in outline only. The decoration came to a sudden stop.

Tomb of Iyenhor [5][98]

Owner

Iyenhor was an overseer, superintendent (and overseer of the department) of the palace guards. He was also a royal chamberlain, sole companion, true nobleman of the king and companion of the house.

Tomb

The tomb is situated to the north of Unis' causeway, south of the mastaba of Akhethetep [1] (reused by Nebkauhor) and immediately to the west of

Figure 2.10 While the decoration on the entrance architrave of Iy's tomb, usually the first to be carved, was finished in reasonably fine relief, the scenes and inscriptions on the northern false door in the forecourt were executed only in paint, now hardly visible. The southern false door is completely blank.

Figure 2.11 Unlike the decoration on the north entrance thickness of Iy's chapel, that on the south thickness is beautifully finished. The figures of Iy, his wife and son, as well as accompanying hieroglyphs, are finely rendered.

that of Niankhpepy [7]. Like that of the latter, the tomb is formed of a descending stairway, an open court and a small chapel cut into the rock below the ground level. The façade was cased with limestone, but, unlike that of Niankhpepy, only the architrave of Iyenhor was inscribed (Figure 2.12). Two false doors are fixed in the west wall of the chapel; the northern one is decorated, the southern is not. A shaft 10.03 metres deep leads to a small burial chamber with a burial pit and a stone lid. The lid was found against the wall of the chamber, but as its edges bear traces of mortar it must have originally covered the pit and been removed by plunderers.

Date

Like his neighbour, Niankhpepy, Iyenhor refers to himself as one who was honoured before Unis. No reference to a later king is found in the tomb, but its proximity and similarity to that of Niankhpepy make it very likely that the two belong to the same date. This is also supported by the request

Figure 2.12 The entrance architrave of Iyenhor's tomb was decorated in fine relief, but the rest of the façade and entrance thickness were left blank.

of 5,000 fowl inscribed on the panel of the false door which appears on a number of false doors of this period.[99]

Suggested date: early Pepy I.

Later treatment

There is no evidence of deliberate damage to any part of the tomb. However, the decoration was abandoned unfinished. Apart from the architrave, the façade and entrance of the tomb is undecorated, and while the northern false door was decorated (Figure 2.13), the southern one was left blank. Of the decoration of the northern false door the excavator wrote, 'This false door was never completed and many of its parts still retain the black lines with which the draughtsman marked the design for the sculptors to work upon, and even this marking out does not appear to have been finished, as one single unit only of the palm-leaf decoration appears upon the cornice.'[100] Two blocks of limestone were placed into the north wall, probably to inscribe an offering list, as is the case in the neighbouring tomb of Niankhpepy [7], but were left blank (Figure 2.14).

Tomb of Niankhkhnum [6][101]

Owner

Niankhkhnum, also called Khenemi and Imi, held the titles royal chamberlain of the palace and superintendent of the palace guards and the rank of sole companion.

Figure 2.13 The northern false door in Iyenhor's chapel was decorated in incised relief which shows no internal details. This, together with the fact that black marking lines are clearly visible, indicates the work was left unfinished.

Tomb

The tomb is located in the immediate vicinity of that of Niankhpepy/Hepi [8] in the Unis cemetery. The only part left of the tomb is the false door at the back of a stone niche. Whether this was the total chapel, or whether there were mud-brick walls which have completely disappeared, is unknown. No associated shaft has yet been found.

Date

The tomb does not provide independent evidence for a precise date. The type of false door with cavetto cornice and torus moulding was introduced in the middle of the Fifth Dynasty, but this is of little use as the location of the tomb in the Unis cemetery would exclude an earlier date. The tomb can only be dated by association with the neighbouring group of small tombs, the closest of which is that of Niankhpepy/Hepi dated to the reign of Pepy I.

Figure 2.14 Two superimposed limestone blocks were embedded in the north wall of Iyenhor's tomb, presumably with the intention of inscribing an offering list, as is the case with the adjacent tomb of Niankhpepy, yet they were left blank.

The poor condition of Niankhkhnum may well be due more to his lower status than to a later date.

Suggested date: The tomb is tentatively dated to early Pepy I.

Later treatment

No evidence of damage to the inscriptions on the false door, but these were obviously left unfinished, with the upper lintel, the panel and the three right jambs totally undecorated, although they may have once been inscribed in paint which has now disappeared (Figure 2.15).

Tomb of Niankhpepy [7][102]

Owner

The name Niankhpepy consistently replaced an earlier name, of which a few traces remain, suggesting that this was Ptahhetep. There is no reason to think

Figure 2.15 Inscriptions on the false door of Niankhkhnum were executed on the lower lintel and on the three left jambs. The rest of the false door is now undecorated, although inscriptions in paint may have once existed.

that Niankhpepy was a usurper, for there is no alteration to the names of the wife and children. It seems much more likely that he was granted the privilege of bearing a new name formed with the cartouche of Pepy.[103] The case of Niankhpepy/Hepi [8] from the same cemetery supports this deduction. After the completion of the decoration of the façade, which according to evidence from the Unis and Teti cemeteries was usually executed first, the decoration of the chapel started. The false door was inscribed in black paint only and was never sculpted. There, the name is consistently written as Niankhmeryre, using Pepy I's name Meryre which he acquired after he abandoned the name Nefersahor.

Niankhpepy was an overseer of the palace guards, guard of Pepy I's pyramid, one who is privy to the secrets of the house of morning, one who is privy to the secrets of the king, overseer of the two districts[104] of the palace; he also held the rank of sole companion. He had a son named Iy who may be the owner of a nearby tomb in the cemetery [4].

Tomb

Situated in the Unis cemetery, to the north of the causeway and to the south of the large mastabas of Nyankhba and Akhethetep/Hemi [1], the tomb is cut in the rock below the ground level and is reached by means of a stairway of five steps leading to an open forecourt which gives access to a small rock-cut chapel. The façade of the tomb was cased with limestone and decorated (Figure 2.16). Two blocks of limestone were embedded into the walls of the chapel, one for the false door and the other for an offering list. While the inscriptions of the false door remained in black paint, those of the offering list were incised. The style of art is fine, but the decoration of the tomb, particularly on the false door, was certainly unfinished. At the bottom of a shaft 8.45 metres deep is a small burial chamber containing a burial pit in which was an elaborately decorated wooden coffin. Human remains were found by the excavator, but no report is available on them.

Date

The tomb owner refers to himself as one who was honoured before the king of Upper and Lower Egypt, Unis. It is likely that he started his career under this king with the name Ptahhetep, a common name at the time. It is uncertain, however, if the tomb was prepared then or at a later date, for the owner was still active early in the reign of Pepy I as indicated by the changes in his name, first to Niankhpepy, then to Niankhmeryre. That officials served under a number of successive kings is also attested in the Teti cemetery (see case studies of Hesi [15], Kagemni [23] and Nikauisesi [35]). The fact that

Figure 2.16 Unlike other guards buried in the Unis cemetery, Niankhpepy has not only the entrance architrave decorated in relief but also both entrance jambs. This may suggest that he started on the decoration of his tomb slightly earlier than the others.

the decoration of the false door was still unfinished in the reign of Pepy I argues against the construction beginning under Unis, for it is unlikely that the decoration would have taken such a long period.

Suggested date: beginning of Pepy I for the building of the tomb; shortly after for the alteration of the name and the inscriptions on the false door and offering list.

Later treatment

There is no evidence of any deliberate damage to the inscriptions of the tomb, but judging by the false door these were certainly left unfinished (Figure 2.17).

Tomb of Niankhpepy/Hepi [8][105]

Owner

On the sarcophagus, usually lowered into the burial chamber before the construction of the mastaba itself, the owner was consistently called Sebekhetep

Figure 2.17 The inscriptions on the only false door in Niankhpepy's chapel were executed in black paint, now barely visible.

with the 'beautiful name', Hepi. On the false door, however, he bears only the names Niankhpepy and the same 'beautiful name', Hepi. This is another example in the Unis cemetery of the tomb owner changing his name during the construction of his tomb, in both cases to Niankhpepy (see also [7]), probably reflecting a favour from the king by allowing him formation of a new name using his cartouche. The owner was a royal chamberlain and overseer of the palace guards and had the rank of sole companion.

Tomb

This small tomb is located in the Unis cemetery to the north of the causeway and in close proximity to the rock-cut tombs of Iy [4], Tjetu [10] and Hermeru [2]. But unlike these its chapel is constructed of limestone blocks above ground and contains a false door formed of a monolithic piece of stone. The upper part of the false door is decorated in relief, but the lower part is only in black paint and is badly effaced (Figure 2.18). The shaft is 8.4 metres deep leading to a medium-sized burial chamber which contains a sarcophagus formed of six pieces – base, lid and four sides, each, with the exception of the base, carrying a line of text in incised relief (Figure 2.19).

Figure 2.18 Although the false door of Niankhpepy/Hepi was fully decorated in paint, only the upper lintel and the figure of the tomb owner on the panel were executed in incised relief. The offering table in front of the tomb owner's figure on the same panel was left as a painted outline only.

Figure 2.19 The sarcophagus of Niankhpepy/Hepi is unusual in that it was formed of six separate pieces. The four sides were each inscribed with a single line on the interior, while the lid was inscribed on the exterior. This photograph shows the back of the sarcophagus.

Date

The change of the tomb owner's name from Sebekhetep to Niankhpepy leaves little doubt as to his date in Pepy I's reign; that is, to the same period as the neighbouring group of tombs excavated in the rock below ground level.
Suggested date: early Pepy I.

Later treatment

Although the front side of the sarcophagus is smashed and the lid is broken into two main parts, this was most probably the work of tomb robbers. Formed of separate and rather thin slabs of stone, this sarcophagus was easily smashed to gain access to its contents. However, there is no attempt at erasing the name on the sarcophagus or on the false door. Yet the decoration of the false door had obviously come to an abrupt halt.

Tomb of Niankhptah [9][106]

Owner

Niankhptah, also called Ithi, was a royal chamberlain and overseer of the palace guards, overseer of all the work of the two workshops, overseer of the two cool rooms [of the palace], one who is privy to all secret works of the king, sole companion and nobleman of the king. Four of his six sons also bear different supervisory levels of the palace guards (Figure 2.20).

Figure 2.20 Niankhptah represented six sons as offering bearers in his chapel. Four of these bear different supervisory titles in the department of the palace guards.

Tomb

This mastaba is situated immediately opposite that of Niankhpepy/Hepi [8] in the Unis cemetery. The chapel is very small but fully constructed of stone blocks. The remains of mud-brick walls suggest that the mastaba had its exterior walls built of this material, but the exact perimeter is uncertain. The entrance jamb and the four walls of the chapel were decorated in relief, including the west wall which is fully occupied by a false door. The shaft descends to a depth of 8.15 metres to open into a burial chamber containing a stone sarcophagus.

Date

The owner held a priesthood of Unis' pyramid and he depicts six sons, four of whom bear names formed with Unis' cartouche. Niankhptah most probably served under Unis, but whether he built his tomb under this king is uncertain. The chair with four lion legs, on which the tomb owner sits, is depicted in tombs containing the cartouches of Niuserre to Teti and rarely that of Pepy I.[107] In the Teti cemetery, this chair last appeared in the mastabas of Nikauisesi [35][108] and Khentika [24],[109] from the very end of Teti's reign and the beginning of that of Pepy I. The same date is also suggested by the relative height of the loaves of bread depicted on the offering table in relation to the seated figure of the owner.[110] In dating this tomb, however, one has to take into account the neighbouring tombs of similar size. Not only is the tomb of Niankhptah close to the rock tombs of Iy [4] and Tjetu [10], but it lies immediately opposite, and is similar in size to, that of Niankhpepy/Hepi [8], all four tomb owners being in the guards' department.

Suggested date: beginning of Pepy I's reign.

Later treatment

There is no evidence of any deliberate damage to the tomb. The fact that all the scenes and inscriptions appear to have been completed might suggest either that Niankhptah built and decorated his tomb before the events which led to the interruption of the decoration of the other tombs, or that he was not implicated in these events. In favour of the latter alternative is the fact that none of Niankhptah's sons had his figure or name erased, although four of them held supervisory levels in the guards. This may suggest that the family continued to be regarded as loyal to the palace.

Tomb of Tjetu [10][111]

Owner

The owner was overseer of the palace guards, priest of the pyramids of Unis and Pepy I and had the ranks of sole companion and nobleman of the king.

Tomb

The tomb is located to the north of Unis' causeway, south of the mastabas of Ihy [3] and Mehu,[112] and within a short distance to the east of the tomb of Iy [4]. It is cut into rock below ground level and formed of a stairway descending to an open court which leads to a small chapel. The façade, entrance and false door are of white limestone, but only the architrave was decorated. The shaft is 7.45 metres deep and leads to a small burial chamber with a burial pit cut into the floor.

Date

Tjetu refers to himself as one who was honoured by Unis. He probably served under this king, but built his tomb under Pepy I in whose pyramid he served as a priest.

Suggested date: early Pepy I.

Later treatment

There is no evidence of deliberate damage to the tomb, but its decoration was certainly abandoned at an early stage. Consistent with the evidence from both the Unis and Teti cemeteries, the architrave was the first part in the tomb to receive decoration. Here, the figures and inscriptions on the left section were executed in relief (Figure 2.21), while those to the right remain in painted outline, as is a line of text above the figures (Figure 2.22). The rest of the façade, entrance and false door are undecorated.

Figure 2.21 The left section of the entrance architrave of the tomb of Tjetu is decorated in well-finished, repeated figures of the tomb owner, with his name and titles inscribed in vertical columns of hieroglyphs.

Figure 2.22 The right section of the same architrave of Tjetu shows traces of figures of the tomb owner and his wife as well as hieroglyphic signs, including the cartouche of Pepy, all outlined in red paint only.

THE TETI CEMETERY

Tomb of Ankh [11][113]

Owner

Ankh was overseer of the guards, overseer of all the king's repasts, overseer of the two fields of offering, royal chamberlain of the palace, and had the rank of sole companion.

Tomb

This small tomb is situated in the second east–west street, constructed of mud-brick in a space between the tombs of Meru [31] and Desi,[114] and used the external walls of both as common walls. The chapel consists of three rooms, occupying a large section of the mastaba. The only decoration in the chapel was on a false door, 1.4 × 0.77 metres, the surface of which was very crudely finished, with the inscriptions very lightly incised and roughly executed (Figure 2.25). No remains of plaster are found on any of the internal or external walls of the tomb. The only shaft of the mastaba descends through the rock to a depth of 6 metres before opening into a relatively large burial chamber, which contained a large, uninscribed and very rough limestone sarcophagus closed with a heavy lid, but completely plundered through a break in the east side.

Figure 2.23 General view of the Teti cemetery looking south. To the left is Teti's pyramid with the northern cemetery of his officials in front of it. To the right are the pyramids of Userkaf and Djoser.

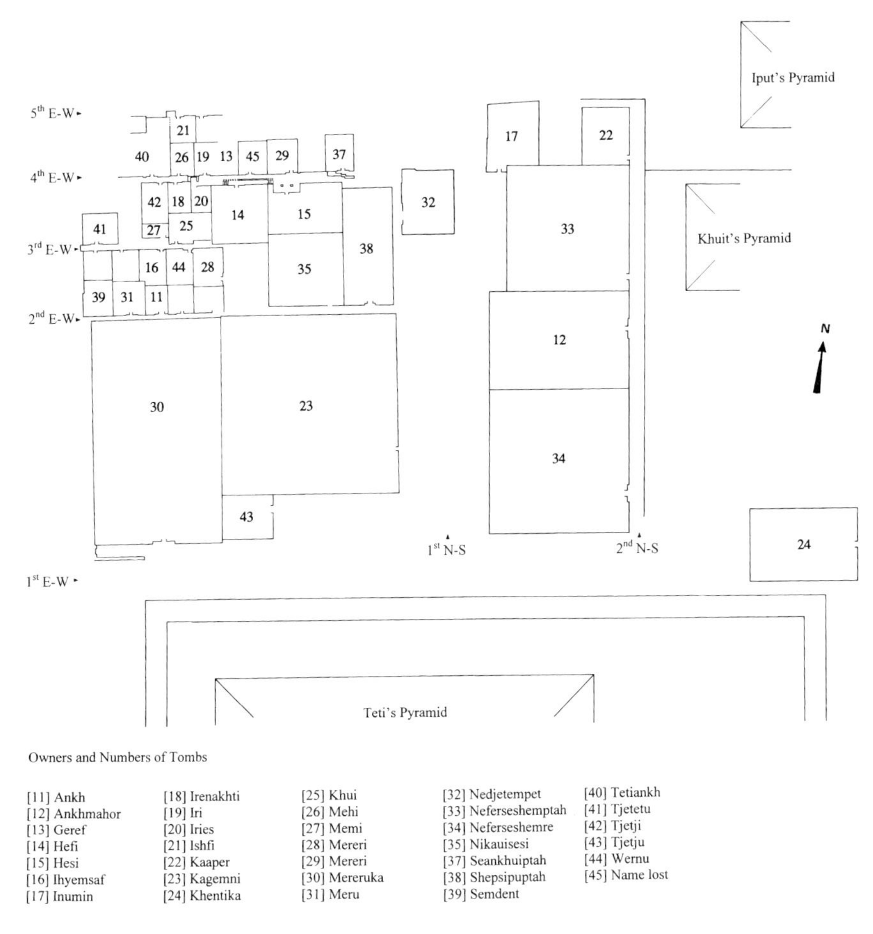

Figure 2.24 Sketch plan of the Teti cemetery showing the location of tombs in the various streets.

Date

The tomb is certainly later than those of Meru and Desi, but not necessarily much later.

Suggested date: very end of Teti, or Pepy I.

Later treatment

There is no evidence of any deliberate damage to the tomb or the inscriptions of Ankh. The state of the false door is not the result of later damage but of being hastily inscribed, the figures barely scratched on the unsmoothed

Figure 2.25 The inscriptions on the false door of Ankh were executed in incised outline, very roughly and hastily finished.

surface. This haste was perhaps also responsible for not covering all the walls with a layer of plaster. The professional work on this tomb appears to have been abandoned at an early stage of preparation, but amateurish work continued on the false door in order to provide the owner with his opportunity of an afterlife, and the fact that the sarcophagus was sealed, even though later broken into, indicates that the tomb owner was actually buried in his tomb.

Tomb of Ankhmahor [12][115]

Owner

Ankhmahor, also called Sesi, was a vizier, overseer of the scribes of the king's documents, overseer of all the works of the king in the entire land, master architect of the king, overseer of the great court, priest of Maat and overseer of all secret hearings. He was also one who is privy to the secrets of the king in his every place, one who is privy to the secrets of all secret commands of the king, overseer of the two fowl pools of recreation and guard of Teti's pyramid. He held the high rank of hereditary prince.

Tomb

This is the second tomb in the second north–south street, the so-called 'Rue de tombeaux'. It is built in the space between the tombs of Neferseshemre [34] and Neferseshemptah [33], and the external north wall of the former and south wall of the latter were used as common walls. The tomb is built of blocks of limestone, with about half its entire area occupied by a chapel formed of five rooms and two larger pillared halls, one of which has a staircase leading to the roof. The decoration in fine relief, with very little colour retained, was completed in all rooms of the chapel, except for the second pillared hall (room VII), which belonged to a son named Ishfi. The main shaft of the tomb is cut into the rock to a depth of 18.4 metres (plus the part constructed of mud-brick within the core of the mastaba to bring the mouth of the shaft to the roof level). It leads to a large burial chamber, the walls of which are lined with limestone blocks and decorated in scenes with the outlines in shallow and rather crude incisions, while the internal details are filled with colours.

Date

The suggested dates of Ankhmahor range from the middle of Teti's reign to the reign of Pepy I.[116] A study of the architectural and artistic development of the tombs in this cemetery now suggests a date in the middle of Teti's reign or shortly after.

Suggested date: mid-Teti, or shortly after.

Later additions

The second pillared hall (room VII) was either originally planned for Ankhmahor's eldest son, Ishfi,[117] or was a later addition by the son himself.[118]

This son, who is also called Tutu, held many titles related to the personal service of the king. He was overseer of the king's repasts, and possibly as such was overseer of the two fields of offering, overseer of the two fowl pools, overseer of all vegetation, overseer of the two granaries and overseer of that which heaven gives and earth produces. But Ishfi was also overseer of the galley of recreation, overseer of the two cool rooms (bathrooms?) of the palace, one who is privy to the secrets of the house of morning and one who is privy to the secrets of the king in his every place.

The decoration of the pillared hall of Ishfi was certainly abandoned at an early stage. All walls and pillars are totally uninscribed, while the decoration on the false door was left unfinished. The hieroglyphs, in incised relief, lack internal details and the lintels, panel and drum are uninscribed – even the essential offering table scene is lacking. However, there is no evidence of any deliberate damage to the door or its decoration (Figure 2.26).

Figure 2.26 A son of Ankhmahor named Ishfi/Tutu built his own chapel as an extension to that of his father. The only decorated part of this chapel was his false door, yet the inscriptions on its upper and lower lintel, as well as the essential offering table scene on the panel, were never executed.

Later treatment

Ankhmahor had a number of sons, all named Ishfi, and probably more than one of them was designated as eldest, which may indicate that Ankhmahor was married more than once.[119] Most of Ankhmahor's sons, as well as one brother, were employed by the department of the palace guards, and at least one of his sons had his image systematically chiselled out from Ankhmahor's chapel (Figures 2.27, 2.28), although the scenes depicting Ankhmahor or other members of his family and retainers were left intact. There is a possibility that the son whose figure and inscriptions were damaged is identical with Ishfi [21] who owned a tomb in the fifth east–west street. It is also possible that the disgrace of the latter resulted in the discontinuation of the decoration of the chapel of his brother/half brother, owner of room VII in Ankhmahor's tomb (Figure 2.26).

Tomb of Geref [13][120]

Owner

Geref, also called Itji, held titles connected to the service of the king, such as overseer of the two cool rooms ('bathrooms') of the palace, overseer of all the king's repasts, overseer of that which heaven gives and earth produces, overseer of the cattle estate, overseer of the two fields of offering, overseer of all vegetation, overseer of the marshlands, keeper of the head ornaments and

Figure 2.27 On the west wall of room II in Ankhmahor's chapel, the tomb owner was depicted with two sons, both named Ishfi. While the figure and inscriptions of the first son are perfectly preserved, those of the second, shown behind Ankhmahor, were chiselled out.

Figure 2.28 Two of Ankhmahor's sons were represented behind him on the east wall of room VI. The figure and inscriptions of the second son were deliberately erased.

priest of Teti's pyramid. He was also one who is privy to the secrets of the king in his every place and had the ranks of sole companion and nobleman of the king. Geref's responsibilities traditionally accompany one of the supervisory levels of the office of the palace guards, but no such title is recorded in his inscriptions.

Tomb

Geref's tomb lies in the fourth east–west street, immediately to the east of that of Iri/Tetiseneb [19]. It was constructed of mud-brick and provided with a limestone false door and entrance architrave. The outline of the mud-brick rectangular offering room, where the false door was placed, is clearly defined, but the rest of the brick work of the mastaba was ruined through the cutting of many later shafts in the area.

Date

The tomb was built in the same street as, and immediately to the east of, those of Mehi [26] and Iri [19], and Geref's architrave and false door bear many similarities to theirs. On the opposite side of the street is the tomb of

Hefi [14], presumably one of the early mastabas in the cemetery. Geref was a priest of Teti's pyramid.

Suggested date: mid to late Teti, or immediately after.

Later treatment

There is no evidence of any deliberate damage to Geref's monuments. However, while the decoration of the architrave seems to have been completed (Figure 2.29), the false door was certainly unfinished. The upper lintel is totally uninscribed, and the remainder of the door is decorated in incised relief with no internal details. The standing figures of the owner at the bottom of each jamb are for the most part left unfinished, in black paint only, and so are the lashings on the torus moulding.[121] No details exist on the cornice (Figure 2.30). The unfinished condition of the false door, which is evident on some small sections, suggests a sudden interruption of the work.

Tomb of Hefi [14][122]

Owner

Hefi, like the owner of the tomb opposite him whose name is now lost [45], was overseer of the great court, a title held by officials likely to be promoted to the vizierate.[123] He was also priest of Maat, superintendent of priests of Ptah, and judge and administrator.

Tomb

This square mastaba was originally free-standing and others, like that of Hesi [15], were built against it later. It lies in the fourth east–west street and was constructed on a naturally elevated area, formed of compacted gravel. Built

Figure 2.29 The entrance architrave of Geref was inscribed with seven horizontal lines of hieroglyphs, all finished with the necessary internal details.

Figure 2.30 The decoration on the false door of Geref shows many degrees of incompletion. Certain parts are in incised relief, others in black paint and the upper lintel is totally undecorated.

of mud-brick, the chapel consists of an entrance corridor, leading to an offering chamber with an inscribed false door, and a second very small room from which a stairway leads to the roof. The shaft descends to the depth of 8 metres in the rock, leading to a burial chamber with an uninscribed stone sarcophagus.

Date

The square shape of the mastaba and the stairway to the roof are attested in the early tombs of the Teti cemetery (Neferseshemre [34], Kagemni [23], Nikauisesi [35]). The depiction of two figures of the tomb owner facing each other in the offering table scene on the false door panel is found in Fifth Dynasty tombs, as for example those of Neferseshemre [34] and Sabu/Ibebi [47],[124] both dated to the reign of Teti. Hefi, Neferseshemre [34] and Wernu [44] provide the only examples of this feature in the Teti cemetery. The pile of loaves of bread on the offering table, reaching to Hefi's shoulders, is characteristic of the Fifth Dynasty, with rare examples under Teti and Pepy I.[125]

Figure 2.31 The decoration in Hefi's chapel is well preserved and shows no deliberate damage, which indicates that the damage was not systematic in the cemetery.

The tomb was presumably one of the earliest in the cemetery, and was certainly earlier than that of Hesi [15] which used Hefi's exterior wall as a common wall.

Suggested date: middle of Teti's reign.

Later treatment

There is no evidence of any deliberate damage to the tomb (Figure 2.31).

Tomb of Hesi – reused by Seshemnefer [15][126]

Original owner

Hesi's career may be divided into two phases, but it appears that his responsibilities during the first phase prepared him for the second. His promotion to the second phase, the vizierate, appears to have taken place late in his career as all associated titles are inscribed only on the pillars and architrave of the portico, but nowhere else in the chapel.

During the first phase Hesi held a large number of scribal and judicial titles, such as overseer of the bureau of the registry, judge and overseer of scribes, overseer of all hearings, priest of Maat, overseer of the great court, overseer of determining cases in the six great courts, and overseer of the apportionments of the god's offerings in the entire land. He also held the titles of guard of Teti's pyramid and controller of a phyle, as well as superintendent of priests of Teti's pyramid. The last title is held only by the most important officials, particularly the viziers. In the second phase he became chief justice and vizier, as well as overseer of the scribes of the king's documents and overseer of all the works of the king.

Hesi's titles and biographical inscriptions emphasize his particular closeness to the king, for he was royal chamberlain, confidant of the king, one who is privy to the secrets of the king in his every place and scribe of royal documents in the presence. He refers to the facts that His Majesty knew his name and his abilities and was discussing matters with him amongst the noblemen even early in his career. Hesi became a scribe for His Majesty ahead of the scribes, and a nobleman ahead of the noblemen. He was allowed special privileges such as access to the great boat of the palace.

Tomb

The tomb lies in the fourth east–west street. It is one of the most economically built as it is in a space available between three already existing tombs, those of Nikauisesi [35] to the south, Hefi [14] to the west and Shepsipuptah [38] to the east, and using one wall of each as a common wall, thus building only one external wall, which is his northern façade. Economy is also evident in the fact that his chapel consists only of a portico and one room, an unusual resting place for a man of his status at this time as he himself remarks by saying: 'I caused one room to be built in this tomb in order that offerings may come forth for me in it, (although) I was capable of building it of numerous rooms.' However, while there was an obvious saving in construction work, the quality of stonework in the portico and the offering room is excellent and the wall surface in both places is covered with scenes in relief of a superb quality. The artist was certainly influenced by the great tombs in the cemetery in selecting his subject matter, but at the same time he shows great originality. For example, while he probably copied the rare scene of the netting of quails during the harvest from the tomb of Mereruka [30],[127] and the mating crocodiles from that of Kagemni [23],[128] the inclusion of certain objects, such as sandals and gloves among the tomb owner's gear during his fishing and fowling trips, and the depiction of mating turtles in the water beneath his boat, is innovative.

Date

On the west thickness of the entrance to the chapel, Hesi outlines the progress of his career under Isesi, Unis and finally Teti when he became royal chamberlain. It was probably at this stage that he built the tomb, as this office was placed at the head of his other titles until he became vizier. When later promoted to vizier he was entrusted with other responsibilities which usually go with the vizierate, but he presumably did not enjoy this office for a long time, as may be deduced from the fact that his burial chamber was left undecorated. After Neferseshemre [34], all viziers of Teti and early Pepy I possessed decorated burial chambers. When Inumin [17] became vizier early under Pepy I he extended his burial chamber into the shaft area in order to gain additional space after casing the walls of the burial chamber with limestone blocks in order to decorate them. In addition, while the reliefs of Hesi's chapel are superb, there is no evidence that they were ever coloured. The last king mentioned in the tomb is Teti. This appears in Hesi's biography, in his priesthood of Teti's pyramid and in the names of his funerary estates. There can be little doubt that the tomb was constructed under Teti, but whether Hesi's short occupancy of the vizierate was under the same king or a successor is uncertain, although the absence of a priesthood of Pepy I's pyramid, as is found with Inumin, for example, is noticeable. Hesi was almost certainly earlier than Inumin, and the latter referred to Pepy I with his early name of Nefersahor.

Suggested date: end of Teti, very beginning of Pepy I.

Later treatment

The name and the figure of the tomb owner have been carefully chiselled out from the inscriptions and scenes inside and outside the chapel (Figure 2.32). This was certainly not through vandalism as only the tomb owner was targeted; all other scenes were left intact (Figures 2.33, 2.34). In a palanquin scene, for example, only Hesi's figure was removed, the palanquin itself and the men who carried it were unaffected (Figure 2.35). The damaged areas were covered with a layer of rough pinkish plaster, perhaps by the new owner of the tomb, but only in the portico and not inside the offering room, perhaps to improve the appearance of the façade or further conceal the memory of the previous owner. Nevertheless, traces of Hesi's name can be discerned in a number of places, and in one instance, above the entrance doorway inside the offering room, the name was left intact. It is uncertain whether the persons in charge of the erasure missed this spot, which is rather difficult to observe by anyone facing the in-coming light from the doorway, or whether they were sympathetic to Hesi's cause (Figure 2.36).

Figure 2.32 Hesi's name and figure were chiselled out everywhere they existed on his external false door. The rest of the inscriptions are absolutely intact.

Reuse of tomb

The tomb was reused by a man called Seshemnefer, a common name during the Fifth Dynasty and the early Sixth, who only held the two titles of sole companion and lector priest. He was content to merely replace his figure,

Figure 2.33 As in other scenes in Hesi's tomb, his figure and name were erased from a spear-fishing scene. The remaining parts of the scene executed in beautiful relief are intact.

name and titles on most parts of the false door inside the chapel where Hesi's figures and inscriptions were erased. But Seshemnefer's reliefs were visibly of far inferior quality (Figure 2.37). More importantly, he inscribed his name and titles on one side of each of the two portico pillars, an inscription which is clear to anyone entering the tomb, and here he stated that the tomb was a boon from the king (Figure 2.38). This declaration by Seshemnefer that he did not usurp the tomb and that it was given to him by the king would indicate that the punishment of Hesi and the loss of his tomb were also by the king's order. But which king? Most probably Pepy I, for whether Hesi was involved in the conspiracy against Teti or that early in Pepy I's reign (see pp. 157 ff.), he would have been punished by Pepy I.

Figure 2.34 A line drawing of Figure 2.33.

Figure 2.35 While all the personnel and equipment in the palanquin scene were left intact, the figure of Hesi seated in the palanquin has been meticulously erased.

Figure 2.36 Despite the care which the artisans showed in erasing Hesi's name, it has survived intact inside the chapel above the entrance doorway.

Figure 2.37 At the bottom of each jamb of the main false door inside the chapel, Seshemnefer added his name, titles and figure after those belonging to Hesi were removed, leaving the surface slightly deeper.

Tomb of Ihyemsaf [16][129]

Owner

The attribution of this tomb to Ihyemsaf, also called Meru, Merugem and Tetiseneb, is only tentative. The chapel originally had two false doors, the northern and larger one of which is missing. Although it is possible for the same tomb owner to have two false doors in his chapel, as in the case of Iries

Figure 2.38 On this entrance pillar Seshemnefer claims that the tomb was given to him by the king. This was probably necessary to avoid any accusation of usurpation.

[20], other chapels seem to accommodate more than one individual; that of Tjetji [42] for example contains three false doors for three different persons (see p. 128). However, Ihyemsaf had titles generally held by officials buried in this part of the cemetery and may well be the tomb owner, or a direct descendant – perhaps an eldest son. Ihyemsaf was overseer of the palace guards, overseer of the department of the palace guards, overseer of the two cool rooms of the palace, controller of clothing and royal chamberlain. He held the ranks of sole companion and nobleman of the king.

Tomb

The tomb is located in the third east–west street, immediately to the west of that of Wernu [44]. Constructed of mud-brick, the tomb has a rectangular chapel, which has two false door recesses, but only the southern, smaller false door (0.73 × 0.44 metres), made of one block of limestone, was found *in situ*. The mastaba contains two burial apartments; the main one descends to a depth of 8.5 metres in the rock and leads to a burial chamber with a burial pit cut into the rock.

Date

The location of the tomb abutting on the west wall of that of Wernu [44], and in part on the north-east corner of that of Meru [31], may suggest that the three tombs were built within a short period of each other. It is also interesting that Ihyemsaf shared two names with his neighbour Meru; these are Meru and Tetiseneb, but unlike him he was not called Pepyseneb or Meryreseneb.[130]

Suggested date: late Teti to early Pepy I if Ihyemsaf was the main owner of the tomb; Pepy I if he was the former's son.

Later treatment

The main false door of the tomb is missing, but no conclusion should be drawn from this fact. Although all the tombs excavated by Macquarie University immediately to the north of Ihyemsaf retained their false doors, that of Ihyemsaf is very close to others excavated earlier in the twentieth century by Zaki Saad,[131] whose finds were not adequately published at the time.

It is important to notice that the decoration of the south false door, that of Ihyemsaf, was certainly left unfinished. The inscriptions on the upper section and the right jambs of the door were incised, but those on both left jambs were in black paint only, which is now mostly effaced (Figure 2.39).

Tomb of Inumin [17][132]

Owner

In his chapel Inumin held a number of positions, including those of overseer of Upper Egypt, overseer of the two treasuries, overseer of the two granaries, overseer of the great court, director of every kilt and chief lector priest, and recorded the highest rank of hereditary prince. He also had a number of titles relating to the personal service of the king, such as confidant of the king in his every place, overseer of the two chambers of the king's adornment, one who is privy to the secrets of the house of morning and one who is privy to the secrets of the king in his every place. He also held the very rarely claimed responsibility of overseer of the protection of every house of the king (Figure 2.40). Presumably later in his career, and after the decoration of his chapel, he was promoted to the office of vizier, with this title now preserved only in the inscriptions inside his stone sarcophagus (Figure 2.41).

Figure 2.39 While the upper section and the right jambs of Ihyemsaf's false door are decorated in incised relief, the left jambs were abandoned after being inscribed in black paint, now hardly visible.

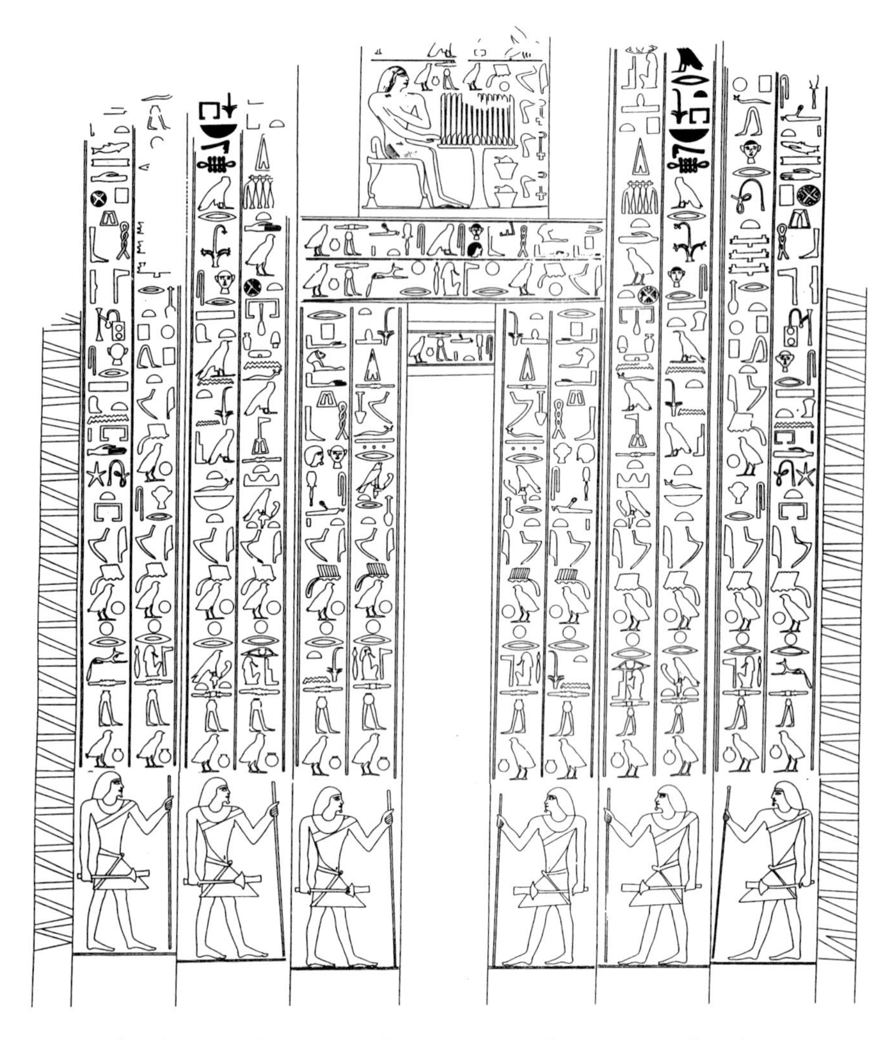

Figure 2.40 The rare title 'overseer of the protection of every house of the king' was recorded on the jambs of Inumin's false door (indicated in bold print).

Tomb

The tomb was built in an available space to the north-west of the mastaba of Neferseshemptah [33] and to the west of that of Kaaper [22]. It partly protrudes into the first north–south street where its façade is located with the entrance opening to the south, almost exactly facing the entrance of Teti's burial apartment, but at a distance. While the external walls of the mastaba were built of mud-brick, the façade and the walls of the five-roomed chapel are constructed of large blocks of limestone, and with the exception of two

Figure 2.41 The title of vizier appears only in the inscriptions inside Inumin's sarcophagus. This was probably a late promotion and does not appear in the decoration of his chapel.

rooms which provide access to the burial apartment, all surfaces were decorated in fine coloured relief (Figure 2.42). The shaft opens into the floor of an inner room and descends to a depth of 13.9 metres where it opens into a medium-size burial chamber with a stone sarcophagus, inscribed on its internal east and north sides. The burial chamber itself was cased with limestone slabs on the four walls, which resulted in reducing its size and requiring its expansion into the shaft area. Half the shaft was accordingly roofed, after the introduction of the large sarcophagus of course, and formed part of the burial chamber. This alteration probably became necessary when Inumin attained the vizierate, for no officials other than viziers had decorated burial chambers in this cemetery. Even the larger burial chamber of Nikauisesi [35], who preceded Inumin as overseer of Upper Egypt, was undecorated.

Date

The date of Inumin's tomb has to be considered in conjunction with that of Nikauisesi [35]. These two tombs, which are within a short distance of each other, have some striking similarities in their architectural design, including the placement of the shaft in an easternmost large, undecorated room inside the chapel, and the building of the west wall of this room partly above the shaft after embedding a large load-bearing stone block across the shaft with its ends wedged in the upper section of the shaft's north and south sides. Inumin almost certainly constructed his tomb together with, or immediately

Figure 2.42 Scenes in Inumin's chapel were executed in coloured relief. Here the tomb owner and his son, Khui, are shown watching a rare and very aggressive desert hunt scene.

after, that of Nikauisesi, and he most probably succeeded him as overseer of Upper Egypt. As Nikauisesi was buried in the eleventh year/count of Teti[133] (that is, presumably towards its end), we may assume that Inumin also built his tomb around that time. On the other hand, the title he records of superintendent of priests of Pepy I's pyramid clearly indicates that he served under this king. In fact a partly preserved inscription inside his chapel shows that a cartouche of Nefersahor, a name which Pepy I used very early in his reign, was chiselled out and replaced in red paint only by the later name of Pepy I, Meryre (Figure 3.1).

Suggested date: end of Teti and early Pepy I.

Later treatment

There is no evidence at all of any deliberate damage to Inumin's tomb and inscriptions. However, the decoration of the façade, probably the last area to be executed after his last promotion to the vizierate, was left partly unfinished (Figure 2.43).

Figure 2.43 The decoration on the façade of Inumin's tomb was left unfinished. The details of the wig, bracelets and anklets of the tomb owner on the left of the entrance were crudely done, while the figure to the right of the doorway is well finished but lacks any identification.

Tomb of Irenakhti [18][134]

Owner

Irenakhti, also called Iri, held only four titles: overseer of the department of the palace guards, superintendent of the palace guards, guard of Teti's pyramid and priest of Teti's pyramid. No honorific titles are recorded on his completely preserved false door.

Tomb

The tomb lies in the fourth east–west street, immediately to the west of that of Iries [20] and opposite that of Mehi [26]. It is constructed of mud-brick and has a corridor chapel. The west wall is cased with decorated limestone and includes two false doors, one of which (1.5 × 6.0 metres) is inscribed, while the other (1.11 × 0.39 metres) is blank. The mastaba contains three shafts; the main one descends through rock to a depth of 7.85 metres and leads to a small burial chamber with a burial pit cut into its floor. The pit has a stone lid, found in place but broken at its south-west corner. Although no human remains existed, the position of the lid suggests that the burial took place.

Date

Irenakhti built his mastaba against the north wall of that of Khui [25], and later Iries [20] built his against Irenakhti's east wall. While Irenakhti falls between Khui and Iries, the three officials need not have been separated by a long span of time. The fact that Khui inscribed on his entrance doorway a priesthood of Pepy I should not automatically indicate that he constructed his tomb under this king. Khui's career could be divided into two stages, only the last of which was certainly under Pepy I (see under the Tomb of Khui, pp. 90–93). The style of art and the type of false door suggest a relatively early date.

Suggested date: mid to late Teti, or immediately after.

Later treatment

While the name of Irenakhti/Iri was left almost intact everywhere it was recorded on his false door, his figure, particularly his face, was attacked in six of the seven times he is depicted on the same monument. Some of Irenakhti's figures suffered more than others, but the greatest damage was inflicted on his image on the false door panel, where he is shown in the especially important scene at the offering table (Figure 2.44). The second false door in this chapel, like that of Tjetetu's [41], is totally uninscribed. By

Figure 2.44 The false door of Irenakhti showing the damage inflicted on the owner's many figures. While damage appears on many parts of his body, that on the face is the most consistent.

comparison with the neighbouring tomb of Iries [20], this false door was presumably intended for Irenakhti's wife, and the lack of any inscriptions on it might suggest that work on the tomb came to an abrupt end.

Apart from the two false doors, the rest of the west wall was cased with limestone blocks and decorated in relief, the condition of which is very intriguing. The lower section of the wall between the main false door and the chapel entrance depicts two rows of offering bearers, the men in the upper row of which are preserved up to the waist only. However, this is not through later quarrying away of the upper part of the wall, which is not uncommon in any cemetery. In fact the course of stone above these figures does exist, but has a rough, undecorated surface and projects between 1 and 2 centimetres from the face of the decorated stone beneath it (Figure 2.45). It would, of course, be illogical for the artist to so completely finish the sculpting of the offering bearers, and the items they carry, up to the waist, before the upper part of the wall was smoothed and prepared for relief. Two explanations of this anomaly come to mind. The first is that the decorated stones are reused from an earlier tomb. However, the fact that the two registers of offering bearers and the accompanying inscriptions clearly represent a complete scene, not parts thereof, with the frieze framing the scene on both

Figure 2.45 The damage to the upper part of the offering bearers scene on the west wall was repaired with new blocks of stone, which have never been dressed or decorated.

sides present and the relief visible even on the remaining parts of the plaster joining the stones, renders this option impossible. The second, almost inescapable explanation is that the scene suffered damage and was restored in antiquity by recasing the damaged part, but work on smoothing and redecorating the new pieces was never achieved. This is not dissimilar to what occurred in the adjacent tomb of Iries [20], where the damaged section on the right thickness of the doorway was also repaired with stone but left undecorated.

A block of stone in the lower section of the southern end of the west wall shows the lower part of a standing male figure, wearing sandals and a short, pointed kilt, who is most probably the tomb owner himself. The wall above this has been filled with very thick mud plaster to compensate for the thickness of the original stone casing, probably during the restoration. The choice between the two different methods of restoration – (a) providing new stone blocks, possibly with the intention of reproducing the original scene, and b) minimizing the damaged appearance by replacing the spoiled casing stones with thick mud plaster covered with a whitewash – presumably depended on the importance of the original scene and the necessity to replace it. A comparison with the decoration of the neighbouring tomb of Iries[135] and others in the cemetery shows that above such rows of offering bearers is usually a representation of the tomb owner seated at an offering table and receiving the gifts they bring. The offering table scene on the panel of Irenakhti's false door was also especially targeted for damage.

Tomb of Iri [19][136]

Owner

Iri, also called Tetiseneb, was overseer of the department of the palace guards, superintendent of the palace guards and guard of Teti's pyramid. But he also was controller of clothing, overseer of the noble places of the palace, overseer of the department of the palace and scribe of royal documents of the palace, and held the relatively modest ranks of nobleman of the king and companion of the house.

Tomb

The tomb is adjacent to that of Mehi [26] in the fourth east–west street, and is constructed of mud-brick. The chapel consists of two small rooms and was provided with a limestone entrance architrave and lintel, plus a false door. The architrave is formed of two blocks totalling 2.38 × 0.52 metres, which bear six lines of text and a representation of Iri and his family. The lintel measures 0.51 × 0.12 metres and the false door 1.45 × 0.69 metres, with the cornice now missing. The main shaft was not excavated.

Date

The name Tetiseneb, the priesthood of Teti's pyramid and the location of the tomb adjacent to that of Mehi [26] and amongst a group of tombs (e.g., that of Hesi [15] and Mereri (Merynebty) [29]), which may be securely dated to the reign of Teti, leaves little doubt that Iri's tomb was also built during this reign, although he might have continued to live under Teti's successors.

Suggested date: late Teti, or shortly after.

Later treatment

The name Tetiseneb was originally written on the entrance lintel, but was later replaced by the phrase 'the honoured one before the great god, Iri' (Figure 2.46). Similarly, the name on the false door has been systematically changed to Iri. Where this occurred the surface is visibly lower than that of the original inscriptions (Figure 2.47). If the architrave did not contain both names, Iri and Tetiseneb, one would have thought that Iri usurped these objects from someone named Tetiseneb. But the architrave clearly demonstrates that Iri was the 'beautiful name' of Tetiseneb and that the two names were for one and the same person (Figure 2.48). The change of name from Tetiseneb to Iri, which no doubt partly spoiled the appearance of both lintel and false door, is therefore unusual and could not simply be explained as a whim of the tomb owner. The insistence on such a change despite the damage it produced may suggest that the owner was trying to hide the name Tetiseneb, or perhaps the cartouche of Teti in particular. This interpretation becomes all the more likely when studied in conjunction with the case of Iri's immediate neighbour, Mehi [26], whose repeated attempt to erase and change the name in a cartouche written on his architrave ultimately required the cutting out of a small piece of stone containing the cartouche and replacing it with a separate piece (see under the Tomb of Mehi, pp. 93–95).

It is curious that the name Tetiseneb has survived once on the architrave, although possibly the same name was chiselled out from the same line in

Figure 2.46 Despite the removal of the name Tetiseneb to replace it by Iri on the entrance lintel, the cartouche of Teti is easily detected.

Figure 2.47 The name Iri is now written seven times on the false door. With the exception of the drum, which was inscribed in the first place with this name, all other six instances clearly replaced an earlier name, most probably Tetiseneb.

Figure 2.48 This architrave proves that the names Tetiseneb and Iri belong to the same person, the latter being his 'beautiful name'. While the name Tetiseneb has survived intact once on the architrave, it is clear that it has been replaced by that of Iri a number of times on the same monument.

the text. That the owner's name may be written more than once in the same line, each time following a title or an epithet, is well attested on other architraves from contemporary tombs in the same street; for example, those of Hesi [15][137] and Mereri (Merynebty) [29],[138] and more importantly that of his immediate neighbour, Mehi [26]. The survival of this single instance on the architrave is difficult to explain; it seems unlikely that it represents an oversight caused by the presence of Teti's cartouche on two other occasions on the same monument in Iri's titles relating to Teti's pyramid. It is possible, however, that Iri wanted drastically to reduce the emphasis on Teti in his name, but deliberately left the two names Tetiseneb and Iri once in this place as a proof that the stonework in his tomb belonged to him and that the erasure of the name was not the result of usurpation. Alternatively, he might not have had the time in the short reign of Userkare to finish off a job which he started and which became unnecessary or undesirable with the accession of Pepy I! It should be noted that the work in this tomb was left unfinished, with the surface of the false door unsmoothed and the internal details of the hieroglyphic signs unachieved.

Tomb of Iries [20][139]

Owner

Iries, also called Iy, held a limited number of titles. He was judge, keeper of the books, priest of Maat, confidant of the king in his every place and one who is privy to the secrets of the king in his every place, and held the ranks of sole companion and nobleman of the king. He appears to have been married three times, as three sons are described as 'eldest son' in his chapel;[140] but only one wife, Qedi, is represented, with two daughters and two sons, presumably hers, carrying offerings to her.

Tomb

The tomb lies in the fourth east–west street, between the tombs of Irenakhti [18] and Hefi [14], and opposite that of Mehi [26] and Iri/Tetiseneb [19]. It is constructed of mud-brick and has a corridor chapel with its entrance and west wall fully cased with decorated stone, which includes three false doors, two for Iries and one for his wife, Qedi. The tomb contains three shafts. The main one, that of Iries, descends in the rock to a depth of 13.7 metres and leads to a burial chamber with a large but undecorated stone sarcophagus. Later an 'antechamber' was built in front of the main entrance to the chapel, blocking the street and resulting in entry to the tomb being through the antechamber. Like Iries' chapel, the west wall of the antechamber was cased with stone, which includes a false door belonging to a man named Tetiankh.

Date

The mastaba of Iries is built against those of Irenakhti [18] and Khui [25], but neither of these must, by necessity, have been constructed after the reign of Teti. It is true that Khui is shown on the façade of his tomb holding a priesthood of Pepy I's pyramid, but this priesthood, as well as other high offices, does not appear in the inscriptions of the chapel and may well represent a promotion received under Pepy I (see under Khui). The style of art and the relative richness of the tomb for the position of Iries does not indicate a date after the reign of Teti.

Suggested date: mid to late Teti, or immediately after.

Later treatment

The real eldest son, the first in the row of offering bearers carrying food to Iries, has had his name carefully erased, but the outline of a cartouche is discernible (Figure 2.49). No deliberate damage at all was inflicted on the son's figure nor on any other individual depicted in Iries' chapel. However, it is important to note that a limited area on the right thickness of the entrance to Iries' chapel shows clear evidence of deliberate damage, which was apparently stopped and even repaired with undecorated stone and pinkish plaster in antiquity (Figure 2.50). It is also likely that whoever caused the damage removed the door lintel and threw it in the tomb's main shaft. The lintel was found broken into a number of pieces at the shaft's floor level near the entrance to the burial chamber, suggesting that it was dumped there when the shaft was still empty. This case resembles that of Ishfi, where both the lintel and the false door were thrown down the shaft. Iries was, however, buried in his tomb; his stone sarcophagus was closed, but later violated, and his skeletal remains are preserved.[141]

Tetiankh, owner of the 'antechamber' in front of Iries' chapel, is puzzling. It is true that the construction of this 'antechamber' blocked the east–west street, but it certainly did not block the entrance to Iries' chapel. It seems unlikely that a total stranger would build his chapel like a vestibule to another, especially since by moving its position slightly to the west he could have avoided Iries' entrance and built an independent monument. Furthermore, no shaft is associated with this individual, and it seems reasonable to think that the three shafts in this mastaba belonged to Iries, his wife Qedi and perhaps Tetiankh; these are the three owners of false doors in the tomb.

Tetiankh's action may well suggest a kind of close kinship, perhaps a father–son relationship, although this remains speculative. This case could be similar to many others in the cemetery, for example those of Mereruka [30], Ankhmahor [12] and Neferseshemptah [33], where the eldest son added his chapel within the perimeter of his father's mastaba and communicating with his chapel. The difference in Tetiankh's case is that no space was available within his father's mastaba, so he had to block the street. Tetiankh held

Figure 2.49 The first of two sons described as 'eldest son', depicted in a row of offering bearers in the tomb of Iries, has had his name chiselled out. Traces suggest that the name contained a cartouche, but the name of the king inside the cartouche is unclear.

the offices of overseer of the department of the guards and guard of Teti's pyramid, and the ranks of nobleman of the king and companion of the house. There is nothing in Tetiankh's decoration which indicates incontrovertibly a date much later than that of Iries himself, and the rather mediocre style of art in his 'antechamber' is indicative of means rather than a date. In this respect if Tetiankh's eldest son, Idy, is the same as the similarly named man shown with a censer in the adjacent tomb of Khui [25],[142] a date after the first half of Pepy I's reign should be excluded for Tetiankh.

It is curious that while the relief on Tetiankh's false door was completed, the decoration of the remaining part of the west wall of his 'antechamber' was left in black outline. Only the lower part of the scene, which includes

Figure 2.50 Evidence of damage and repair in antiquity to the right entrance thickness of Iries' chapel.

Figure 2.51 A small part of the decoration on the west wall of Tetiankh's chapel was executed in rough relief, with the remainder of the scenes and inscriptions abandoned and in black outline only.

Tetiankh's name, the son's figure and a very few hieroglyphs, is executed in rough, incised relief (Figure 2.51). There is no deliberate damage to Tetiankh's own inscriptions or figures, but if he is the eldest son of Iries, whose name, but not figure, was erased from the latter's chapel, the erasure of the name in this case would indicate disassociation rather than punishment.

Tomb of Ishfi [21][143]

Owner

Ishfi, also called Ishfu, held the professional titles of overseer of the department of palace guards, superintendent of the palace guards and one who is privy to the secrets, but had the honorific titles of hereditary prince, count, sole companion and nobleman of the king. Considering Ishfi's relatively modest responsibilities, it is astonishing that he held the rank of hereditary prince, not held by any of his equals. Even Weni, the most trusted official of Pepy I, did not reach the rank of count until he became overseer of Upper Egypt under Merenre,[144] and it is uncertain if he ever reached the rank of hereditary prince even though he became a vizier at the end of his career.[145] Neither should we think that Ishfi was claiming a rank which he did not enjoy, for, if so, he could have claimed other more prestigious functional positions, or at least the highest responsibility within his department – that is, overseer of the palace guards rather than the slightly lower overseer of the department of the palace guards.

The name Ishfi is attested elsewhere only in the tomb of Ankhmahor [12][146] in the same cemetery. Ankhmahor had a number of sons, all apparently named Ishfi,[147] at least one of whom had his figure and inscriptions systematically erased from his father's tomb. It should also be noted that members of Ankhmahor's family, including his sons, were in the palace service as guards. One is therefore justified in seeing a link between Ishfi the owner of the erased figure in Ankhmahor's chapel and the owner of the tomb in the same cemetery where the name and figure were also chiselled out from the decoration of the false door. In this case the unexpected rank of hereditary prince could be explained as a special honour which he received, perhaps from his mother. Neferseshemptah, son of Neferseshemptah [33] the owner of the adjacent tomb to that of Ankhmahor [12], also reached the rank of hereditary prince, although his responsibilities did not justify it, and his father did not hold it. Yet his mother, Seshseshet, was a king's daughter, possibly of Teti.[148] It is true that no figure of a wife survives in Ankhmahor's chapel, but this may be due to the chance of preservation, or to the wife's death and burial elsewhere before Ankhmahor's tomb was built or decorated. It remains possible that Ankhmahor, like his neighbours, also viziers, Kagemni [23] and Mereruka [30], was also married to a princess. However, despite his superior rank, the tomb of Ishfi does not reflect greater means than those available to his equals in the profession at the time.

Tomb

Constructed of mud-brick in the fifth east–west street, the tomb of Ishfi was provided with two elements in stone, an entrance lintel and a false door, both inscribed in fine relief. The main shaft has a total depth of 9.7 metres and leads to a small burial chamber which, rather than having a limestone sarcophagus, has a burial pit cut into its floor and provided with a stone lid.

Date

The tomb of Ishfi abuts on the tombs of Mehi [26] and Tetiankh and Hesy [40] in the fourth east–west street and uses parts of their walls as common walls. Ishfi must therefore have been later than the other two, but not necessarily much later. Mehi is dated to the transitional period Teti–Pepy I,[149] and his neighbour Hesy to early Pepy I.[150]

Suggested date: early to mid-Pepy I.

Later treatzment

The false door and the entrance lintel of Ishfi were found in the burial chamber of the main shaft. Although broken into five pieces, all parts of the false door were present, which suggests that it was thrown down into the shaft when this was still empty, and perhaps even pushed inside the burial chamber. The lifting up of such a large (1.55 metres high × 0.96 metres wide) and heavy object from the chapel floor to the roof of the mastaba, where the mouth of the shaft opens, must have required effort and determination. The name and figure of the owner have been chiselled out wherever they existed on the false door, although parts of the name may still be seen (Figure 2.52). On the other hand the entrance lintel, where his other name, Ishfu, is recorded, was left intact. This brings to mind the cases of the vizier Hesi [15] and the chief physician Seankhuiptah [37], who also had their names left intact at least once in their tombs. Was this accidental or deliberate?

Tomb of Kaaper [22][151]

Owner

Kaaper's career may be traced in two stages, with marked advancement in both his honorific and functional titles. Nowhere in his offering room or on his sarcophagus are inscribed the ranks of hereditary prince and count, or the particularly important administrative offices of overseer of the scribes of the king's documents and overseer of all the works of the king. These titles, which usually accompany the office of vizier, do, however, appear on the entrance inscriptions which are far superior in quality to the rest of the decoration. This presumably represents a late promotion, perhaps even to the vizierate, although this title is not found in the surviving inscriptions. However, it should be borne in mind that the entrance lintel is missing and the inscriptions on the south entrance jamb are completely damaged.

Tomb

The tomb of Kaaper is the fourth, and possibly last, in the second north–south street, known as the 'rue de tombeaux'. It is formed of seven rooms constructed of mud-brick with the entrance to the chapel and the west wall of the offering room built with large blocks of limestone and decorated in relief, but showing no colour. The main shaft descends through the native rock to a depth of 14 metres, above which retaining walls of mud-brick

Figure 2.52 Broken into separate pieces all of which were found in the shaft, a false door of Ishfi shows a deliberate effort to remove his name and figure wherever they existed.

brought the mouth of the shaft to the roof level. The burial chamber is undecorated, but contained a large stone sarcophagus inscribed for Kaaper.

Date

The date of Kaaper has recently been discussed by the present writer,[152] where a comparison was made with the tomb of Idu at Giza (G7102). It was also noticed that, like other officials who lived in the transitional period between Teti–Userkare–Pepy I, Kaaper did not record any title related to a king's pyramid.

Suggested date: end of Teti–early Pepy I.

Later treatment

The decoration on the south jamb of the tomb entrance has suffered deliberate damage. But unlike other tombs in the cemetery where the figures and names of the tomb owners, or others depicted in their tombs, were chiselled out very carefully and without affecting the background of the scene, here the whole surface, not only the name and figure, was roughly chiselled out in the upper part, but was suddenly interrupted and was not continued on the other jamb or inside the offering room (Figure 2.53). The significance of this is not clear; does it represent a lighter punishment, or a change of verdict? It is also noteworthy that no attempt was made at repairing the damage. On the other hand Kaaper was certainly buried in his tomb, for although his sarcophagus was broken into and no human remains were found, the lid was placed over the chest and sealed with plaster, indicating that the burial took place.

Tomb of Kagemni [23][153]

Owner

A chief justice and vizier, Kagemni held many other titles associated with the office, such as overseer of the scribes of the king's documents, overseer of all the works of the king, overseer of the six great courts, overseer of all hearings,

Figure 2.53 After the decoration of the two entrance jambs of Kaaper in beautiful relief, the scenes and inscriptions on the left jamb were chiselled out. For some reason, though, the damage was interrupted before it was completed.

over-seer of the two bureaux of the registry, overseer of the two houses of gold, overseer of the two treasuries, overseer of Upper Egypt, overseer of commissions in the entire land and overseer of the entire land of Upper and Lower Egypt. He had many important religious duties, including that of the high priest of Re and the stolist of Min. Some of Kagemni's responsibilities were in the service of the king, including overseer of the two chambers of the king's adornment, director of the mansions of the White and Red Crowns, keeper of the head ornaments, overseer of all commands of the king and confidant of the king, foremost of his two banks (river banks). Kagemni was married to a king's daughter, possibly of Teti, and held the rank of hereditary prince.

Tomb

This is the largest mastaba in the Teti cemetery, measuring 32 x 32 metres and therefore square. Entirely constructed of limestone, the mastaba has a chapel which occupies almost one-third of its total area. This is formed of six rooms, a pillared hall, a series of five magazines, two chambers to contain boats, a serdab and stairway to the roof. The walls of the chapel rooms are decorated in very fine relief. The shaft is accessible from the roof and descends to a total depth of 24 metres, 21 of which are excavated into the rock. It leads to a large burial chamber, the walls of which were lined with limestone and decorated. The chamber contained an inscribed stone sarcophagus, into which was placed an inscribed wooden coffin.

Date

Kagemni's biographical inscription states that he began his career under Djedkare, then served under Unis and continued under Teti, when he was promoted to the vizierate.[154] The mastaba is believed to have been constructed early in Teti's reign,[155] and this is consistent with its location close to the pyramid, with its entrance in the preferred eastern façade, and its square plan and its stairway leading to a shaft accessible from the roof.

Suggested date: early Teti.

Later treatment

There is no evidence of any deliberate damage to the figures or the inscriptions of Kagemni himself. However, a number of his offering bearers had their figures and labels completely chiselled out (Figure 2.54). The fact that these individuals are mostly depicted at the head of the rows of offering bearers may suggest some kind of relationship to the tomb owner, or at least emphasize their hierarchical importance. Such front positions are frequently reserved for sons and family members of the tomb owner. Although there is definite evidence of erasure in Kagemni's tomb, no final conclusions can be drawn from it until its full publication.[156]

Figure 2.54 While there is nothing in the tomb of Kagemni to suggest that his figures and inscriptions have been attacked, those of a number of individuals depicted in his tomb have been deliberately chiselled out.

Tomb of Khentika [24][157]

Owner

Khentika, also called Ikhekhi, was chief justice and vizier and held a long list of titles including overseer of all the works of the king, overseer of the two granaries, overseer of the two districts of the palace, chief lector priest, director of every kilt and overseer of the guards. He held the important priestly titles of superintendent of the pyramids of both Teti and Pepy I, and the ranks of hereditary prince, count and sole companion.

Tomb

The tomb is situated to the north-east of the temenos wall of Teti's pyramid, and is fully constructed of limestone blocks. The chapel, formed of twelve rooms, and a serdab occupied the whole area of the mastaba. Eight of the rooms were decorated in fine relief. The main shaft opens into the floor of one of the rooms and descends to a depth of 17.54 metres, leading to a large burial chamber lined with limestone blocks and decorated. It contained an inscribed stone sarcophagus.

Date

Khentika is one of the well-dated individuals. He started his vizierate, built and decorated his chapel under Teti, but continued his career under Pepy I. Inside his chapel Khentika inscribed a priesthood of Teti's pyramid, and only on the façade, presumably the last to be decorated in such large tombs, does he mention a priesthood of Pepy I's pyramid. Also, a son of Khentika seems to have changed his name from Tetidjedi to Pepydjedi, probably on the accession of Pepy I.

Suggested date: late Teti–early Pepy I.

Later treatment

Khentika is an interesting case because he almost certainly served in the top position of vizier at the end of Teti's reign and continued to hold the office early under Pepy I. This means that he lived under Userkare, who is not mentioned in Khentika's tomb or in any other tomb in the cemetery, but we are not informed of his role in the administration or in the events under this king.

Khentika's false door is found in room VII. Two more false doors are found in room III, both also inscribed for Khentika/Ikhekhi. By examining the titles on these two false doors, James rightly noted that there are many titles there which are attributed to Khentika elsewhere in the main mastaba. He also noticed that the title 'overseer of linen/clothes', which is recorded on these false doors, appears also in a subsidiary burial chamber in the mastaba, which belongs to a man also named Khentika. James correctly suggested that there are two individuals with the name Khentika, but did not suggest any probable relationship between the two men.

That we are dealing with two separate individuals is almost certain. Not only are their titles different in many ways (see below), but also no official in this cemetery, or elsewhere, provided his chapel with three false doors for the same individual. Furthermore, the so-called subsidiary shaft in room III is directly in front of these two false doors and leads to a burial chamber lined with stone blocks and decorated, with the name Khentika recorded as its owner.[158] The owner of the two false doors was directly involved in the service of the king, for he was inspector of the robing room, one who is privy to the secrets of the house of morning, superintendent of the king's house, overseer of linen/clothes, director of the two thrones, and held priesthoods in the pyramids of both Teti and Pepy I, but only the rank of count.

To establish the relationship between the owner of room III and the main tomb owner we have to bear in mind that the use of a part of someone else's tomb must have been restricted to close family members. In this cemetery, all the cases are of a son using part of his father's mastaba or chapel, as for example in the case of Meryteti son of Mereruka [30], Neferseshemptah son of Neferseshemptah [33], Ishfi son of Ankhmahor [12] and possibly Tetiankh son of Iries [20]. That Khentika/Ikhekhi of room III was also the son of the vizier of this name may be implied from the depiction of a man named Ikhekhi, bearing the titles sole companion and lector priest, in a relatively large size opposite the seated figure of the tomb owner in his chapel.[159] James has already noted that it is unusual to find someone bearing someone else's 'beautiful name' in the latter's tomb.[160] However, two other such cases do exist in the Teti cemetery and both belong to sons of tomb owners. These are Mereruka's son, Meryteti [30], who like his father bears the 'beautiful name' Meri,[161] and Neferseshemptah's, who carried both his father's name and the 'beautiful name' Sheshi [33].

There is no evidence of deliberate damage to the figures or inscriptions of the vizier Khentika or to those of his similarly named son. However, in the vizier's offering room, the figures of the first and fourth offering bearers, carrying the forelegs of animals towards his seated figure at an offering table, appear to have been erased (Figure 2.55).[162] The identity of these men is impossible to establish at present, but the first position in the offering bearers' row is usually reserved for a son. The scenes in Khentika's chapel are by no means complete, and the fact that the identity of the erased figures is unknown should not exclude the possibility that one of them was the tomb owner's son. But if this is correct, then this son is different from the Khentika/Ikhekhi who owned a room in his father's chapel and whose false doors are undamaged. This might be a similar case to that of Ankhmahor's children.

Tomb of Khui [25][163]

Owner

Khui's career can be divided into two stages. The first stage is attested inside his chapel on the false door and the thicknesses of the entrance doorway, probably the first to be decorated,[164] where he is described as lector priest, elder of the robing room, one who is privy to the secrets of the house of morning, one who is privy to secret commissions, with the rank of sole companion. In the second stage, which is recorded only on the façade of his tomb, he became overseer of all secret hearings and one who is privy to all secret commands,

Figure 2.55 In a very long row of offering bearers represented in Khentika's chapel, the figures of the first and fourth men have been chiselled out. Their advanced positions in the row suggest their importance or their relationship to the tomb owner.

but more importantly he also became overseer of Upper Egypt. Khui was, in addition, guard of Teti's pyramid and priest of that of Pepy I.

The eldest son of Inumin [17], who is buried in the near vicinity, was called Khui and held the title overseer of the department of the palace guards, a title also held by Khui's own son, shown in his tomb. Since Inumin became overseer of Upper Egypt, possibly at the end of Teti's reign following the death of Nikauisesi [35], and was made vizier early under Pepy I,[165] it seems likely that Khui, owner of this tomb, was the son of Inumin and that he succeeded his father when the latter attained the vizierate. One may even surmise that this Khui was the same as the similarly named official whose two daughters married Pepy I and who was also sent with his wife Nebet to govern Upper Egypt from Abydos where they were buried (see discussion under 'Later treatment').

Tomb

The tomb is situated in the third east–west street, opposite that of Wernu [44]. It is constructed of mud-brick, has a chapel formed of two very small rooms, and was provided with a stone false door (1.58 × 0.88 metres) and stone casing for the façade and entrance doorway. All stone elements received decoration in relief; that on the entrance area is fine but the craftsmanship on the false door is mediocre. The mastaba has one shaft which descends to a depth of 7.6 metres in the rock, leading to a relatively small burial chamber with no stone sarcophagus provided nor a burial pit cut into its floor. This rather inadequate burial apartment was presumably prepared during Khui's early modest career.

Date

Khui held offices in the pyramids of both Teti and Pepy I. There is nothing in the location of his tomb or in his inscriptions which points to a date beyond the reigns of these two kings. Furthermore, if he was the son of Inumin, as seems likely, and constructed his tomb before succeeding his father as overseer of Upper Egypt, presumably early under Pepy I, the building of his tomb would have taken place late under Teti, while the stone carving and decoration of the façade would have been under Pepy I when Khui became overseer of Upper Egypt.

Suggested date: end of Teti–early Pepy I.

Later treatment

There is no evidence whatsoever of deliberate damage to Khui's tomb. This is of great significance as it shows that those who were on Teti–Pepy I's side (as evident in Khui's promotion by Pepy I) escaped any kind of destruction to their tombs. On the other hand, it is impossible to judge whether Khui was buried in this tomb or at Abydos, assuming that he was one and the same person as Khui of Abydos. If there had been a stone sarcophagus or a burial pit with a lid we would have been able to judge whether a burial took place, even if it were later violated, but as burials could also take place directly on the floor of the burial chamber we cannot be sure. Nevertheless, the burial apartment is so unusually miserable for a man who became the overseer of Upper Egypt that one wonders if it was ever used.

Tomb of Mehi [26][166]

Owner

The only professional titles held by Mehi, also called Mehnes, are in the guards department. He was overseer of the guards, overseer of the department of the palace guards and superintendent of the guards, and had the honorific titles of sole companion and king's nobleman of the palace.

Tomb

Constructed of mud-brick in the fourth east–west street, the tomb of Mehi has a chapel formed of one room. The entrance was provided with a fine limestone architrave, which when complete could have been over three metres in length, with seven lines of text containing traditional offering formulae and repeating the fact that he was honoured by the king. The chapel contains two false doors, a large one (1.6 × 0.68 metres) for Mehi and a small one (0.65 × 0.50 metres) for a female relative named Khenti. Some of the details of the inscriptions on Mehi's false door were left unfinished and the decoration of the torus moulding barely begun. The upper part of the shaft built of mud-brick is partly damaged, but the shaft descends through the rock to a depth of 7.65 metres, where it opens into a relatively small burial chamber, with a burial pit cut into its floor and a stone lid. The cutting of the burial pit is unfinished, with all four sides incomplete and uneven. This, together with the fact that the cleanly cut lid (2.6 × 1.15 × 0.30 metres) was found to the east of the burial pit, resting exactly on two long, narrow blocks of stone laid parallel to each other (each 2 × 0.30 × 0.20 metres) as if waiting to be moved into place, as well as the complete absence of human remains, suggests that the burial chamber may never have been used.

Date

Mehi refers to himself as being honoured in front of Teti, and it may be safely assumed that the tomb was mainly constructed under this king, although Mehi may have lived beyond this reign. Evidence from the neighbouring tombs supports such a date, for Mehi's tomb is in the same east–west street where the tombs of Hefi [14], Hesi [15], Mereri [29] and Seankhuiptah [37] are located.

Suggested date: late Teti, or shortly after.

Later treatment

The architrave of Mehi presents us with a very curious case. Its seven lines of inscription are executed in fine incised relief with no apparent errors or corrections. However, a small piece of stone, cut exactly to replace the top right corner of the central block (the architrave was presumably formed of, or broke into, three blocks), contains nothing except the cartouche of Teti. This piece is thinner and of poorer quality stone than the main block. Furthermore, slight differences in the shape of signs and the absence of internal details suggest that the name of Teti was executed by a different hand (Figure 2.56). In such a fine and otherwise error-free text, it seems hardly plausible that the only error originally made coincided with the only instance of the name of the reigning king attested, not only on the architrave but in the tomb in general. Also, a correction, if needed, could have simply been made after covering the original error with plaster, instead of spoiling the appearance of the architrave by cutting and replacing a part of it. In all probability the name of Teti has replaced that of another king whom Mehi also served, and space may well admit the name of any of Teti's immediate predecessors or successors. Unis appears as a remote possibility, given the location of the tomb in the Teti cemetery and the absence of such references to Unis in this cemetery. Moreover, the fact that Unis was held in special reverence after his reign[167] makes it improbable that his name would be removed with such insistence from the tomb of an official who once served him. That the original name was that of Pepy I may also be confidently excluded, since it would make no sense for an official to inscribe the name of the reigning monarch and then to replace it with that of his father. The conclusion is therefore compelling that the name Teti replaced that of Userkare, which Mehi hastened to remove, thereby declaring his loyalty to

Figure 2.56 The small piece of stone containing the cartouche of Teti is certainly a later alteration to the entrance architrave of Mehi. The stone is thinner than the original block and the handwriting is slightly different from that in the main text.

Teti, most probably after the accession of Teti's son, Pepy I. This action of Mehi is in agreement with the curious fact that the tombs of officials who served under both Teti and Pepy I, such as Khentika [24][168] and Inumin [17],[169] are completely silent about Userkare, who is not mentioned even in biographies of officials who most certainly also served under him.[170] But whether the name of Userkare was the original name on the architrave is also doubtful, for evidence from all neighbouring tombs suggests that they were built and decorated during Teti's reign. In fact it is unlikely that officials of Userkare continued to construct their tombs in the Teti cemetery among all the officials who served Teti. It seems therefore more plausible that Mehi changed his allegiance more than once. Teti was probably written in the original text, then was erased and replaced by Userkare, which was once more replaced by Teti. It was probably the last change that necessitated the use of a separate piece of stone on which the cartouche was written.

To what extent Mehi's actions were successful is uncertain. It is true that there is no evidence of any deliberate damage to his tomb inscriptions, but on the other hand he was unable to complete the decoration of his false door and it is questionable whether he was actually buried in his burial chamber.

Tomb of Memi [27][171]

Owner

Memi was a chief lector priest, elder of the robing room and one who is privy to the secret of the god's word. He had the rank of sole companion.

Tomb

A small mud-brick tomb built in the third east–west street against the west wall of Khui's tomb [25]; the only decoration is on a finely inscribed limestone false door. The mastaba has one shaft which despite the small size of the chapel opens into its floor and descends to a depth of 8.05 metres in the rock, leading to a medium-size burial chamber with no sarcophagus or burial pit.

Suggested date: possibly mid-Teti to Pepy I.

Later treatment

There is no evidence of any deliberate damage to the tomb.

Tomb of Mereri [28][172]

Owner

Mereri was overseer of the palace guards, overseer of the two districts of the palace, overseer of the two cool rooms (bathrooms?) of the palace, overseer of the two chambers of the king's adornment, overseer of all that heaven gives and earth produces, overseer of the two houses of gold, overseer of the two treasuries, senior lector priest, and one who is privy to the secrets of the house of morning. He held the ranks of count and sole companion.

Tomb

This is a stone-built mastaba which was originally free-standing and later formed the south-east corner of the entrance to the third east–west street. It lies at a short distance from the north wall of Mereruka's tomb [30] and the west wall of that of Nikauisesi [35]. The tomb consists of a three-roomed chapel; two rooms are decorated in fine relief and the third is undecorated and has a stairway leading to the roof. It presumably also contained a serdab, now damaged. Two false doors, both belonging to Mereri, are found – an exterior one in the eastern façade and an internal one in the offering room which is axial to the first. The shaft opens into the floor of the offering room; it descends to a depth of 14.95 metres and leads to a burial chamber with a stone sarcophagus inscribed on the outside and inside with the name and titles of the owner. The lid was closed, but the sarcophagus was plundered through a hole made by tomb robbers.

Date

In their examination of the tombs in the vicinity Davies *et al.* suggested that 'several, including Mereri, may well be contemporary with the larger mastabas in the area which are dateable [*sic*] to Teti and Pepy I'. They further suggest that 'it is likely that the tomb of Mereri, its entrance on the favoured eastern side, was the earliest'.[173] Other features in Mereri's tomb are consistent with an early date. Like the early tombs in this cemetery (Neferseshemre [34], Kagemni [23] and Neferseshemptah [33][174]) that of Mereri is squarish rather than truly rectangular in shape, and it has one false door in its eastern façade and another inside the chapel. Also, like the early tombs (Neferseshemre, Kagemni, Ankhmahor [12], Hefi [14], Mereruka's wife [30] and Nikauisesi [35]), it has an internal stairway leading to the roof. However, Mereri's burial apartment shows an architectural transition from a stage where the mouth of the shaft opened into the roof of the mastaba and was reached by a stairway, to a stage where the shaft opened into the floor of one of the rooms of the chapel, and accordingly no stairway was needed. In Mereri's case the shaft is inside the chapel, but the stairway still exists, and in this respect it is comparable only to the neighbouring mastaba of Nikauisesi [35], whose death is recorded as having taken place in the eleventh count/year (of Teti) – that is, presumably at its very end.[175] Like Nikauisesi, Mereri sits on a chair shown with four, rather than two, bull's legs.[176]

Suggested date: mid to late Teti.

Later treatment

The examination of the decoration inside and outside Mereri's chapel gives a clear indication that the work was never fully finished, particularly in the details. While Mereri's name was almost always left intact, his figure sustained damage, most commonly to his face and ankles but occasionally to other parts of his body, including his neck, wrists and waist (Figures 2.57, 2.58). Interestingly, Mereri's face was left intact in all seven figures on the internal false door. The figures and inscriptions of both his sons, the eldest, the superintendent of the palace guards, Mereri, and the younger, the under-supervisor of palace guards, Haishtef, also received some damage, more consistently in the case of the eldest.[177]

Tomb of Mereri – reused by Merynebty [29][178]

Original Owner

Mereri was overseer of weapons, overseer of the noble places of the palace, superintendent of the king's house, guard of Teti's pyramid, and held the rank of sole companion.

Figure 2.57 While the name of Mereri was left clearly legible, deliberate damage was inflicted on his figure, particularly to his face and ankles. This scene shows Mereri's figure at an offering table on the panel of the external false door.

Figure 2.58 Repeated figures of Mereri on both sides of his false door show systematic damage to his face and ankles.

Tomb

Constructed of mud-brick in the fourth east–west street, the tomb of Mereri has a one-roomed chapel which contains a single, relatively small limestone false door. The entrance was provided with an architrave finely inscribed with seven lines of hieroglyphs containing traditional offering formulae as well as the owner's name and titles and emphasizing the fact that he was honoured before Teti. The tomb contains a serdab and one shaft 9.15 metres deep, leading to a burial chamber with a burial pit cut into its floor and covered with a stone lid.

Date

Mereri mentions the fact that he was honoured before Teti, and there is no reason for dating the construction of the tomb later than this reign, but we do not know whether the owner outlived Teti. The fact that the tomb is exactly opposite that of Hesi [15], whose biographical inscriptions date him

Figure 2.59 The name of Mereri has been systematically erased from the inscriptions on his entrance architrave.

to the reign of Teti, and in the proximity of many other tombs from the same reign, supports such a date.

Suggested date: late Teti, or immediately after.

Later treatment and reuse of the tomb

The name and figure of Mereri have been carefully erased on both entrance architrave (Figure 2.59) and false door, and it was with difficulty that we were able to detect parts of the name. The erased parts on the false door have been smoothed in order to receive the inscriptions of a new owner, a woman called Merynebty who only held the titles guard and acquaintance of the king. However, not only were her inscriptions rendered in black paint, as against relief, but they were never inscribed on the left jambs of the false door (Figure 2.60).

The burial chamber was found disturbed, broken into from both its entrance and from the south-east corner of the chamber itself through a tunnel made from a nearby tomb by tomb robbers (Figure 2.61). The lid still covered the burial pit, but was broken at the corner. The human remains found in the pit are predominantly those of an elderly woman, with a very few male bones, which perhaps found their way there when the tomb robbers dug the tunnel between this burial chamber and that of a neighbouring tomb.

Tomb of Mereruka [30][179]

Owner

In addition to the office of chief justice and vizier Mereruka held numerous other titles including that of overseer of the scribes of the king's documents, overseer of all the works of the king, overseer of the six great courts, overseer of the two granaries, overseer of the two treasuries, overseer of the two

Figure 2.60 Following the erasure of Mereri's figures and inscriptions in relief on his false door, Merynebty added hers in black paint. These were never completed.

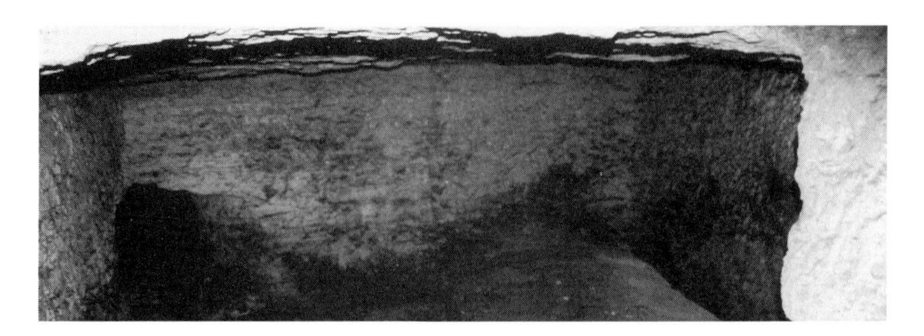

Figure 2.61 Merynebty's burial chamber, showing the lid of the burial pit and the opening of the robbers' tunnel in the inner left corner of the room.

houses of gold; he also had many religious responsibilities, including that of the high priest of Re and the stolist of Min. Many of his titles indicate his direct service in the palace, and one may assume that these were duties he performed before his promotion to the vizierate. Among these are he who is privy to the secrets of the house of morning, overseer of that which heaven gives and earth produces, overseer of the king's harem, overseer of the two cool rooms of the palace, overseer of the two fields of offering, overseer of the two chambers of the king's adornment, and confidant of the king in his every place. It may also be of particular significance that Mereruka held the two titles of overseer of the protection of every palace and overseer of the house of weapons. Mereruka was married to an eldest daughter of a king, possibly of Teti himself, and had the rank of hereditary prince.

Tomb

The tomb lies in the first east–west street opposite Teti's pyramid. It is large in size, fully constructed of stone, with almost its entire structure occupied by a multi-roomed chapel. This is clearly divided into three sections; the largest belongs to Mereruka himself while the two other sections belong to his wife, the king's daughter, Seshseshet, and their son Meryteti. Each of the sections has its own burial apartment. That of Mereruka has a shaft 14.5 metres deep, leading to a very large burial chamber, its walls lined with limestone blocks and decorated. A large, inscribed limestone sarcophagus was also provided.

Date

It is generally agreed that Mereruka served under Teti, whose daughter he married. The position of the tomb shows that it was built after that of Kagemni, but perhaps not considerably so.[180]

Suggested date: mid to late Teti.

Later treatment

The family of Mereruka has been studied by Nims,[181] who shows that Mereruka's eldest son was Memi, whom he probably had by an earlier marriage than that to Princess Waatetkhethor/Seshseshet, who became the mother of Meryteti. The last was probably born after the original reliefs of Mereruka were completed, since his figure was inserted later. Meryteti was described as king's son of his body, presumably being a grandson of Teti. He was allocated a section in his father's mastaba, where a chapel was added with its entrance cut through the scenes of Mereruka's pillared hall (Figure 3.2). It has been suggested that rivalry seems to have erupted, presumably after Mereruka's death, between Memi, later called Pepyankh, and Meryteti. Memi was able

Figure 2.62 Mereruka with two sons. The eldest, Pepyankh, has his name, but not his figure, erased, although this could still be read.

temporarily to usurp the tomb of his younger half-brother, but the latter succeeded in regaining his tomb and presumably in punishing his elder half-brother, becoming a vizier under Pepy I, with whose pyramid he is closely associated. In five of the six times Memi is represented in his father's chapel, his name has been erased, although traces of the name are evident.

Two scenes in the pillared hall showing Mereruka with his sons are of particular interest. Depicted between two sons, Mereruka holds their hands, the son to the fore, Pepyankh the eldest, had his name erased (Figure 2.62). On the west wall, Mereruka is also accompanied by two sons, but unlike that on the north wall the composition of the scene does not bring the figures in direct and close contact. The figure of the son at the front, probably the same Pepyankh, although the name is not preserved, was completely erased (Figure 2.63). Whether the erasure of Pepyankh's names and figure was due to his attempt to usurp his brother's chapel as hitherto believed, or the result of his involvement in the events at the end of Teti's reign for which many others were similarly punished, is uncertain. The nature of the punishment suggests that the latter alternative is more likely.

An examination of the offering bearers depicted in Mereruka's chapel also shows that some of these have their names and figures chiselled out (Figure 2.64). It is possible that these, like Memi, were involved in some activities for which they were later punished.

Figure 2.63 As the figures of the two sons are separated from that of Mereruka, it was possible in this instance to completely erase that of the eldest son.

Tomb of Meru [31][182]

Owner

The career of Meru, also called Tetiseneb, Pepyseneb and Meryreseneb, appears to fall into certainly two or possibly three stages:

1 As recorded on the false door only the name Meru and titles related to Teti's pyramid or temple are attested. Here he bears titles similar to those of his neighbour, Semdent: overseer of the palace guards, overseer of messengers and guard of Teti's pyramid, controller of clothing, overseer of the two cool rooms of the palace, overseer of that which heaven gives and earth produces, overseer of all vegetation, overseer of the cows' house, overseer of the two districts of the palace, and the ranks of sole companion and nobleman of the king.

2 In the wall decoration inside the chapel none of the titles related to feeding and clothing the king is attested, but those of guards and the overseer of the two cool rooms of the palace persist and new ones were added: one who is privy to the secrets of the house of morning, lector priest and priest of Hathor. Offices in the pyramid of Teti and the temple of Pepy are recorded, as are the names Tetiseneb and Pepyseneb.

3 On the façade, Meru acquires the new name Meryreseneb and the titles chief lector priest, sem-priest, director of every kilt and, for the first time, the rank of count.

Figure 2.64 Some of the offering bearers of Mereruka, particularly those shown at the head of rows, also had their names and figures removed.

Tomb

A square mastaba of mud-brick construction, the façade and a two-roomed chapel are cased, perhaps at a later stage, with small blocks of limestone joined with plaster. The false door, in two halves with a vertical joint, is 1.72 × 1.12 metres and made of a rather poor-quality stone. All the surfaces of the chapel and entrance area are decorated. The shaft descends through the rock to a depth of 7.92 metres and leads to a relatively small burial chamber containing an uninscribed stone sarcophagus.

Date

There can be no doubt that Meru lived under Teti and Pepy I; he held offices in the pyramid of the former and in the temple of the latter, and the names

Tetiseneb and Pepyseneb were presumably acquired or granted during his services under the two kings. A fourth and last name, Meryreseneb, appears only on the façade, west of the entrance to the tomb, and may help in limiting the date. We know that Pepy I changed his name from Nefersahor to Meryre (i.e. beloved of Re) early in his reign, perhaps as a policy statement, and officials in this cemetery and elsewhere immediately started to use the new name. Inumin [17], made vizier early under Pepy I, went as far as chiselling out the name of Nefersahor and replacing it with Meryre in his tomb in the Teti cemetery. Not only is the name Meryreseneb completely absent in all the decoration inside the chapel, but the figure of the tomb owner was never finished on the west side of the façade where this name was written (Figure 2.65).[183] The decoration of the façade was probably left until last, as can also be implied from examining the tomb of Inumin, but artistically it was the best in the tomb; this is also the case, for example, in the tombs of Nikauisesi [35] and Kaaper [22]. It could therefore be assumed that Meru died shortly after the new name, Meryre, was adopted by Pepy I.

While Meru presumably died early under Pepy I, he probably built his tomb under Teti, as can be seen by examining the progress of his career. In fact, on the façade, the last part of the tomb to be decorated, Meru summarizes his career, or perhaps explains all the changes in his names and titles. On the east side he calls himself Tetiseneb and describes himself as sole companion, overseer of the two cool rooms of the palace, overseer of the palace guards, and guard and overseer of messengers of Teti's pyramid. On the west side he calls himself Meryreseneb and lists his latest responsibilities, which include chief lector priest, sem-priest, director of every kilt and the high rank of count. The two sides of the entrance seem to illustrate Meru's career under the two kings he served, but it seems likely that his tomb was built under the first king and modified under the second. It is also improbable that such a prime location in this restricted cemetery would have remained empty until the reign of Pepy I, and the same applies to the tombs of Semdent [39] and Ankh [11] which are built against the west and east walls of that of Meru.

Suggested date: Teti for the construction of the tomb, but Pepy I for its completion.

Later treatment

The tomb of Meru is now covered by drifting sand and is difficult to examine without reclearance. However, Lloyd *et al.*, who recorded the tomb, make some interesting remarks on the condition of the scenes, which may have been related to Meru's career. Throughout the tomb many signs were unfinished, with their details not incised; numerous alterations and revisions in scenes suggest that either the blocks were reused from an earlier tomb or that the artists/craftsmen changed their minds on the decoration and lacked the time to remove all of the anomalies. More important, however, is the

Figure 2.65 Parts of Meru's decoration were unfinished. The facial details of the tomb owner's figure on the west side of the façade were never sculpted.

existence of many damaged parts in the scenes which in the opinion of Lloyd *et al.* may be due partly to natural destruction, though in many cases it is the result of deliberate slighting. This applies also to Meru's figure in the main table scene in the offering room, where 'the head has been partly destroyed and the entire figure pitted with chisel marks'.[184]

Tomb of Nedjetempet [32][185]

Owner

Nedjetempet, also called Titi, was the mother of the vizier Mereruka. She appears in his chapel and her tomb is close to his. She was a priestess of both Neith and Hathor and had the rank of acquaintance of the king.

Tomb

Located in, and partly blocking, the first north–south street, this relatively large mastaba is constructed of mud-brick, except for the entrance lintel and drum, as well as the false door, which are of good quality limestone and finely inscribed. The chapel is formed of three rooms, an open court and a stairway to the roof. The mastaba contains a large number of shafts, eleven in total; although one or two may have been added after the tomb was first built, the rest form part of the original design and may have been allocated to other members, perhaps brothers, of Mereruka's large family. The main shaft, that of Nedjetempet, is cut into the floor of the open court and descends to a depth of 14.6 metres, leading to a large, uninscribed burial chamber with a massive limestone sarcophagus, inscribed in black paint on three of its internal sides. The sarcophagus was broken into from its east side, but the skeletal remains of the owner were left *in situ*.

Date

In addition to the fact that Nedjetempet was Mereruka's mother, the architecture of the tomb can help with the dating. The architect was certainly influenced by the design of the neighbouring mastabas of Nikauisesi [35] and Shepsipuptah [38]. Like the former, that of Nedjetempet had a stairway leading to the roof, but a shaft opening into the floor of the chapel rather than from the roof of the mastaba, and, like Shepsipuptah's, its façade was decorated with a panelling of compound niches. The false door and the painted scenes on the walls of two rooms are fine in style.

Suggested date: mid to late Teti.

Later treatment

There is no evidence of any deliberate damage to the tomb.

Tomb of Neferseshemptah [33][186]

Owner

Neferseshemptah, also called Sheshi and Wedjahateti, held titles related to the administration of justice, such as overseer of the great court, judge and administrator, judge and superintendent of the scribes connected with the petitions and one who is privy to the secrets of all judgments. He was also guard and superintendent of priests of Teti's pyramid. Although he was married to an eldest daughter of the king, Seshseshet, he did not hold high ranks, being only a royal chamberlain.

Tomb

The tomb is situated in the second north–south street, the so-called 'rue de tombeaux', immediately to the north of that of Ankhmahor [12]. In its final form, it consisted of seven rooms, all believed to have belonged to the same tomb owner.[187] However, an examination of the westernmost decorated room and its false door suggests that it belonged to the tomb owner's son. The external walls of the mastaba were constructed of mud-brick, but all walls of the chapel as well as the façade were built of large blocks of limestone. The original chapel contained three decorated rooms, with a fourth one added later by the son. The main shaft has been cleared by the Egypt Exploration Society, but no information on this is available at present.[188]

Date

Based on the fact that Neferseshemptah was described as a priest of Teti's pyramid in the eastern section of the chapel and as a priest of the pyramids of both Teti and Pepy I in the westernmost room, it was concluded that he began decorating his tomb in the reign of Teti, but completed it under Pepy I.[189] A careful examination of the art and titulary in the two sections of the tomb shows no similarity whatsoever. The only similarity is in the names; yet both Neferseshemptah and Sheshi were common names at the time, and naming a son after his father was equally common in all periods. It seems much more likely that the inner, westernmost room belonged to the similarly named son of Neferseshemptah. The square shape of the tomb, like those of Kagemni [23] and Neferseshemre [34], suggests an early date and an examination of the area where this mastaba joins that of Ankhmahor [12] indicates an earlier date for that of Neferseshemptah.

Suggested date: early to mid-Teti's reign for the construction of the tomb and early to middle Pepy I for the addition/decoration of the son's room.

Later treatment

A man represented as the first in two rows of offering bearers in Neferseshemptah's chapel had his figure and inscriptions carefully chiselled out (Figure 2.66). The remaining traces of the inscriptions clearly identify him as 'son', with part of the name visible Nefer . . . Ptah. All other figures and inscriptions in the chapel are intact and very well preserved. Since the decoration of the westernmost room, belonging to a Neferseshemptah/Sheshi, was similarly erased, it is reasonable to think that this room belonged to the same disgraced son (Figure 2.67). That a son was allocated a section in his father's chapel, or that he added rooms in the available space within the latter's mastaba, is hardly unparalleled in the cemetery. This was done in the neighbouring tomb of Ankhmahor [12],[190] and but also in those of Mereruka [30][191] and probably Khentika [24].[192]

Neferseshemptah (the son) had a completely different career from that of his father and, unlike the latter, was very much in the direct service of the king. Among his titles are confidant of the king, foremost of his two banks (river banks), overseer of the two chambers of the king's adornment, overseer

Figure 2.66 The figure and inscriptions of the son of Neferseshemptah, shown as the first offering bearer in a register below the seated figure of his father, have been erased.

Figure 2.67 In his own chapel, added to that of his father, the son of Neferseshemptah, also named Neferseshemptah, had his inscriptions and figures systematically damaged.

of all that heaven gives and earth produces, overseer of the two cool rooms of the palace, keeper of the head ornaments, overseer of the noble places of the palace, overseer of the two districts of the palace, one who is privy to the secrets of the king in his every place. Neferseshemptah also held some important administrative offices, as, for example, overseer of the two houses of gold, director of every divine office and director of every kilt. In addition he was an overseer of the guards, guard of Teti's pyramid town and under-supervisor of priests of the pyramid towns of both Teti and Pepy I. His rank was that of hereditary prince.

Tomb of Neferseshemre [34][193]

Owner

Neferseshemre, also called Sheshi, was a vizier with all the other responsibilities that go with the office, such as being overseer of the scribes of the king's documents, overseer of all the works of the king, overseer of the six great courts, etc. He also held, perhaps earlier in his career, titles related to his service in the palace, including overseer of all the king's repasts; as such, he was overseer of all vegetation and overseer of that which heaven gives and earth produces. But he was also overseer of the two chambers of the king's adornment, overseer of the two cool rooms (bathrooms?) of the palace, overseer of the residence, and superintendent of priests and guards of Teti's pyramid. He held the high rank of hereditary prince.

Tomb

This is probably the earliest tomb in the cemetery. It lies immediately to the north of Teti's pyramid and to the west of those of his queens and is the first mastaba in the second north–south street, known as the 'rue de tombeaux'. The mastaba is totally constructed of large blocks of limestone, and is square in shape like other mastabas erected early under Teti, as for example that of Kagemni [23]. Only about one-third of the mastaba area is occupied by a chapel formed of four rooms, a large pillared hall with a staircase leading to the roof and a serdab. The burial chamber is reached through a vertical shaft 21 metres deep and was blocked by a portcullis before the shaft was filled, but unlike all viziers of Teti and early Pepy I buried in this cemetery, Neferseshemre's burial chamber was left undecorated. As the walls of the pillared hall were in rough stone and also undecorated, compared for example with those of his immediate neighbour Ankhmahor [12],[194] it seems possible that Neferseshemre died before the work on his tomb was completed. While the upper courses of the walls in the other rooms have disappeared, and with them any possible decoration, it is fortunate that the entrance to the tomb, the four faces of each of the six pillars in the pillared hall, and the false door in the offering room are decorated, mostly well preserved, and give adequate details about Neferseshemre and his family.

Date

There seems to be a general agreement that Neferseshemre's tomb was one of the earliest, if not the first, to be constructed in the Teti cemetery.

Suggested date: early to mid-Teti.

Later treatment

There is no evidence at all that the name and figure of Neferseshemre were deliberately damaged. However, four small figures shown in front of the tomb owner on the west faces of pillars 1 and 5 and the east faces of pillars 3 and 5 of the pillared hall have been chiselled out (Figure 2.68). The erasure also includes the names and titles inscribed above each figure, with the exception of the name of Teti's pyramid as part of the original titles which were left intact. Evidence shows that the damaged areas were repaired with plaster in antiquity (Figure 2.69). The fact that in three surviving fragments the erased

Figure 2.68 Standing in front of Neferseshemre was one of his sons holding his staff. His figure, name and part of his title were carefully removed. The undamaged part of his title gives the name of Teti's pyramid and the son was probably a guard in this pyramid.

figure holds Neferseshemre's staff suggests a father–son relationship, and like two other sons of the tomb owner, these held positions as guards of Teti's pyramid. The surviving inscriptions do not allow us to determine whether all four damaged figures represent one or more sons, but the fact that each of the other sons, including the eldest, Hekaib, are depicted only twice on the faces of these pillars, may suggest that the four damaged figures belonged to two sons. It is important to emphasize that the date of the erasure of the figures is unknown and may well have been during Neferseshemre's life or long after his death.

Figure 2.69 To repair the damage done to the tomb of Neferseshemre by the erasure of the figures of his son/s, the affected area was plastered in antiquity.

Tomb of Nikauisesi [35][195]

Owner

Nikauisesi, also called Isesy, was overseer of Upper Egypt, overseer of all the works of the king, overseer of the two houses of gold, chief of the great ones, chief lector priest and keeper of the head ornaments. He had the highest rank of hereditary prince.

Tomb

The tomb lies at the entrance to the second east–west street immediately to the north of that of Kagemni [23]. It is large, squarish in shape and fully constructed of good quality blocks of limestone. The chapel, formed of five rooms, a serdab and an open court with stairway leading to the roof, occupies most of the area of the mastaba. The façade and four of the chapel rooms are decorated in fine reliefs. The shaft[196] opens into the floor of a large, undecorated room inside the chapel. The west wall of this room was built above the western side of the shaft, resting on two large limestone beams wedged in ledges cut into the rock at the top of the north and south sides of the shaft. This design was copied only by Inumin [17] in this cemetery. The shaft descends to a depth of 19.6 metres, leading to a large but undecorated burial chamber, which contained a massive uninscribed limestone sarcophagus, found with its lid correctly placed and plastered, but with the burial violated through a hole in the east side of the sarcophagus. Nikauisesi's skeletal remains were found *in situ.*

Date

This is one of the most soundly dated individuals buried in the Teti cemetery. Like his immediate neighbours to the south and north, Kagemni [23][197] and Hesi [15],[198] Nikauisesi probably started his career under Isesi. He is presumably the official of this name depicted on the causeway of Unis,[199] and again mentioned in a royal decree of Teti.[200] The location of Nikauisesi's tomb, the use of stone on a large scale, the squarish area of the mastaba, the use of a stairway to the roof, the relative chronology of other tombs built against Nikauisesi's (Shepsipuptah [38] and Hesi), the artistic details in the chapel (for example, the necklace and amulet worn by the tomb owner and the type of chair shown with four lion legs)[201] are indicative of a date around the middle of Teti's reign. The date of Nikauisesi's burial is recorded in his tomb as the eleventh count/year (most probably of Teti)[202] (Figure 2.70).

Suggested date: middle of Teti's reign for the building of the tomb and end of the same reign for the death of the owner.

Figure 2.70 A very rare inscription giving the date of burial of Nikauisesi. The date was inscribed in black paint below the tomb owner's figure in a fowling scene. It was probably written by the owner's son, who also added his figure immediately above the inscription in rather poor relief.

Later treatment

The scenes on parts of three walls of the offering room were erased when these walls were used to form the upper section of a late, intrusive shaft. However, this action is considerably later in time and was not an attack against the tomb owner or any of his depicted relatives. Other than this 'accidental' damage, and the usual deterioration or loss of decorated blocks, there is no deliberate damage to the figures or inscriptions of Nikauisesi, his sons, or retainers. It is interesting that none of them held office in the guards department, and Nikauisesi himself died before Teti.

Tomb of Rawer [36][203]

Owner

Rawer was chief justice and vizier, overseer of Upper Egypt, director of every kilt, treasurer of the king of Lower Egypt, chief lector priest and elder of the *Senut*-house. He had the rank of hereditary prince and the epithet of beloved of the god. The last epithet is infrequent and probably indicates a special relationship with the king, being probably the 'god' referred to in the epithet. The name Rawer is attested once more in the cemetery as the eldest son of Shepsipuptah [38]. As the latter was married to a king's daughter, perhaps of Teti, it seems possible that the choice of the vizier Rawer for the post was based on his kinship to the royal house, whether he was the son of the princess or of a different wife of Shepsipuptah.

Tomb

The tomb lies to the south-east of the funerary temple of Teti. Its superstructure, built of stone, is very small (6.83 × 4.3 metres) considering the position of its owner, and was surrounded by a paved courtyard with temenos walls on at least three sides. The chapel is formed of one room with its entrance and all four walls decorated in relief, including two false doors both for Rawer. The shaft is 6.9 metres deep, ending in three small chambers with no stone sarcophagus.

Date

There is no biographical inscription or even the cartouche of any king to use in dating this tomb. However, the date of Rawer has been the subject of a detailed study, and from the position and size of the tomb and the style of relief a date after Teti is suggested. As viziers of Pepy II, unlike those of Pepy I, were buried in his cemetery, this leaves us with the reign of Pepy I as the most probable date for Rawer. A comparison of the tombs of all possible viziers of this king would place Rawer towards the end of the reign. Because the name of a vizier has been erased from the Dahshur decree of Pepy I dated to the 21st count/year, it is tempting to link Rawer, whose name and figure were damaged in his tomb, to this disgraced vizier of Pepy I's decree.[204]

Suggested date: late Pepy I.

Later treatment

The decoration of Rawer's chapel has been deliberately damaged; his name was chiselled out every time it was inscribed, but with varying degrees of thoroughness. Surviving parts of the name allow us to reconstruct it with certainty, and in one instance, on the left thickness of the entrance to the chapel, the name is preserved almost in total. Parts of Rawer's figures were also attacked. This is particularly evident on the face, hands and feet, and is more regular on the large representations of the tomb owner than on the small figures depicted on the jambs of the false doors (Figure 2.71). Figures of Rawer's offering bearers frequently received a similar treatment.

Figure 2.71 The name of Rawer has been erased eight times on this false door, but various parts of it remain legible.

Tomb of Seankhuiptah [37][205]

Owner

The tomb owner, who also bore the name Hetepniptah, was the chief physician of Upper and Lower Egypt, overseer of the messengers and guards of Teti's pyramid, overseer of the two districts of the palace, and was also confidant of the king, foremost of his two banks (river banks), one who is privy to the secrets of the king in his every place, one who is privy to the secrets of what one sees, one who is privy to the secrets of all commands. Thus he combined medical expertise with guard duties and was trusted and close to the king.

Tomb

It lies in the fourth east–west street, immediately to the north of Shepsipuptah's tomb [38] and like the latter has niched panelling on its eastern external wall. The mastaba is built of mud-brick, but stone is used in the entrance recess of the façade, for the doorway, for the stone lining of the offering room and for its roofing slabs. All the stone surface of the walls outside and inside the tomb is decorated in relief of a fine quality, and that inside the offering room is also coloured. Some of the details of the scenes, such as the water lines and the fish under the boats in the fishing and fowling scenes, are rendered in paint only, a great deal of which is still preserved. Unlike most other tombs in this street, this tomb has a two-roomed chapel, although only one room is decorated, and like that of Mereri [29] it had a serdab. The shaft descends into the rock to a depth of 9.7 metres, leading to a large burial chamber, 5.3 × 3.7 metres, which contains a roughly cut and badly damaged stone sarcophagus.

Date

The location of the tomb immediately to the north of that of Shepsipuptah [38], who was probably married to Teti's daughter, the similarity of the external niched walls of the two tombs and their proximity to the tomb of Hesi [15], whose biography clearly indicates that his tomb was constructed under Teti, suggest that Seankhuiptah built his tomb almost at the same time as the other two. There is nothing in his titulary which refers to a king other than Teti.

Suggested date: reign of Teti, probably late, for the construction and decoration of the tomb.

Later treatment

The name and figure of Seankhuiptah have been deliberately chiselled out. However, the removal of the figures on the façade and entrance is more thoroughly executed than inside the chapel, where the outlines, frequently in red paint, are reasonably clear (Figures 2.72, 2.73, 2.74, 2.75). The names Seankhuiptah and Hetepniptah were even less meticulously removed, and instances of both names have survived in full or in part, both outside and inside the chapel, including immediately above and on both sides of the entrance doorway and on the drum. Considering the amount of chiselling work which the removal of the figures and names required, one wonders if the surviving instances of the names were out of negligence or deliberate! The wife's figure was obviously not targeted, her figure was in one place left intact, while in another it was chiselled out with that of her husband. Her inscriptions were partly affected, but interestingly the damaged section was apparently rewritten in black outline. Like Hesi's case [15], the damage to this tomb does not seem to be the work of vandals, but of those executing specific orders.

Figure 2.72 The façade of Seankhuiptah shows repeated figures of the tomb owner, six on the architrave and one on each of the jambs. While these have been systematically erased, as was his name, the latter curiously escaped any damage in the most obvious place in the centre of the architrave above the doorway.

Figure 2.73 The figure of Seankhuiptah in the palanquin has been erased, but the palanquin itself and the men who carry it are intact.

Tomb of Shepsipuptah [38][206]

Owner

Shepsipuptah did not hold many titles. He was keeper of the head ornaments, overseer of the two districts of the palace and lector priest, and held the ranks of count and sole companion and the high priestly office of superintendent of priests of Teti's pyramid. His importance may be due to the fact that he was married to a king's daughter, perhaps of Teti, named Seshseshet (Figure 2.76).

Tomb

This is the first tomb in the second east–west street. Built of mud-brick, with panelling of compound niches on both east and north external walls, this mastaba has a chapel of four rooms, two of which appear to have been decorated with painted scenes on mud plaster. It has a large limestone false door, placed in a stone niche. No other stone elements exist in the chapel, but the entrance area, which could have included such elements, is now badly

Figure 2.74 Seankhuiptah's figure in the spear-fishing scene was chiselled out, but that of his wife, Khentkaues, is intact.

damaged. The main shaft descends into the rock to a depth of 16.25 metres, leading to a large burial chamber with a massive stone sarcophagus which was broken into from its north side.

Date

The tomb was built against the east wall of Nikauisesi's mastaba [35] and later Hesi [15] built his against the north-west angle of Shepsipuptah's. He is therefore later than Nikauisesi and earlier than Hesi.

Suggested date: middle of Teti's reign, or immediately after.

Later treatment

There is no evidence of any deliberate damage to the tomb.

Figure 2.75 While the offering table and the accompanying inscriptions were left intact, the seated figure of Seankhuiptah and his name were removed.

Tomb of Semdent [39][207]

Owner

Semdent, also called Semdenti, was overseer of the palace guards, controller of clothing and overseer of the king's repasts in all his places. In association with the last office he also held the titles of overseer of all that heaven gives and earth produces, overseer of the marshlands, overseer of the cows' house,

Figure 2.76 Part of the wall scenes in Shepsipuptah's chapel showing his wife, Seshseshet (a daughter of Teti), and his eldest son, Rawer.

overseer of the two fields of offering and overseer of all offerings of the king. He was also one who is privy to the secrets of the king in his every place and a true nobleman of the king.

Tomb

The tomb is located at the western end of the second east–west street and is constructed of mud-brick with limestone casing the entrance. The chapel consists of three rooms, the walls of which were decorated with paintings on mud plaster which have now completely disappeared, while the main offering room is dominated by a large limestone false door, 2.62 metres high × 1.72 metres wide, fully decorated in incised relief. The shaft descends through the rock to a depth of 7.8 metres and leads to a burial chamber which contained an uninscribed stone sarcophagus, in which was placed an inscribed wooden coffin, fragments of which still exist.

Date

The date of Semdent's tomb presents some difficulties. The fact that its partly preserved east wall abuts the west wall of Meru's tomb [31] meant that Semdent was later than Meru. As the latter was also called Tetiseneb, Pepyseneb and Meryreseneb, this would exclude a date before the middle of

Pepy I's reign for Semdent, a date which I accepted in an earlier publication, and which now seems doubtful, although by no means impossible. The location of Semdent's tomb in a prime position immediately to the north of Mereruka's tomb [30] suggests an earlier date. This relatively small cemetery appears to have been fully divided and allocated to officials during the reign of Teti, with later constructions blocking streets or partly fitted between existing tombs. It is of course important to reconcile this with the fact that Semdent's neighbour, Meru, had names and titles which definitely associate him with Pepy I. However, a study of the decoration of Meru's chapel suggests that he was promoted later in his career, a promotion which may have enabled him to provide his chapel with stone lining where the names and titles referring to Pepy appear (see under Meru's case study). This does not necessarily mean that the original building of the tomb was not earlier, and if so should not be taken as evidence for dating Semdent to the reign of Pepy I or later.

There is nothing in Semdent's inscriptions that would independently date him after the reign of Teti. In fact, his false door would be almost impossible to reconcile with a date under Pepy I, let alone late in this reign, when tombs and false doors grew much smaller than those of Teti's officials. Semdent's false door (2.62 × 1.72 metres) is particularly large, almost identical, for example, to that of the vizier Neferseshemre from the beginning of Teti's reign (2.63 × 1.7 metres),[208] and slightly smaller than that of the vizier Hesi from the end of the same reign (2.8 × 1.7 metres),[209] but certainly larger than that of any of his equals in the cemetery in general[210] and of many important officials of Pepy I elsewhere.[211] The standard of relief and some details, for example the relatively low back of the chair and the short loaves of bread in relation to the height of the seated figure, seem to be characteristic of Teti's reign.

Suggested date: mid to late Teti.

Later treatment

The figures of Semdent as shown on his false door have not suffered any damage. His inscriptions also remain intact, except for the name which was repeatedly chiselled out, although the degree of erasure varies in different parts, and, as is usual in such cases where one or more instances survive intact, the name, written in small characters at the bottom of both outer jambs has suffered little damage (Figure 2.77). The interpretation that the damage was 'presumably the subject of the wrath of enemies soon after interment'[212] seems questionable. The restriction of the erasure to the name and nothing else, including the figure of the deceased himself, and a comparison with other tombs where different but equally systematic damage is found, suggest that these represent the execution of certain punishments, different for each individual.

Figure 2.77 Although the name Semdent has been chiselled out from most places on the false door, it survived intact in two instances where it was written in small characters at the bottom of the outer jambs. The rest of the inscriptions, as well as the figures, are very well preserved.

Tomb of Tetiankh and Hesy [40][213]

Owner

The tomb has two false doors, each placed in a separate room. The larger room and larger false door belong to an official named Tetiankh with the titles sole companion and lector priest; but as the upper half of the false door is missing the full responsibilities of the owner are unknown. The second false door belongs to Hesy who was overseer of Upper Egypt, director of every kilt and overseer of that which is within the boundaries, and held the rank of sole companion. As Tetiankh had the innermost room, usually reserved for the owner's offering room, he may well be the main tomb owner.

Tomb

The tomb lies in the fourth east–west street, immediately to the west of that of Mehi [26] and opposite that of Tjetji [42]. Constructed of mud-brick, the tomb contains five rooms, or more probably four rooms and an open court, and two false doors each in a separate room. Nine shafts are cut into the floor of the different rooms; the main shaft of which (shaft IX) has not been cleared.

Date

A study of the connections between this tomb and that of Mehi shows that the building of the two tombs progressed simultaneously. Both tombs were earlier than that of Ishfi [21] which used their external walls. The plan of the chapel is similar to that of Shepsipuptah [38], and the false door of Hesy with its elongated panel is characteristic of the reign of Pepy I.[214] The absence of the ranks of count or hereditary prince for an overseer of Upper Egypt is noteworthy. The same is attested in the case of Khui [25] who held a similar post under Pepy I, and the overseer of all the works of the king, Nekhebu of Giza, from the same reign.[215] Perhaps Hesy was Tetiankh's son, as a number of sons used rooms in their fathers' chapels in the Teti cemetery at this particular time, and it is possible that he succeeded Khui [25] as overseer of Upper Egypt.

Suggested date: mid to late Teti for Tetiankh; Pepy I for Hesy.

Later treatment

There is no evidence of any deliberate damage to the tomb.

Tomb of Tjetetu [41][216]

Owner

Tjetetu, also called Iwenmin, was overseer of the guards, overseer of the department of the palace guards, and guard and priest of Teti's pyramid. He also appears to have had responsibilities related to the Egyptian frontiers, as overseer of every secret word belonging to the entry of the foreign land and one who is privy to the secrets of the king in every secret command belonging to the entry of the foreign land. Tjetetu had the ranks of sole companion and nobleman of the king.

Tomb

The tomb of Tjetetu is located at the western end of the third east–west street. It was constructed of mud-brick, and provided with a stone-cased entrance recess and two stone false doors in the chapel, only one of which was inscribed. The rest of the chapel walls are plastered, with parts decorated in paint. There are two burial apartments. That of the owner has a shaft which descends to a depth of 7.2 metres in the rock and leads to a rather large burial chamber with a burial pit cut into its floor and provided with a stone lid. The wife's (?) shaft is 5.7 metres deep in the rock and leads to a small burial chamber, probably unfinished.

Date

Tjetetu was both a priest and a guard of Teti's pyramid. His sons are named Tetiankh and Intef, the latter bearing the same name as that of Wernu's son [44]. There is nothing in the art style or the inscriptions which make a date after Teti's reign preferred.

Suggested date: mid-Teti to early Pepy I.

Later treatment

There is no evidence of deliberate damage to Tjetetu's tomb, but this was left in an obviously unfinished state. The walls of the chapel were covered with mud plaster, then coated with yellow plaster on which scenes were painted. The work in this chapel was certainly abandoned in different stages of completion, the north wall and half of the west wall have mud plaster only, while the remaining walls have the additional coat of yellow plaster. The painted scenes on part of the west wall were finished in the usual brilliant colours, those on the east wall, except at the northern end, are only roughly outlined in red paint and guidelines are still visible (Figure 2.78). The northern false door, although completely inscribed in incised relief, was left in an unfinished state with many signs lacking internal details and, except for the left outer jamb, the lines bordering the hieroglyphic inscriptions are outlined only in black paint. The southern false door, perhaps belonging to the wife, although of large dimensions (1.72 × 0.92 metres) and slightly smaller than the northern one, has a rough and unfinished surface and is totally uninscribed (Figure 2.79). One wonders why such a valuable limestone false door was provided if

Figure 2.78 The decoration in painting on the east wall of Tjetetu's chapel was left unfinished, with figures in outline, colours not added and guidelines still visible.

it was to be left undecorated and why the painted scenes on the walls and the inscriptions on the northern false door were unfinished. Work on the tomb seems to have come to a sudden halt.

Tomb of Tjetji [42][217]

Owners

The chapel in this tomb contains three false doors belonging to three men, whose relationship to each other is unknown. Here the tomb is tentatively attributed to Tjetji, owner of the northernmost and largest of the three false doors. He held the titles of royal chamberlain of the palace, overseer of the noble places of the palace and priest of Maat. The other two individuals, Nebemdjeri and Kagemni, were chief physicians and lector priests and held the rank of sole companion.

Tomb

The tomb lies in the fourth east–west street, immediately west of that of Irenakhti [18]. Apart from the three limestone false doors, the mastaba and its

Figure 2.79 The northern false door belonging to Tjetetu was almost certainly left unfinished and his southern false door, presumably belonging to his wife, was left undecorated.

corridor chapel are constructed of mud-brick. It has three shafts, the main one of which descends in the rock to a depth of 7.95 metres and leads to a small burial chamber which contained neither a stone sarcophagus nor a burial pit.

Date

The mastaba started as a single project with that of Memi [27]. It used the west wall of Khui's mastaba [25] and later Irenakhti [18] built his against that of Tjetji. There is no evidence in the decoration that helps assign the tomb to a precise date within the Sixth Dynasty, and its date relies mainly on the relative chronology of this group of tombs.

Suggested date: mid-Teti, or later.

Later treatment

There is no evidence of any deliberate damage to the tomb.

Tomb of Tjetju [43][218]

Owner

Tjetju was a chief justice and vizier and held numerous titles, such as overseer of the six great courts, overseer of all the works of the king, overseer of the two treasuries, overseer of the two granaries, etc. He also occupied offices related to his service to the king or the palace – for example, superintendent of priests, and guard of Pepy I's pyramid, director of every divine office, overseer of the Residence, overseer of the two chambers of the king's adornment and one who is privy to the secrets of the house of morning.

Tomb

This is a small tomb constructed in an angle formed by the mastabas of Mereruka [30] and Kagemni [23] in the first east–west street. It is built of stone, has a one-roomed chapel and one shaft leading to a burial chamber with an inscribed stone sarcophagus.

Date

The titles Tjetju held in the pyramid of Pepy I, and the fact that a jar lid bearing the name of the same king was discovered in the burial chamber, would suggest a date under Pepy I. The small size of the tomb is in total agreement with the trend of tombs of this period and should be compared for example with that of Rawer. The date in the First Intermediate Period proposed by some[219] is totally unjustified.

Suggested date: late Pepy I.

Later treatment

There is no evidence of any deliberate damage to the tomb.

Tomb of Wernu [44][220]

Owner

Wernu held a large number of priesthoods, but he was also a guard of Teti's pyramid, confidant of the king in his every place, one who is privy to secret commissions and one who is privy to the secrets of the house of morning.

Tomb

The tomb of Wernu was presumably constructed of stone against the west exterior wall of Mereri's mastaba [28], but only its chapel now remains. This is formed of one corridor-like offering room with its walls and false door decorated in relief ranging from moderate to good quality, but in many parts unfinished. The main shaft descends in the rock to a depth of 7.7 metres and leads to a burial chamber which contains an uninscribed stone sarcophagus.

Date

In discussing the dating of this group of tombs Davies *et al.* suggested that Mereri [28] may well be from the reign of Teti or Pepy I, but that others, 'including Wernu, are certainly later, perhaps considerably so, but for none does there seem to be evidence which points incontrovertibly to a date later than the end of the Sixth Dynasty'.[221] In fact there is nothing in the architecture or the decoration of Wernu's tomb which indicates a considerably later date than that of Mereri. The fact that one tomb is built against another should not by necessity indicate a huge gap in time between the two. In the immediate vicinity, Nikauisesi built his tomb, then Shepsipuptah constructed his tomb against that of Nikauisesi and finally Hesi built his against that of Shepsipuptah, all most certainly within the relatively short reign of Teti.

Wernu's false door is large (2.2 × 1.05 metres), formed of a single block of good limestone and very similar in pattern to the outer false door of Mereri.[222] The interior of the chapel is decorated with a number of themes in relief, which although of varying quality was presumably beyond the means of any equal of Wernu after the reign of Teti. From the reign of Pepy I onwards such decoration seems to have been affordable only by the viziers, higher officials and provincial governors. Artistically, the representation of lotus flowers and buds floating on the water beneath the tomb owner's boat in the fishing and fowling scenes[223] is characteristic of the Fifth Dynasty and early Sixth,[224] and the depiction of the tomb owner at either side of an offering table[225] is attested elsewhere in this cemetery only in the tombs of Neferseshemre [34] and Hefi [14], two of the earliest officials to construct their tombs in the area.[226]

Suggested date: mid to late Teti.

Later treatment

The relief work in Wernu's chapel was certainly left unfinished, with figures in different stages of completion. Wernu's inscriptions and name were not attacked, but his face and in particular his eyes have been deliberately damaged, although in some instances his figure remained intact. Sporadic damage of a deliberate nature was also observed in the figures of his offering bearers. More important, however, is the complete erasure of his son's figure and inscriptions. Two panels flanking the false door in the west wall each depict Wernu with a son. While the damage to Wernu's face is similar in both cases, the figure and inscriptions of his eldest son, his beloved, the palace guard, Intef, on the left panel were intact, while those related to the son on the right panel are completely chiselled out, with only the bird he held in his hand now visible (Figure 2.80). There is no reason to believe that the two figures belonged to the same son, most probably not. Nor could one be certain that the erased son was not also designated as eldest, for having more than one eldest son, probably the result of different marriages, was not infrequent.[227] The fact that one of Wernu's sons was employed as a palace guard makes it likely, although by no means certain, that the other was employed in a similar profession. It is noticed that his immediate neighbour, Mereri [28], also had two sons in this same department. At the southern end of the west wall, Wernu is shown receiving offering bearers. He is accompanied by a small figure of a son which has also been chiselled out in the same manner as that on the panel. It seems likely that the two erased figures belonged to one and the same son.

Tomb of . . . (name lost) [45][228]

Owner

The only surviving inscriptions are on a part of an entrance architrave, still *in situ*. These inscriptions do not show the name of the owner and his titles are also obviously incomplete. He was overseer of the great court, director of scribes of petitions, and judge and administrator.

Tomb

Located in the fourth east–west street, this tomb is adjacent to that of Mereri (reused by Merynebty) [29]. It is built of mud-brick, and has a one-roomed chapel with an undecorated false door, and a finely inscribed architrave above the entrance of which only a small part is preserved. The shaft is 9.2 metres deep leading to a small burial chamber which contains a stone sarcophagus.

Figure 2.80 The scene on the right panel next to the false door shows the damage to Wernu's face and the complete erasure of the figure and inscriptions of his son.

Date

There is very little independent evidence for dating this tomb; its date relies therefore on that of the neighbouring tombs (Hefi [14], Hesi [15] and Mereri [29]), all of which appear to belong to the reign of Teti.

Suggested date: reign of Teti, probably at its end.

Later treatment

Because most of the architrave is missing and only the right part preserved, which, as usual, contains the beginning of lines of offering formulae, claims of moral goodness and list of titles, we do not know the owner's name, nor are we certain whether his name has been erased like many others in the same street. However, the only false door in the chapel was left rough and totally undecorated (Figure 2.81). This is unusual for a man who was 'overseer of

Figure 2.81 The preserved part of this entrance architrave does not record the name of the tomb owner, and the false door inside the chapel is not only uninscribed but has never been smoothed in preparation for inscriptions.

the great court', a title which was held by officials prior to their promotion to the vizierate![229] The decoration of this tomb most certainly came to an abrupt stop, perhaps for the same reason which caused many tombs in this street (Mehi [26], Iri [19] and Geref [13]) to be left unfinished.

NORTH SAQQARA

Tomb of Merefnebef [46][230]

Owner

Merefnebef, also called Unisankh and Fefi, was a vizier who did not hold many of the traditional titles usually associated with this office, such as overseer of all the works of the king, treasurer of the king of Lower Egypt, etc. He held some responsibilities related to the personal service of the king such as keeper of the head ornaments and one who is privy to the secrets of the house of morning, was also guard and priest of Teti's pyramid and had the ranks of hereditary prince and count. The vizierate might have been a late promotion which is recorded on the façade.

Tomb

This recently discovered tomb by the Polish expedition lies to the west of the Step Pyramid and is relatively small, formed of an open court leading to a rock-cut chapel 6.46 × 2.43 metres, which is fully decorated in relief and painted. A shaft 18 metres deep leads to a burial chamber containing a stone sarcophagus with a lid.

Date

The excavator tentatively proposes that Merefnebef spent the first part of his career under Teti, became vizier under Userkare and was dismissed by Pepy I.[231] In the absence of a full publication of the tomb it is impossible to be more precise, but a range of dates from the end of Teti's reign to the end of that of Pepy I seem possible.

Suggested date: Pepy I.

Later treatment

The tomb owner was married to at least four wives, perhaps even six, and the excavator suggests that there is some evidence of family feud. More important, however, is the evidence that at least one of Merefnebef's sons had his figures and inscriptions systematically chiselled out from the tomb (Figure 2.82). There is no deliberate damage to the tomb owner's figures in the currently published data.

Tomb of Sabu [47][232]

Owner

Sabu, also called Ibebi, was overseer of all the works of the king and director of artisans, and he held an unusually large number of priesthoods of various gods as well as of the pyramids of both Unis and Teti.

Tomb

The mastaba is situated at North Saqqara, with its exact location uncertain. It is built of mud-brick with a large false door and two side panels, each made of a single block of limestone and fully decorated in relief. No further information on its architectural features is available.

Date

Sabu's inscriptions specifically date him to the reign of Teti, and a date in the latter part of this reign has already been proposed.[233]

Suggested date: late Teti.

Figure 2.82 While the figures of Merefnebef, one of his wives, Seshseshet, and one of his sons named Fefi are well preserved, the figure and inscription of the second son were carefully removed.

Figure 2.83 Sabu with his son standing in front of him. The figure and inscriptions of the latter have been carefully removed.

Later treatment

There is no evidence of any damage to the figure or name of Sabu himself. However, a son of Sabu and another offering bearer, who may also have been a son, had their figures and accompanying inscriptions systematically chiselled out (Figure 2.83).

3
THE INVESTIGATION

The choice of the Teti cemetery

There is nothing unusual in a king starting a new cemetery for the building of his pyramid and the tombs of his officials; every king did this. But the move of Old Kingdom kings from one site to another, sometimes separated by miles, and the return of later kings to earlier cemeteries, is curious. Following the use of Saqqara by Djoser, the royal burials moved to Zawiyet el-Aryan, Maidum, Dahshur, Giza, Abu Rawash, back to Giza, then back to Saqqara by Userkaf, followed by a move to Abusir by his Fifth Dynasty successors until Djedkare/Isesi, or perhaps Menkauhor, returned to Saqqara where the remaining monarchs of the Old Kingdom chose to be buried. Surely these moves were not without reasons, nor were they haphazard; some dynastic, political or religious motives may well have been behind each of the moves.

Teti's choice of his cemetery was no exception; in fact, more than any other king he must have had very strong grounds for his selection. The site is simply too restricted, being bound to the north by the First and Second Dynasty tombs, to the east by the steep slope of the plateau, to the west and perhaps the south by the already existing Fifth Dynasty tombs. So close is Teti's pyramid to the tombs of Kaemheset, Kaemsenu and Pehernefer, immediately to the west of his cemetery, that some of their excavators presumably felt obliged to date them to the Sixth Dynasty,[234] although others questioned if they should not be dated to the Fifth.[235] The location of these tombs still influences modern scholars in their attempt to date them. Klaus Baer, for example, clearly states that 'one would expect the mastabas in this area largely to date from the Sixth Dynasty',[236] and finally dates all three tombs to this dynasty.[237] A recent reclearance and examination of these tombs (the design of the chapels, the size of the mud-brick used, the style of the false doors, the artistic and inscriptional evidence) leaves little doubt that they belong to the Fifth Dynasty, and therefore certainly antedate the building of Teti's pyramid itself. These most probably represent some of the north-easternmost mastabas in the extended cemetery of Userkaf. The planners of Teti's cemetery appear to have been well aware of the strict limitations of the site and the lack of any possibility of further expansion should Teti's reign last long and require more land for the tombs of new officials, an important factor which seems to have usually been taken into account in selecting sites for other pyramids. With the absence of such a possibility, Teti's official cemetery was from the beginning fenced by an enclosure wall, divided and allocated. That a funerary complex of a king be surrounded by an enclosure wall (for example that of Djoser) is understandable, as no future expansion was necessary, but the same did not usually apply to official cemeteries around other pyramids. Teti's cemetery appears to have been already full, or at least fully allocated, before the end of his reign. Even his last vizier, Khentika [24], was assigned an awkward site for his mastaba, outside the main official cemetery and squeezed between the king's mortuary temple and the queens' funerary complexes. This important fact has to be taken into account when dating the officials buried in Teti's cemetery in general.

The plan of the cemetery was simple (Figure 2.24). The king's pyramid and its mortuary temple, attached to the east side, occupy the southern section with the rest of the cemetery to the north and thus in front of the entrance to the king's burial apartment. The north-east part of the cemetery, opposite the mortuary temple, contains the queens' funerary complexes, arranged on a north–south axis. The first from north – that is, the furthest from the king – is that of Iput, followed by that of Khuit, with the area further south still covered by a mound of debris. Abutting on the east side of Iput's funerary complex is a rather small mastaba belonging to a king's eldest son named Tetiankh,[238] and it is uncertain if other tombs of members of the royal family exist in this unexcavated area. It is also uncertain whether Tetiankh, who held some administrative titles, including that of overseer of Upper Egypt, was assigned this area because of his royal kinship or because the western half of the cemetery, reserved for officials, was already fully occupied or apportioned. This western half was well but tightly planned, with two main streets and a number of smaller ones. The first east–west street is a main street separating the king's complex from the cemetery to its north, and the first north–south street is a large one in front of the entrance to the king's burial apartment and dividing the official cemetery into two unequal parts. The eastern part is separated from the queens' monuments by the second north–south street, at the south end of which is the entrance to the whole cemetery,[239] while the larger, western part was divided by four narrow east–west streets (the second to the fifth streets). Towards the end of Teti's reign, presumably as a result of the shortage of space, the large streets began to be used for building tombs, leaving much narrower passages instead, and starting from north to south, thus beginning with the more distant area from the pyramid. In this way the mastabas of Inumin [17] then Nedjetempet [32] were constructed in the first north–south street, followed perhaps by the now unnamed mud-brick structures. The first east–west street was also used for building later tombs, some probably from the end of Teti's reign or shortly after.[240] The narrow east–west streets were obviously not suitable for such projects, but in one instance the fourth east–west street was totally blocked by the construction of the small chapel of Tetiankh as an extension to the chapel of his father(?), Iries [20].

In the publication of the individual tombs in the cemetery there was a tendency by many scholars, and to a certain extent by the present writer, to date some of the tombs to a period later, even considerably later, than the reign of Teti. Three factors appear to have influenced such late dates: (a) sometimes two or three tombs show clear evidence that they were built one against the other, and accordingly one later than the other; (b) the style of art in some chapels is of inferior quality to that found in the main mastabas of Teti's viziers; (c) the inscriptions of some tombs show cartouches of kings who came to power after Teti. With the completion of the excavation and recording of the cemetery, the dating of the tombs, on which the history and events of the period are based, should be reconsidered. That a tomb was built against another surely demonstrates its later date, but how much later? Later tombs were built against the external walls of earlier ones, perhaps even before the total completion of the construction or the decoration of the latter. We do not have to think of a period of years separating two successively built tombs; it may have been only a few months or even days. The inferior style of art is not necessarily a criterion for a late date, but much more likely due to lesser means and the reliance on less adequate craftsmen. Scholars in the past were only too willing to place any Old Kingdom art which deviates from the traditional masterpieces of the period into a later time, even in the First Intermediate Period, which has now become illogically crowded with contradictory evidence.[241] The date of these so-called late monuments should be reconsidered. With regard to cartouches inscribed in tombs of the cemetery, it is true that some show names later than Teti, but these are by no means frequent and invariably refer to the same king, Pepy I/Nefersahor/Meryre. The main question that we should raise, however, is whether these tombs were constructed under Pepy I or were simply completed and decorated under this king.

With the completion of the excavations in the Teti cemetery we are in a better position to examine this problem carefully. We should divide the tombs where Pepy I appears into those which formed parts of the original layout of the cemetery and those which were later additions in marginal locations or blocking streets or parts thereof. We should also examine whether Pepy's cartouche appears in the names or titles of the tomb owner himself, or in that of a son, and whether the inscriptions including Pepy's name form part of the original decoration of the chapel or of later additions and alterations, usually showing a different hand or type of relief.

Only two tombs which clearly formed parts of the original design of the Teti cemetery show the name of Pepy I in the inscriptions of the tomb owner himself. These are the tombs of Meru [31] in the second east–west street and Khui [25] in the third street. Both Meru and Khui mentioned their priesthoods and other offices in the pyramids of Teti and Pepy I, and Meru changed his name from Tetiseneb to Pepyseneb and then to Meryreseneb,[242] changes which were probably linked to the accession of the new king or to the latter's acquisition of a new name. However, the examination of the decoration programme in the two tombs shows that neither of them had the name of Pepy in the initial stage of the decoration and that this appears to have been used in a later stage, when Meru's chapel, for example, unlike those of his equal contemporaries and neighbours, was cased with stone blocks and decorated.[243] Pepy's name appears in Khui's tomb only on the façade, presumably the last area to have been decorated, and the same area in Meru's tomb records the later name of Pepy, Meryre (see p. 103). There is nothing unusual in an official serving under two or more kings, and considering the relatively short reign of Teti (not much more than eleven years),[244] it is surprising that evidence for such cases is not more common. This in itself might hint at troubles in the transition from Teti to Pepy I.

Priesthoods of Pepy I's pyramid were also held by another two original tomb owners, Khentika [24] and Inumin [17]. Both men constructed their mastabas in marginal positions, which suggests that they were built when the cemetery was already fully occupied or at least fully allocated. Khentika was assigned a spot at the extreme eastern end of the cemetery away from tombs of other officials, and Inumin partly blocked the first north–south street. When we take into account that both men were viziers, the most powerful administrative officers in the country, we must conclude that by the time they built their tombs, no better, more conventional sites were available in the cemetery. Khentika was almost certainly a vizier in the last years of Teti and he held the same office under Pepy I, presumably at its beginning.[245] Inumin was overseer of Upper Egypt and was elevated to the vizierate early under Pepy I. A cartouche in the tomb with the early name of Pepy I, Nefersahor, was chiselled out and replaced, in red paint only, by the later name, Meryre (Figure 3.1).

Sons sometimes owned rooms or sections in their fathers' chapels. The cases in question are those of Neferseshemptah son of Neferseshemptah [33], Ishfi son of Ankhmahor [12], Meryteti son of Mereruka [30], Tetiankh (son of ?) Iries [20] and Khentika son of Khentika [24]. The well-preserved case of Meryteti clearly demonstrates that the doorway to his chapel was created by removing already decorated blocks from the north wall of Mereruka's pillared hall (Figure 3.2).[246] This means that work on the son's chapel began after that of the father was completed; that is, late in Teti's reign at the earliest. In this case, as well as in some others (Neferseshemptah and Khentika), it is not surprising to find that the son lived and held office under Pepy I.

The preceding discussion was necessary in order to demonstrate that late in the reign of Teti his unusually small and fenced cemetery was already fully occupied. Even the viziers of this time had to be content with less than ideal

Figure 3.1 Inumin went as far as erasing Pepy I's early name, Nefersahor, and replacing it with the new name, Meryre.

spots. Sons constructed their chapels in the empty space within the external walls of their fathers' mastabas, and, in the case of Tetiankh, son of Iries, just adjacent to his father's chapel which resulted in blocking the street. These actions by the sons are very rare outside the Teti cemetery. When Wepemnefert of the late Fifth Dynasty allowed his son to cut a chapel within his mastaba at Giza, a will with fifteen witnesses was inscribed on its wall,[247] and when Djau of Deir el-Gebrawi built a single tomb for himself and his father, he left an inscription explaining that this was not through the lack of means to build a second tomb, but because of his desire to be with his father in the same place.[248] Whether Djau's filial affection was the only reason behind his action is open to question, but in the four cases at Saqqara no justification whatever was given for using part of the father's mastaba. The only reason for such use that one can think of is the lack of other available space in the cemetery. The same lack of space was probably responsible for the location of the tombs of some of Pepy I's viziers in most unconventional spots in the Teti cemetery. For one reason or another (see p. 173) Pepy I preferred his officials, including the viziers, to be buried away from his own cemetery, and some of them were therefore buried in the Teti cemetery. In addition to the viziers Khentika, Inumin and Meryteti (son of Mereruka), who have already been discussed, Tjetju [43] built his chapel in an unusually elevated level in an angle formed by the external walls of the mastabas of Mereruka and Kagemni,[249] and Rawer [36] built his in the south-east corner of the pyramid, far from everyone else.[250]

The conclusion that towards the end of Teti's reign the cemetery was fully occupied has serious implications, for it would mean that the cemetery was presumably planned as a single project. Land was allocated for each official by the king, and this is specifically stated by Iri/Tetiseneb [19] (Figure 2.48).[251] But as each official paid for the construction of his tomb, a claim made, for example, by Iri/Tetiseneb and Mehi [26] (Figure 2.56),[252] the starting time or the speed of progress must have differed from one individual to another according to their means and responsibilities. Iri tells us that he

Figure 3.2 The incomplete figures on both sides of the door to Meryteti's chapel indicate that the door was opened into the north wall of Mereruka's pillared hall after the decoration of this wall was completed.

paid one stonemason, but that he did the work (possibly the brick work) with his own hands, together with his children and brothers. In such circumstances the building projects began and finished at different times, resulting in some individuals being able to abut their tombs against the already finished exterior walls of others, but at no time do these appear to be separated by any considerable time. With the exception of the limited number of officials whose tombs were built in awkward locations (Khentika [24], Tjetju [43], Rawer [36])[253] and those who added a chapel within their fathers' mastabas, all of whom were no later than Pepy I, the rest of the tomb owners most probably served under Teti and participated in the events of his reign. That a few of these outlived him to also serve under his successor(s) does not contradict this conclusion.

The site of the Teti cemetery was, as has been argued above, very restricted. There was no available space for the tombs of any future generation(s) of officials should the king live longer, nor was there a suitable location within sight for the cemetery of his successor(s), who accordingly had to move away to south Saqqara. With this being the case, there must have been some reasons, other than the suitability of the site, for Teti's choice of his cemetery.

Establishing the motives behind any decision is not, however, an easy matter: this could be influenced by a web of causes and effects interplaying upon each other, with perhaps the most obvious cause being in reality the least important, and the major cause being hardly apparent. Nevertheless, this should not stop us from seeking explanations for major decisions and actions.

Since the site of the Teti cemetery was far from being ideal, its selection may well have been dictated by the king's desire to be in the proximity of other particular royal monuments in this area. The closest to Teti's pyramid is that of Userkaf, followed by that of Djoser and finally that of Unis, all four pyramids being almost aligned along one north-east to south-west axis. Userkaf and Teti share the claim of being founders of what we, following Manetho, call dynasties. Djoser was the first to change the shape of the royal burial place into a pyramid, even though formed of steps, which may presumably indicate more than a mere progress in architecture and the use of stone. Unis is peculiar, for he does not seem to belong to the Fifth Dynasty, nor was he the founder of the Sixth.[254] Perhaps he attempted to establish a dynasty, but left no male heir and the honour of achieving this went to Teti. Yet Unis, like Djoser, revolutionized royal burials, being the first to inscribe his burial chamber with the Pyramid Texts, a tradition which was followed by the remaining Memphite kings. It is possible that the positioning of these four pyramids represented a kind of declaration of similar policies/beliefs by their owners. In this case Teti's choice of his site to the north-east of that of Userkaf rather than to the south-west of that of Unis may be explained as an attempt to associate himself with the group, and at the same time to somewhat distance himself from his immediate predecessor and indeed father-in-law, in order to avoid any confusion as to the real founder of the dynasty.

The monarchy and the sun cult

Like the owners of this group of pyramids, Djoser, Userkaf and Unis, Teti did not use Re as an element in his name. Considering the popularity of this element among kings of the late Fourth (Djedefre, Khafre and Menkaure), the Fifth (e.g., Sahure, Neferirkare, Niuserre) and Sixth (Userkare, Meryre, Neferkare) Dynasties, the absence of such an element from all four royal names in this group might have been more than a mere coincidence. We should not, however, think of this as a rejection of the sun cult by these kings, for they kept the 'son of Re' title, which is sometimes written inside the cartouche of Teti.[255] On the other hand, like the names of kings, individual names formed with Re as an element became conspicuously rare. After Teti's very early vizier Neferseshemre [34], who must have been so named long before Teti's reign, not a single tomb owner in this cemetery had Re in his name until the end of Pepy I's reign, when Rawer [36] held the vizierate. By that time, however, Pepy I himself had changed his name from Nefersahor to Meryre. In fact one can notice a trend towards the end of the

Fifth Dynasty, perhaps starting with Menkauhor's reign, to bear names formed with that of a deity other than Re. Names such as Ptahhetep, Akhethetep, Sebekhetep, etc. became particularly popular in this period. When we think that the end of the Fifth Dynasty and the founding of the Sixth followed the unprecedented rise in the visibility and possibly the power of the cult of Re, and perhaps its priesthood in the preceding period, with each king building a sun temple in addition to his own funerary complex, one wonders if what we have here was a reaction by Teti and the last kings of the Fifth Dynasty before him against this trend. However, for this to be true it has to apply also to Userkaf, whose pyramid is among this group, closest to Teti's, but who built a sun temple.

A study of the reign of Userkaf is outside the scope of this book, but a brief look at the transition from the Fourth to the Fifth Dynasty shows that this was not without problems. After the introduction of the title 'son of Re' late in the Fourth Dynasty, probably under Djedefre, this king was followed by Khafre and Menkaure, then by Shepseskaf. The last king did not have Re in his name, moved out of Giza to South Saqqara, did not build a pyramid but rather a sarcophagus-shaped tomb, the so-called Mastabet Faraon, and with him the dynasty came to an end. Userkaf's name has the same resonance as that of Shepseskaf, with the meaning 'powerful/noble is his ka'. The two names most probably glorify the ka of the king himself, and we have no reason to believe that they refer to the ka of Re. Royal names do not seem to be selected at random, and occasionally appear to represent a kind of declaration of policy. However, frequently a compromise has to be made in politics everywhere and Egypt was probably no exception. Userkaf later built a sun temple, but at Abusir, not at Saqqara where he had his pyramid. The Westcar Papyrus was composed probably as political propaganda establishing a strong bond between kings of the Fifth Dynasty and the cult of Re. But as this papyrus referred to the first three kings of the Fifth Dynasty, Userkaf, Sahure and Neferirkare, as triplets (a disputed fact) it could not have been composed before the reign of the third king Neferirkare, when the cult of Re was well entrenched.[256] Userkaf's sun temple shows a number of stages and probably expansions,[257] perhaps forced on him; but he was able to remain on the throne. A similar compromise was probably made later by Pepy I, who adopted the name Nefersahor at the beginning of his reign, but later changed it to Meryre, 'beloved of Re'.

Teti's appointment of two of his viziers, Kagemni [23] and Mereruka [30],[258] to the position of high priest of Re was very unusual and curious. This office was presumably held successively by the two viziers, since Kagemni was earlier than Mereruka, and was later held by Ibi, son of the vizier Khentika [24],[259] and between them they cover almost the entire reign of Teti.[260] Kagemni and Mereruka, and to some extent Khentika, possessed the richest and most impressive mastabas in the cemetery and, with Neferseshemre [34], were allocated the most prestigious sites, immediately in front of the king's funerary complex. Furthermore, both Kagemni and Mereruka were married to daughters of a king, presumably of Teti himself; we have no information on Khentika's wife. Did the appointment of the king's son-in-law to the office of the high priest of Re represent an elevation of the status of this post to a new height, or an attempt to bring it more under his control? The evidence suggests that the latter alternative is more likely.

Not only were the burials of the priests of the sun cult in the late Old Kingdom poor,[261] and names of officials formed with Re as an element exceedingly rare, but not a single funerary estate bearing the name of a king formed with Re was recorded in the Teti cemetery. Two scenes of female offering bearers with estate names inscribed in front of them are well preserved in the mastabas of Mereruka [30] and Hesi [15].[262] In the former, and of fifteen names containing cartouches, eight are those of Teti, five of Unis and one of Ikauhor.[263] The complete list of Hesi shows eighteen estates, fourteen bearing names formed with that of Teti, three with Unis and one with Userkaf (Figure 3.3).[264] When these names are compared to others listed in late Fifth Dynasty mastabas, where the names of Sahure, Neferirkare, Niuserre and Djedkare figure prominently,[265] the absence of royal names formed with Re in the Teti cemetery is striking. Furthermore, a total lack of Fifth Dynasty royal names in Sixth Dynasty tombs would have been comprehensible considering the change of dynasties, but restricting these names to those of Userkaf, Ikauhor and Unis is puzzling. Even if Userkaf and Unis formed part of this group of four pyramids, the inclusion of Ikauhor (Menkauhor), the only Fifth Dynasty king, other than the first and last – Userkaf and Unis – in the list of estates in Mereruka's tomb, is curious. No pyramid has yet been identified with certainty for Menkauhor/Ikauhor. Berlandini argues that he was the owner of a ruined pyramid to the east of that of Teti.[266] Her suggestion is questioned by Malek because of the absence of any significant Old Kingdom evidence, such as contemporary tombs in the area. He proposes other possible locations for this pyramid, which would have been more convenient, being away from the steep heights of the eastern edge of the Saqqara plateau.[267] The location of the funerary complexes of Teti's queens may lend support to Berlandini's suggestion, for if the area to the east of these was empty of earlier buildings it would have been of considerable advantage to construct them further to the east, thus allowing for more space in the desperately limited cemetery of Teti's officials. The area to the east of the Teti cemetery is covered by a high mound of sand and debris and needs systematic excavations before a conclusion on the presence of Menkauhor's pyramid is reached. But if it were there, which is possible, it would add yet another king to the group – Unis, Djoser, Userkaf and Teti – who built their pyramids on one axis and who had no Re in their names. However, Menkauhor built a sun temple known only from inscriptions and it is uncertain whether it was at Saqqara or at Abusir, like its predecessors.

Figure 3.3 Funerary estates of Hesi were named after Userkaf, Unis and Teti.

From Unis to Teti

Whether the transition from the Fifth Dynasty to the Sixth was plagued by a struggle for power between the priesthood of Re and the monarchy, and/or by some dynastic troubles, is uncertain. Following Menkauhor, the location of whose pyramid is still disputed, Djedkare/Isesi moved to South Saqqara. But whether by Menkauhor or Djedkare, the decision to abandon the site of Abusir, which had become associated with the sun temples, must have been for good reason(s). Although Isesi adopted the name Djedkare, 'the ka of Re is stable', he did not build a sun temple, and with him this Fifth Dynasty tradition came to an end. His successor, Unis, instead inscribed his burial chamber with the so-called Pyramid Texts, a new tradition which continued to the end of the Old Kingdom. The Pyramid Texts speak of a hereafter in the company of both Re and Osiris for the dead king, and it might be significant that Osiris appeared also in the offering formulae written in the tombs of officials under Djedkare or Unis. This rise in the importance, or the visibility, of Osiris, when viewed together with the abandonment of the construction of sun temples, may well have represented a challenge to the power of the priesthood of Re. Furthermore, the Pyramid Texts guaranteed a safe passage in the hereafter for the king, and their inscription in his burial chamber perhaps made him less dependent on the priesthood for his future well-being.

The relationship between Djedkare and Unis, and the latter and Teti, is far from being certain, but the evidence suggests no break between their reigns, and some of Teti's officials proudly recorded in the most obvious places in their tombs their services under the three kings. Examples of these officials are the viziers Kagemni [23][268] and Hesi [15][269] (Figure 3.4), and most probably the overseer of Upper Egypt Nikauisesi [35], whose name commemorated Djedkare/Isesi and who may well be the official with this name depicted on the causeway of Unis.[270]

Teti's mother was Queen Seshseshet, and her name became extremely popular at the time.[271] Although her name is known from many sources, no tomb for her has yet been found, and her relationship to Unis, if any, is not known. Teti, however, married Princess Iput who was described as 'daughter of the king of Upper and Lower Egypt, wife of the king of Upper and Lower Egypt and mother of the king of Upper and Lower Egypt',[272] referring to Unis, Teti and Pepy I, respectively.

On the surface, Teti's succession to the throne appears smooth, but in reality might have been less peaceful. His Horus-name, Seheteptawy, 'He who pacifies the Two Lands'[273] strongly hints at problems he had to deal with and advertises his policy. Names formed with Sehetep. . . 'He who pacifies . . .' appeared again, but always in periods of difficulties. Amenemhat I, founder of the Twelfth Dynasty, for example, had the name Sehetepibre, 'He who pacifies the heart of/is Re', and we know that the transition from the Eleventh Dynasty to the Twelfth was not without internal and possibly external problems. The opposition at Thebes, which was probably loyal to the Mentuhetep family of the Eleventh Dynasty, might even have forced Amenemhat to move his capital to El-Lisht in the north.[274] The evidence shows that, like Teti, an attempt had been made on Amenemhat's life, but whether it was successful or not is disputed.[275] The name he adopted, Sehetepibre, was used later a number of times, always at times of internal difficulties – for example during the Hyksos period.

To investigate whether Teti's accession was accompanied by some problems one needs to examine the evidence – not only from his cemetery but also from that of his predecessor, Unis. The latter cemetery, however, has not so far received the attention it deserves, although recent attempts to remedy this situation are being made.[276] Two tombs in the Unis cemetery seem to provide information on the problem under consideration; these belong to Akhethetep/Hemi [1] and Ihy [3]. Both men occupied the highest administrative position in the country, that of vizier, and it seems possible that they were contemporaries. Earlier studies have demonstrated the presence of two viziers in the capital, one for Upper Egypt and the other for the Delta.[277] An examination of the layout of the Unis cemetery shows the existence of three main rows of major tombs on an east–west axis. The middle one contains the tombs of the queens Nebet and Khenut, while the northern and southern ones were reserved for viziers and others who were likely to be promoted to

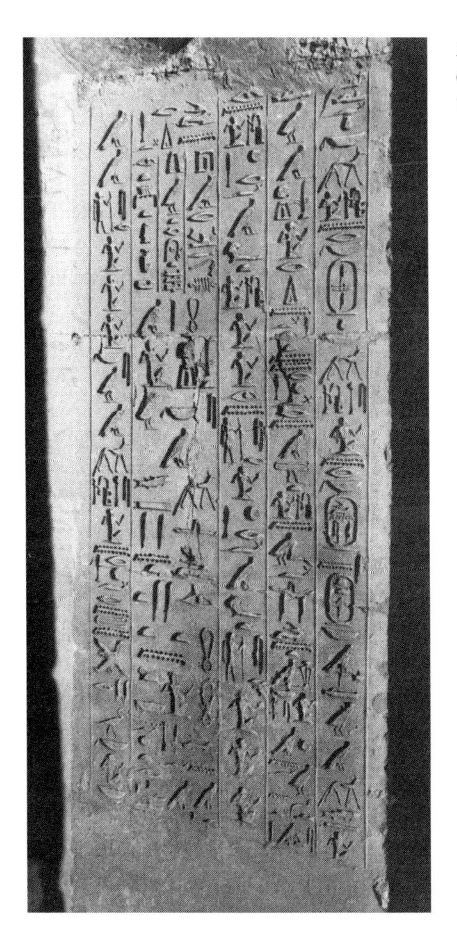

Figure 3.4 On the thickness of his entrance doorway Hesi recorded his career under Djedkare/Isesi, Unis and Teti.

this office. The northern row seems to have progressed eastwards, thus the tombs were built in the order Iynefert, Unisankh and Ihy [3]. The southern row, close and parallel to the causeway, progressed westwards as did the causeway itself, and therefore the tomb of Niankhba was followed by that of Akhethetep/Hemi [1]. It is likely that Ihy and Akhethetep/Hemi shared the vizierate, and the fact that the latter held the office of overseer of Upper Egypt suggests his responsibility for this part of the country, while Ihy might have been in charge of the Delta. It is interesting that Akhethetep's tomb is located in the southern row of tombs, while that of Ihy is in the northern row, perhaps representing Upper and Lower Egypt.

It is striking that both viziers lost their tombs, which were assigned to new owners. Akhethetep's tomb was given to a prince named Nebkauhor, with the 'beautiful name' of Idu, who was designated as eldest king's son of his body, while Ihy's tomb was given to a king's daughter of his body, called

Seshseshet, with the 'beautiful name' Idut. In both tombs the work relating to the new owners appears to have been executed in a great haste (Figure 2.2). The figures and inscriptions, including the titles, of Akhethetep were in most parts left intact, with only the name and one or two epithets erased at the end of certain lines in order to add the new name, Nebkauhor, and the designation of eldest king's son of his body. This was less than perfectly done; the new inscriptions were carelessly added and the name of the original owner was allowed to survive in a number of instances. In the case of Ihy, and because the new owner was a woman, his figures and titles had to be erased and replaced by her figure and epithets. There is a vast difference in the quality of his and her reliefs, hers being mediocre and very shallow (Figure 2.8). The name of Ihy could still be detected in the scenes of the chapel, and on the sarcophagus walls in the burial chamber, certainly less visible to the viewers, the name and titles have survived almost intact.

We do not know the crime for which Akhethetep and Ihy lost their tombs, and perhaps their lives, but as their tombs were assigned to members of the royal family, it is reasonable to deduce that the punishment was ordered by the king. The exact identity of the new owners is also uncertain. That they shared the same 'beautiful name', only with the addition of the feminine *t*, Idu and Idut, may be more than a mere coincidence; the two may have been brother and sister. They were both designated as king's son/daughter of his body, and Idu was described as 'eldest'. However, whether they were the children or grandchildren of the king is impossible to tell with our present information, and whether they were related to Unis or Teti has been equally uncertain. Because they were buried in the Unis cemetery it was tempting to associate them with this king. On the other hand, it is possible that they were related to Teti and that they died prematurely, before his cemetery was laid out and tombs built for them. This can explain not only their burial in the cemetery of Teti's predecessor, but also in tombs originally built for others, after hastily making alterations to suit the new occupants. That Idut died young is evident in her consistent representation with a pigtail and disc hairstyle, characteristic of young age,[278] and in the fact that she is shown once in a boat trip accompanied by her nurse.[279] As the figures of Akhethetep were not erased and replaced by those of Nebkauhor, the latter's maturity, or lack of it, cannot be assessed. And being a royal relative, even the titles he perhaps held[280] are not necessarily indicative of age.

The names of these two members of the royal family are of some interest in this regard. Idut bore the 'great name' of Seshseshet, a name held by Teti's mother as well as by all his daughters whom he gave in marriage to his top and most trusted officials (see p. 153). While the name Seshseshet might have also been used under Unis,[281] it seems more likely that Seshseshet/Idut was another daughter of Teti who died young at the beginning of his reign. It is also possible that the same scenario applies to Nebkauhor/Idu, whose name, Nebkauhor, has the same resonance as that of Teti's son and successor Pepy I who came to the throne under the name 'Nefersahor' and changed later to Meryre. If Nebkauhor was also a son of Teti his name may add to the evidence suggesting a determined policy by this king to distance himself from the power of Re.

Whether related to Unis or Teti, Idut must have died and been buried under Teti; a man named Tetiankh appears in the reliefs cut in Ihy's chapel when these were altered for Idut's use.[282] As Nebkauhor did not alter the scenes of Akhethetep's chapel, no cartouche later than that of Unis exists in the chapel; yet the absence of a later cartouche does not in itself disprove a later date. The tombs of Ihy and Akhethetep were certainly most spectacular, and having been 'confiscated' from their original owners they were unlikely to remain unallocated for a long time.[283] However, the reuse of a tomb was not befitting members of the royal family, and when two officials, including a vizier, in the Teti cemetery lost their tombs, these were reallocated to much more modest officials [15, 29]. In the cases of Idu and Idut it may well have been a matter of urgency. From the above discussion it appears that the two viziers, Ihy and Akhethetep, were disgraced and lost their tombs, presumably the equivalent of a 'perpetual death' sentence, at the end of Unis' reign, or the beginning of Teti's, and their tombs were reassigned shortly after to two members of the royal family, probably of Teti. The cause of the disgrace of the last two viziers of Unis is not known, nor is the cause of the premature death of the two royal children, but the possibility of a violent transition of power to the new dynasty should not be easily dismissed.

If Teti faced some internal problems, or opposition to his accession or rule, these were unlikely to have been publicized. For dynastic reasons, and for the preservation of the dogma of divine kingship, such problems had to be dealt with in secret. The many titles referring to important officials of the palace as 'He who is privy to the secrets of . . .' suggest that all affairs of the palace, the king and the royal family were officially conducted in secrecy. It is astonishing that Weni, for example, was later allowed to record in his autobiography and publicly advertise the trial of Pepy I's queen, which, as he specifically stated, was held in secrecy and which even the viziers and the higher officials were excluded from attending (Figure 1.1).[284] It is true that Weni wrote his biography in the following reign, under Merenre, who was not the son of the disgraced queen, but the very act of divulging such a royal secret is puzzling. Perhaps the fact that he was sent to Abydos, where he constructed his tomb, far from the central government, encouraged him to do so. With the usual secrecy surrounding the monarchy we should not expect to find direct evidence of problems under Teti. Nevertheless, indirect and circumstantial evidence, in the form of the type of officials with whom the king surrounded himself, statements made by these officials, new titles appearing at the time, etc., should be investigated.

High level of security

Teti seems to have drastically increased the number of guards of his palace and pyramid. The office of 'guard' was first introduced late in the Fifth Dynasty,[285] but the number of occupants, as far as we know, was far more restricted than that under Teti. Furthermore, at no other time were the holders of this office, particularly in its supervisory levels, overseers, superintendents, etc., so clustered in the cemetery of a reigning monarch. Presumably this reflects the desire of the king for these men to be close to him in the hereafter as well as in life. This appears also in the other responsibilities these 'guards' had, for they were in charge of one or more of the following departments: the king's repasts, his clothing, his ornaments, the palace cool rooms (bathrooms), etc. In addition to the tombs of the higher officials, including the viziers and overseers of Upper Egypt, etc., the rest of the cemetery is occupied by the tombs of individuals employed in the personal service of the king and who, in addition, were almost always 'guards'. Security appears to have become of paramount importance, not only for the king but also for his top officials and supporters. A striking example of this may be seen in the case of the vizier and son-in-law of the king, Mereruka [30], who was depicted in an outdoor activity, carried in a palanquin and accompanied by a number of men. Seven of them bore no titles other than that of a guard or one of its supervisory levels, and all seven were his brothers.[286] The appointment of Mereruka's brothers as guards was not exceptional, for the sons and relatives of most individuals buried in the Teti cemetery were absorbed in the same department, which must have become overcrowded with its employees.

Although the king's trust must have always been an essential factor in the appointment or the promotion of an official to an important position, it has never been so emphatically and systematically expressed as in the Teti cemetery. Many officials refer to themselves as 'confidant of the king', literally 'He who is in the heart/mind of the king',[287] and even though this title/epithet appeared before Teti's reign, presumably in the latter part of the Fifth Dynasty and perhaps linked to some difficulties then,[288] it has never been so frequently bestowed as evidenced in the Teti cemetery. Many officials also mention some distinction or honour received from the king, but the clearest example of this is found in the short but completely preserved autobiography of Hesi [15], who says:

> I was a judge and scribe in the time of Isesi. I was a judge and superintendent of scribes in the time of Unis. It was Teti, my lord, who promoted me as a judge and administrator, and who promoted me as royal chamberlain. His Majesty caused it to be done for me because His Majesty knew my name when selecting a scribe because of his ability, and without any backer. He remembered the one who spoke to him wisely.

> I became a scribe for His Majesty ahead of the scribes. I became a nobleman for His Majesty ahead of the noblemen. His Majesty had allowed that I accede to the great boat of the palace, that I be welcomed to the roads and that gifts be made, as if for a royal chamberlain, while I was only a judge and administrator. Never the like was done for any equal of mine. Likewise, His Majesty was discussing matters with me amongst the noblemen, while I was only a judge and superintendent of scribes, because His Majesty knew the name of he who was more distinguished than any servant. (Figure 3.4)[289]

The only reason given by Hesi for the exceptional treatment he received and for placing him ahead of all others was that the king knew his name and ability and remembered him as one who spoke to him wisely. But how such a junior official was able to be noticed by the king and to speak to him directly we are not told, and what 'wisdom' came out of his mouth that the king remembered we do not know. It must have been something of special importance to the king, and surely the usual way up the career ladder at that time appears to be through the personal trust and favours of the king.

While some favouritism and nepotism might be found in every government, they appear at their extreme under Teti. In addition to individuals like Hesi, who received royal favours for not very obvious reasons, four owners of large tombs – Kagemni [23], Mereruka [30], Neferseshemptah [33] and Shepsipuptah [38] – were married to princesses, probably daughters of Teti. The wives of the owners of some other impressive tombs – for example, Ankhmahor [12], Kaaper [22], Nikauisesi [35] and Khentika [24] – were not depicted in their chapels. Perhaps they died before the tombs were built and were accordingly buried elsewhere, but we cannot be certain that none of them was also a royal relative. The unprecedented need to be so surrounded by adherents and security, as may be clearly deduced from the evidence in the Teti cemetery, may hint at some kind of expected danger, or at least at some concern on the part of the king.

Such a concern may also be inferred from Teti's introduction of the title 'overseer of the protection of every house of the king/palace' (Figure 2.40). The first holder of this post was Mereruka [30],[290] followed by Khentika [24][291] and finally Inumin [17].[292] All three men were viziers, but not necessarily when first appointed to the position of 'overseer of the protection of every house of the king'. Inumin, for instance, recorded this position in his chapel, which he apparently decorated before becoming a vizier, a title which appears only in the inscriptions on his sarcophagus. Mereruka became a vizier and built his mastaba around the middle of Teti's reign but he may well have been responsible for the protection of the king's houses earlier, for this responsibility is not claimed by Teti's earlier viziers, Neferseshemre [34] and Kagemni [23]. If the protection post was introduced at the beginning of Teti's reign it could mean that his accession was not as peaceful as we thought, but if it started in the middle of the reign, it may suggest that some difficulties occurred in the first half of the reign which necessitated the creation of such a post. At some stage in his reign, probably at its beginning, Teti must have felt insecure or somehow threatened in order to initiate this position and consistently to entrust it to the highest administrator in the country, the vizier – or at least reward its holder with the vizierate.

Some other titles of Mereruka, the first holder of the position of protection, need to be examined. In addition to the usual administrative responsibilities associated with the vizierate, as well as some religious titles and those representing personal services to the king, Mereruka held two interesting titles, 'overseer of the house of weapons' and 'overseer of the king's harem'.[293] Holders of the first title seem to be responsible for the weapons in general, not only during wars, and as such one of them is shown in the temple of Sahure accompanying the king in a desert hunting expedition, where the king is shooting wild animals with bow and arrows and the official carrying a quiver full of arrows.[294] This title in all its forms, 'overseer of weapons', 'overseer of the house of weapons' and 'overseer of the two houses of weapons', is not very common, and although attested in the Fourth Dynasty,[295] evidence suggests a concentration of its holders in the period from the middle of the Fifth Dynasty to the early part of the Sixth,[296] almost all being buried in the capital cemeteries of Giza and Saqqara.[297] It is intriguing, however, that between the reigns of Djedkare and Teti the responsibility of weapons was entrusted to viziers – Seshemnefer III and Sendjemib/Inti under Djedkare, Sendjemib/Mehi under Unis, and Mereruka under Teti. These viziers appear to have been among the most distinguished ones of the Old Kingdom. Seshemnefer III, for example, was given the title 'king's son of his body' although neither his father, Seshemnefer II, nor his mother, Henutsen, appear to have royal blood;[298] Sendjemib/Inti inscribed in his tomb the text of two letters from Djedkare, and received some of his tomb equipment from this king. His son, Sendjemib/Mehi, succeeded him in the office and either built, or more likely completed, the tomb for him.[299] Mereruka [30] was also given the rare title of 'fosterchild of the king',[300] and his mother Nedjetempet [32] was given a separate tomb in the cemetery[301] rather than a burial in her husband's tomb at Giza.[302] The fact that she became the mother-in-law of Teti's daughter does not explain the special treatment, for three other daughters of the king were married to his officials, Kagemni [23], Neferseshemptah [33] and Shepsipuptah [38], yet none of their mothers, if they were alive at the time, received such a privilege. The question should be asked: why was the responsibility of the house of weapons given to the highest official in the country, and to men who seem to have been particularly close to the king, in this period in particular? After Mereruka the position was given to a lesser official, Mereri [29][303] and was never held by a vizier for the remainder of the Old Kingdom.

Mereruka was also 'overseer of the king's harem', an unusual title for a vizier. But it is interesting that Sendjemib/Inti was 'overseer of the houses of the king's children'.[304] The responsibility for the house of the king's harem or for that of his children might appear in the first instance as the job of a caretaker or butler, but it is not.[305] The importance, and possibly the sensitivity, of the royal harem might appear in the later appointment of Weni, the most trusted official of Pepy I, to the charge of it.[306] Weni revealed to us the secret trial of Pepy I's wife within the royal harem (Figure 1.1), but we do not know the crime committed, nor if precedents existed. However, the multiple marriages and the large number of children of different mothers that the Egyptian kings had, no doubt provided fertile ground for internal strife and intrigues. This problem was presumably compounded when a king with no royal blood acceded to the throne by marrying the daughter of his predecessor, for in such a case the real eldest son by an earlier marriage was likely to compete with the son of the princess for the throne, each probably supported by his mother and a group of officials. An example of this may be seen in the later case of Amenemhat I, founder of the Twelfth Dynasty, and his son and successor, Senusert I. In a unique piece of literature, believed to be composed on behalf of Senusert I by a royal scribe, Amenemhat I, presumably after he was assassinated, was made 'to speak from the grave', giving instructions to his son Senusert I, saying:

> Beware of subjects who are nobodies,
> Of whose plotting one is not aware.
> Trust not a brother, know not a friend,
> make no intimates, it is worthless.
> When you lie down, guard your heart yourself,
> for no man has adherents on the day of woe . . .
> He whom I gave my trust used it to plot.

Amenemhat then speaks of an attack by his guard while he was asleep – 'weapons for my protection were turned against me' – and hints at the role played by women of the palace in the plot.[307] Amenemhat I therefore warned his son against brothers, intimates, guards and women. No such direct evidence, as in the case of Amenemhat I, has survived from the reign of Teti. Yet the analysis of the indirect evidence from his cemetery suggests that his reign was not free from similar problems and that the king took the utmost and unusual measures of security and protection.

End of Teti's reign

As argued above, the small cemetery to the north of Teti's pyramid appears to have been planned and apportioned as a single project. Although a limited number of sites were allocated later, these were in awkward locations, partly or fully obstructing certain paths. It has also been noted that although the building of tombs in this cemetery progressed at different times and possibly at different speeds, there is no reason to think that any of the tombs occupying a 'proper' allotment were built after Teti's reign. While our evidence frequently allows us to date the building and/or decoration of a tomb, it seldom permits us to establish the time of the owner's death. One exception in this regard is Nikauisesi [35], in whose tomb the date of his burial was recorded as 'the eleventh count, first month of inundation season, day 20. Burial in the necropolis of the hereditary prince, the treasurer of the king of Lower Egypt, Nikauisesi' (Figure 2.70).[308] It has already been argued that this date refers to the eleventh count under Teti, the highest so far known and probably one of the latest to be undertaken by this king. It has also been argued that the count was annual in this period and not biannual as many suggested, and accordingly Teti could not have reigned for much longer than eleven years.[309]

With such a relatively short reign it should be expected that a good portion of Teti's personnel would have outlived him, but the probability of this should theoretically be less among individuals appointed to the top administrative positions, whom one would expect to be of mature age. The viziers Neferseshemre [34], Kagemni [23], Ankhmahor [12] and Mereruka [30] ended their careers before Teti's death, but we do not know whether they died or if retirement from office existed in ancient Egypt, although the first alternative seems much more likely. It is now believed that beginning with the reign of Djedkare there were two viziers serving simultaneously in the capital and that their functions may have been divided on a geographical basis,[310] which may explain the embarrassingly high number of viziers who served during the relatively short reign of Teti. None of the four above-mentioned viziers had his personal figures or inscriptions in his tomb chapel deliberately damaged, although the figures of their sons or retainers were frequently targeted.

With the end of Mereruka's career, whether he died or, less likely, retired, he was presumably succeeded by Khentika [24]. The tombs of these two officials bear great similarities in design concept. Another vizier buried in this cemetery who could have shared the office with Khentika is Hesi [15]. This was towards the end of Teti's reign, when his trusted officials and in-laws, upon whom he clearly relied in the earlier part of his reign, were already dead and their offspring with royal blood must have been still too young to replace them. A change of policy appears to have been introduced. The accumulation of responsibilities, and accordingly power, as was given to Mereruka, was never repeated, and his duties were distributed amongst a number of officials, none of whom was at the administrative level of a vizier. Thus the office of 'overseer of the protection of every house of the king' was given to Inumin [17] (when he was overseer of Upper Egypt and before becoming a vizier under Pepy I), the office of 'overseer of (the house of) weapons' was given to Mereri [29] who had a tomb opposite that of the vizier Hesi, and the office of 'overseer of the royal harem' was assigned to an official named Ibi, who had his two false doors fitted into the west wall of a small room leading to the offering chamber of Nedjetempet [32], mother of Mereruka.[311] The date of Ibi is uncertain, but could not have been much later than that of the original building of Nedjetempet's mastaba, when the chapel was still perfectly clear and accessible.[312] Ibi must have been related to Nedjetempet and accordingly to Mereruka. The fragmentation of the responsibilities originally exercised by Mereruka should not reflect on his loyalty, and indeed his son, Meryteti, became a vizier under Pepy I. However, it may indicate a reduced level of trust by Teti in his remaining personnel and his reluctance to put too much power into the hands of any of them, as he once did with his son-in-law Mereruka. This apparent lack of trust proved to be well justified.

Was Teti assassinated?

There is no contemporary source referring to the assassination of Teti, and Manetho's statement, written almost two thousand years after the event, mentioning that Teti was murdered by his bodyguards, remains our only report on the matter. Although Manetho's statement should not be accepted at face value, it should equally not be rejected because of the absence of direct evidence to support it. Concealing such an event, even by a usurper to the throne, was essential for the preservation of the dogma of divine kingship. Yet we do not know if there were any contemporary sources (similar, for example, to the Instructions of King Amenemhat I to his son Senusert) which were available to Manetho but are now lost to us. The indirect evidence from the Teti cemetery should be considered.

The people who were theoretically in the best position to assassinate the king were those closest to him – that is, his guards and other personnel employed in his personal services. The majority of these were buried in front of his pyramid.[313] If Teti was actually murdered, the fate of the assassins and those who helped them or had been slack in their duties of protection would have depended on the identity of the successor. If this was a usurper who benefited from their action it would probably be expected that these individuals be rewarded, or at least not punished. If, on the other hand, the successor was a son, the culprits' penalties would almost certainly be severe.

We know that Teti was succeeded by Userkare, but the latter's relationship to Teti is disputed. Some see him as a usurper, and with the name Userkare ('The ka of Re is powerful') may have led the opposition to the current regime with the view of returning the sun cult, and its priesthood, to its previous supremacy. Others consider him as a legitimate king, mentioned in the Abydos and the Turin king lists, or 'as a stopgap ruler who would have overseen the regency of Queen Iput, Teti's widow, while her son was still too young to come to the throne'.[314] Userkare's mention in the king lists is totally unrelated to the way he acceded to the throne; a king who ruled over Upper and Lower Egypt was considered worthy of an entry. Furthermore, kingship is for life in ancient Egypt and no examples of 'stopgap' rulers are known. Certainly no such person is mentioned in king lists during the long minority of Pepy II who was reportedly appointed at the age of six, and a regent does not enjoy the royal titulary. Some scholars think that Userkare was a son of Teti by a wife whose damaged tomb lies in the partly unexcavated area in the Teti cemetery, between the pyramid of Queen Khuit and the mastaba of Khentika [24].[315] While this suggestion is not impossible, it cannot be proven without further excavations in this area. Nevertheless, even if Userkare was a son of Teti by a secondary wife perhaps from an earlier marriage, he succeeded to the throne by supplanting the heir apparent, Pepy I, son of Idut, the daughter of Unis. This in itself is a usurpation of the throne. The short reign of Userkare, probably not much more than one year,[316] the very limited monuments belonging to him,[317] and most importantly the total absence of any reference to him in a personal name, or that of an estate, or in a title, including any related to a funerary cult, in the tombs of many officials who served under Teti and Pepy I, and therefore under Userkare (e.g. Khentika [24] and Inumin [17]), strongly suggest that Pepy I, probably for good reason, wished to wipe out any memory of this king. In fact, if Userkare was the son of a minor queen of Teti then this might explain the perhaps deliberate destruction of her tomb.

Goedicke's suggestion that Userkare reigned for a long period of between 20 and 33 years, is not supported by contemporary evidence, but his assumption that Pepy I considered his reign as beginning with the death of his father Teti[318] might have some validity. However, Pepy I's apparent desire to obliterate the memory of Userkare should not automatically mean that Teti was murdered or that Userkare was the conspirator. It may be argued that Userkare simply took advantage of the young age of the heir apparent, Pepy I, and declared himself king after Teti's death from natural causes. This is not impossible, but highly unlikely, for if this was the case then Pepy I's reprisal when he regained the throne would have been directed against Userkare and perhaps a limited number of the top officials who helped him achieve his goal. Instead, the great majority of individuals known to us who were attached to the palace in various capacities were punished.

Egyptian history is full of examples of punishments in the form of erasure of names and figures from monuments. Not only did private individuals suffer in this manner but royalty also was sometimes subjected to similar treatment by their disgruntled successors, for instance as seen on the monuments of Hatshepsut and Akhenaten. Many cemeteries offer examples of tomb owners whose names and figures have been chiselled off their monuments, but these are usually isolated cases, most probably as a result of a serious offence committed by an individual owner. However, the Teti cemetery remains unique in that the majority of its tombs show evidence of deliberate destruction of names and figures, and because most of these appear to belong to a limited period of time. Such actions could not be attributed to vandalism, for they are well targeted and executed, usually restricted to the name and/or the figure or to parts of the body. The chiselling out was generally done with precision and only to the name or the figure, leaving the rest of the inscription or scene intact. In some cases where accidental damage occurred to a figure or inscription of a person who was not meant to be erased (for example, the inscriptions belonging to the wife of Seankhuiptah [37] (Figure 2.74)), these were restored in black paint. The impression one gets is that the people in charge of the erasure were executing very specific orders. But what does such damage represent?

In a later conspiracy which took place at the end of Rameses III's reign we learn from surviving papyri that this was organized in the harem by a second wife attempting to secure the throne for her son. The plot failed, twenty-eight were brought to trial and seventeen were executed. Five judges were arrested for collusion or for having relationships with the accused women; one was condemned to commit suicide, three had their ears and noses cut off, and the last was reprimanded.[319] Such a documented case informs us of the type of punishment inflicted for a crime of this sort. Yet, bearing in mind the Egyptian beliefs in a perpetual hereafter, any punishment would theoretically be ineffective unless it is also everlasting, for there is little point in inflicting a punishment, including a death penalty, if the person will live forever in the afterlife. The individual's name formed an essential aspect of their personality, distinguishing one from others. Remembrance and pronouncing the name was important for the survival of the deceased, and it was necessary to call the name for the dead person to come and receive the most needed earthly sustenance in the form of offerings. The name was usually written many times in the tomb, or on the same object, as for example on the false door, in order to be visible and to guarantee its survival. Tomb owners needed their memory to remain in the minds of future generations. This is clear in many burials from the later periods – Djehutirekh says 'O you who are alive on earth, who shall come here to this desert; all you who come to offer in this graveyard: pronounce my name with abundant libation, Thoth will favour you for it.' Petosiris says: 'I built this tomb in the necropolis, beside the great souls who are there, in order that my father's name be pronounced, and that of my elder brother. A man is revived when his name is pronounced.' The teachings written in the Insinger Papyrus explain the wisdom behind this desire to commemorate one's name as: 'The grace of the god for the man of god is his burial and his resting place. The renewal of life before the dying is leaving his name on earth behind him.' With such a belief, erasing someone's name would not only condemn them to oblivion but also eliminate their chances of receiving offerings and threaten their very essence. It was also believed that the tomb owner's ka ('life force') could enter his statue or his figure in a scene of fishing, fowling or watching daily life activities and relive the pleasant moment.

Thus erasing his figures would deprive him of such opportunities. It seems likely that the damage to the name and/or figure in a tomb was also accompanied by a punishment in real life, thus the punishment was 'perpetual'. The consistent damage to the face and feet of Mereri in the scenes of his tomb may well have been accompanied by the cutting of his nose, ears and feet in real life.

It is unfortunate that a study of the human remains from these tombs could not be more informative. Records of earlier excavations are not as complete as one would wish. The lack of, or at least inadequate, mummification practised at the time meant that only skeletal remains survived, from which it is frequently impossible to establish any bodily mutilation or the cause of death. Many tombs have been reused in later periods, and thus we cannot always be certain that the remains belonged to the original owner. One of the important questions is: was a disgraced person actually buried in his tomb? Some of the tombs of such individuals were found empty of any human remains. But that does not necessarily indicate that the owner was deprived of the use of his resting place; frequently tomb robbers removed and/or destroyed the body to prevent it from taking vengeance on them, and many tombs of people who were certainly not punished were equally empty of human remains. When the tomb of a disgraced man was allocated to another (for example, Hesi and Seshemnefer [15]), even if the body was found, which is rarely the case, it would be almost impossible to attribute the remains to either of the owners with any degree of certainty. One example in the Teti cemetery can fortunately be useful in answering this question; this is Mereri, who was disgraced and his tomb reallocated to a woman named Merynebty [29]. In the burial pit, which was found still closed, even though the lid was broken at the corner and the contents very disturbed, the almost complete remains of a woman, and only a very few bones of a male, were found. As this burial chamber was broken into by tomb robbers tunnelling through from a neighbouring burial chamber, the few male bones are likely to be intrusive, pushed from the latter chamber through the tunnel and the break in the lid of the burial pit. The body actually buried in the pit was that of a woman.[320] This may well suggest that individuals who lost their names and figures, as did Mereri [29], were also deprived of the use of their tombs for a proper burial.

The damage inflicted on scenes and inscriptions varies from one tomb to another; some lost only the name, as did Semdent [39], others both name and figure, as did Hesi [15], Mereri [29] and Seankhuiptah [37]. Some tomb owners did not lose their entire figures, but these show systematic damage to certain parts of the body – the hands, legs, nose and ears, as for example in the case of Mereri [28] and Irenakhti [18]. Evidence suggests that individuals whose figures were partly mutilated were allowed the use of their tombs and were actually buried in them. This seems in total agreement with the Egyptian justice system. The king had to maintain justice, 'Maat', or at least he had to be seen to do as much. Every criminal was entitled to a trial. Pepy I's queen was tried, even though in secret, and the conspirators against Rameses III were tried by a court of twelve judges, and the dishonest judges were also tried. The different types of damage inflicted on the names and figures of the tomb owners in the Teti cemetery were not haphazard, but probably represented different punishments for different levels of involvement in perhaps the same crime; thus punishment had to fit the crime. The number of tomb owners punished and the titles they held suggest involvement in a major crime in/against the palace, since the common factor among them is that they were all employed in the personal service of the king. It is important to note that not every tomb shows damage to the name and/or figure of the tomb owner himself (this is different from the damage to the inscriptions or figures of his sons or retainers, which could have been done at a later stage). Two categories of officials escaped any such deliberate damage; those who ended their career, or more likely died, before the end of Teti's reign (for example, Neferseshemre [34], Kagemni [23], Mereruka [30], Ankhmahor [12], Neferseshemptah [33] and almost certainly Nikauisesi [35]) and those who were not in the personal service of the king (for example, Nedjetempet [32], Tetiankh and Hesy [40] and Hefi [14]). This may well suggest that the punishment was for some offence directly related to the king, probably at the very end of Teti's reign.

A bunch of conspirators

While evidence for punishment is found in most tombs of the Teti cemetery, it is particularly evident in the tombs located in the fourth east-west street. We know that the sites for the tombs were allocated by the king (Iri/Tetiseneb [19] clearly states this),[321] but we are not sure of the criteria by which the lots were assigned to different individuals. In all cemeteries where successive generations of officials were buried there is an obvious preference for tombs belonging to members of the same family to be in the same vicinity. This was presumably out of desire to be close to people they loved; Djau of Deir el-Gebrawi goes as far as saying that he built a single tomb for both himself and his father in order to be with him in one place so that he could see him every day.[322] However, the Teti cemetery, as already argued, appears to have been designed as a single project, with very limited later additions. Owning tombs in the same street, and the frequent use of an exterior wall of a neighbouring tomb as a common wall, might suggest some kind of comradeship, and not improbably family relationship, between these tomb owners. Nevertheless, although the sites in the Teti cemetery were occupied within a short period of each other, the proximity from the pyramid may offer a criterion for a relative dating. But we should always bear in mind the possibility of a later tomb added in an available space. In this respect tombs in the fifth and last street from the pyramid, like that of Ishfi, may well be dated to the beginning of Pepy I's reign. Tombs in the fourth street were probably built later under Teti, and this is almost certain in the case of Hesi [15], for instance, who used the exterior wall of Shepsipuptah [38], who in turn abuts on Nikauisesi's mastaba [35]. The last probably constructed his mastaba around the middle of Teti's reign.

Many tombs in the fourth east–west street provide strong evidence for a date under Teti. In addition to holding offices in the pyramid of Teti and bearing a name formed with that of Teti, Iri/Tetiseneb [19] says that it was 'the king' who granted him the site of his tomb.[323] The reference to 'the king', without the need to mention his name in this cemetery and in the context of this statement, almost certainly signifies Teti. Mehi [26] specifically wished that 'his honour remain before Teti'.[324] Hesi [15] left a short, but complete, biography outlining his career under Djedkare, Unis and finally Teti, and there is no mention of a later king in his titles or in the names of his funerary estates (Figure 3.4).[325] Mereri [29], like Mehi, wished that 'his honour remain before Teti', and he also mentioned that he was an 'honoured one before Teti, may he be given life forever'. Both Hefi [14] and Seankhuiptah [37] held priesthoods in Teti's pyramid, and the architecture of their tombs suggests a date under this king. The absolutely square shape of Hefi's mastaba [14], the presence of a stairway leading to the roof and the depiction of the tomb owner on the panel of the false door at either end of the offering table are all characteristics of the earliest tombs built in this cemetery (for example, Neferseshemre [34], Kagemni [23] and Neferseshemptah [33]). The tomb of Seankhuiptah [37] shares with those of Shepsipuptah [38] and Nedjetempet [32] an unusual architectural feature for the Sixth Dynasty, a series of compound niches in one of the external walls. Shepsipuptah was married to a princess, possibly a daughter of Teti, and Nedjetempet was the mother of the vizier Mereruka [30], who ended his career late under Teti. The evidence strongly suggests that all the tombs in this street were constructed before the end of Teti's reign.

To establish whether these officials outlived Teti, two tombs offer indirect, but significant evidence. On the architrave of Mehi [26] he is described as honoured before Teti;[326] yet the name of Teti is written on a separate piece of stone which, although cut exactly to replace a removed small section of the architrave, is thinner and of poorer quality than the main block and also appears to have been inscribed by a different hand (Figure 2.56). It seems possible that the cutting and removal of the original part caused the breakage of the large block down the middle, or at least it weakened it, resulting in the breakage when the architrave fell down from its place. The inscriptions on the small block were almost certainly meant to replace a previous error, but it is astonishing that the only error in such a fine piece of work coincided with the name of the reigning king. Furthermore, errors could simply be corrected by erasing the signs or covering them with plaster and adding the new signs, rather than by such a drastic action as was taken here. The context of the inscription makes it clear that the cartouche of Teti replaced another name of a king – but who was he? It would be unlikely for an official building his tomb in the Teti cemetery to mention only that he was honoured before Unis then to change it to Teti, nor is it logical to remove the name of Teti and replace it for no reason with that of the same king. It is also unlikely that the original name was that of Pepy I, and that in his reign Mehi replaced his cartouche with that of his father. The only possibility left is that the removed name was that of Userkare, but it remains highly unlikely that the building and decoration of Mehi's tomb was undertaken during the short reign of this king. What appears to be more probable is that the original inscription contained the cartouche of Teti, which was chiselled out and replaced with that of Userkare during the latter's reign. When Pepy I came to the throne, it was impossible to return to the original name of Teti without chiselling much deeper, spoiling the appearance of the architrave and rendering the first change all the more obvious. Thus the name was cut and replaced on a different stone.

The tomb of Mehi's immediate neighbour, Iri/Tetiseneb [19], provides more evidence to support the above deduction. Iri built his tomb against that of Mehi [26], and the two were probably colleagues working in the same profession in the palace. Six or seven[327] times on his false door, Iri's name replaced an earlier name which was meticulously chiselled out, causing the areas on which the new name is written to be appreciably deeper and rougher than those of the remaining inscriptions (Figure 2.47). The same thing was done on the entrance lintel, but there traces of the original name are clearly visible. The name Tetiseneb was replaced by the phrase 'the honoured one by the great god, Iri' (Figure 2.46). It is tempting in such cases to conclude that the monuments were usurped from an earlier owner, except that both names, Tetiseneb and Iri, occur on the entrance architrave of the same tomb, Iri being his 'beautiful name' (Figure 2.48). On this architrave, the name Tetiseneb was written twice in the same line (line 6) of the text. In the first instance it was completely removed and replaced by the name Iri, in rough outline only. In the second instance the erasure of the cartouche of Teti, in the name Tetiseneb, appears to have just begun. Iri, obviously for strong reasons, wanted to conceal his real name Tetiseneb 'Teti is healthy' and to replace it by 'his beautiful name' Iri, even though this clearly spoiled the appearance of his monument. Once more, Iri, like his neighbour Mehi, appears to have taken extreme measures to disassociate himself from King Teti. However, his title as guard in the pyramid of Teti was not damaged, presumably because, except in very unusual circumstances, the cult of the dead king had to be maintained. But bearing an official title in Teti's funerary cult was obviously less personal than being named Tetiseneb.

The above two cases of Mehi and Iri strongly suggest that they outlived Teti, that they transferred their allegiance, most probably to Userkare, and later declared their loyalty to Teti – at least Mehi did, presumably when his son Pepy I came to the throne. This in itself, if true, may indicate that the accession of Userkare was not smooth and that he was probably not considered as a legitimate successor to Teti. Iri's erasure of his name, Tetiseneb, stopped short of completely removing the last instance of the name. One wonders if this was due to the lack of time; if so, then Userkaf's reign must have been particularly short, perhaps even shorter than the one to two years usually assigned to it.[328] Whether Mehi and Iri were successful in regaining Pepy I's confidence seems doubtful. Although there is no evidence of deliberate damage to their tombs, the work on their false doors seems to have come to an abrupt end, both being left unsmoothed, with very few, unfinished internal details in the signs. The fact that Mehi's burial pit was also unfinished, with its lid resting on parallel blocks of stone as if waiting to be rolled over the pit, and the complete absence of human remains, might suggest that the burial did not take place.[329]

This same unfinished condition is observed in many of the neighbouring tombs. Geref [13], Iri's immediate neighbour to the east, had the upper lintel of his false door left uninscribed, the remainder of the door was decorated in relief with no details, and the standing figures of the owner at the bottom of the jambs were mostly in black paint only (Figure 2.30).[330] Further east is the tomb of an official whose name is lost [45], and it was not necessarily deliberately damaged. Only about one-third of his architrave is preserved *in situ*, and no part where the name was written has survived. Although the inscriptions on the architrave were finely finished, the only false door in the chapel was rough and totally uninscribed (Figure 2.81).[331] This tomb definitely shows that the decoration of the architrave was undertaken before that of the false door, a conclusion supported by the unfinished condition of the false doors of Mehi [26], Iri [19] and Geref [13], despite the fact that the decoration of their architraves was complete. The unfinished work on these four neighbouring tombs, including in one instance leaving the only false door in the tomb uninscribed, could hardly be due, in all cases, to the premature death of the owners. It appears more likely that the decoration of the tombs was progressing simultaneously and was interrupted suddenly.

Facing the tombs of Mehi and Iri in the same street are those of Irenakhti [18] and Iries [20]. The figure of Irenakhti, particularly his face, was attacked in six out of the seven times he is depicted on the northern false door (Figure 2.44). The smaller, southern false door, perhaps belonging to his wife, was never inscribed, and the scenes on the west wall of the chapel show clear evidence of deliberate damage and later restoration, which was abandoned at an early stage (Figure 2.45). This damage and incomplete repair is also found in Iries' chapel (Figure 2.50), although his own figure was left intact. However, the name of his eldest son was attacked, but this could have been at a somewhat later date (Figure 2.49).

While two tombs to the west of the above-mentioned group, those of Tjetji [42] and Tetiankh [40], show no evidence of any deliberate damage, three other tombs in the eastern end of the street have suffered the most drastic damage attested in this cemetery. These are the tombs of the vizier Hesi [15], the overseer of weapons Mereri [29], and the chief physician of Upper and Lower Egypt Seankhuiptah [37]. The three individuals appear to have been contemporaries, most probably at the end of Teti's reign. Hesi and Mereri received what seems to be the harshest punishment; their figures and names have been chiselled out, smoothed over and in the case of Hesi covered with plaster (Figures 2.32–2.37, 2.59, 2.60).[332] Furthermore, their tombs were reallocated to others, the only ones to be so treated in the cemetery.[333] Hesi's tomb was given to a lector priest called Seshemnefer, who left an inscription in an obvious place on the two portico pillars stating that the tomb was a boon from the king (Figure 2.38).[334] This inscription clears Seshemnefer from any accusation of usurpation, and since the tomb was given to him by the king, then the punishment of Hesi must have also been by the king. Mereri's tomb, on the other hand, was given to a woman named Merynebty who held the titles of acquaintance of the king and guard, the only female guard attested in this cemetery (Figure 2.60).[335] The fact that in the burial chamber of this tomb the human remains are predominantly those of a female may suggest that it was Merynebty who actually used the tomb (see p. 99). It is interesting to notice that Mereri was the only official other than Mereruka [30] to be in charge of weapons, and it seems that after Mereruka this responsibility was divorced from the vizierate.

The third individual in this group is the chief physician Seankhuiptah [37]. The involvement of the chief physician in what appears to have been a plot in the palace brings to mind the Instruction of Ankhsheshonq, a literary papyrus from the Ptolemaic period, but possibly copied from an earlier source. Ankhsheshonq, a priest of Re at Heliopolis, was visiting his friend Harsiese, the chief physician, at Memphis. During his long stay with him, Harsiese confides in Ankhsheshonq that he, some councillors, generals and grandees of the palace have agreed to murder the king. Their conversation was overheard by a servant who reported it to the king. The physician and the other conspirators were executed, and Ankhsheshonq was sent to prison for having failed to inform the king. In the prison he composed his instructions for his son.[336] This literary piece is not mentioned here to suggest any similarity of events, but in order to indicate who, according to the Egyptian way of thinking, was able or likely to plot against the king, and certainly the chief physician was one. The decorations of Seankhuiptah were treated somewhat differently from those of Hesi [15]. Although the figures of both tomb owners were chiselled out, those of Hesi were completely hidden by smoothing and plastering them, while the shape of Seankhuiptah's figures were allowed to survive (Figures 2.72–2.75), even the original red outlines being still visible.[337]

The name of Hesi [15] could be detected with great difficulty in some areas, but it has survived once intact above the entrance doorway inside the chapel

(Figure 2.36).[338] As the incoming light makes it difficult to observe the inscriptions in this spot, it may be argued that the survival of the name in this instance was an accidental omission. However, the name of Seankhuiptah [37], although systematically erased, can be read in a number of places, and was left intact in the most obvious spots: in the centre of the architrave above the entrance doorway (Figure 2.72)[339] and on the entrance drum.[340] As the damaged names of the tomb owners throughout the cemetery have survived in full or in part so that in almost all cases we can read them, we can conclude that either the people responsible for the erasure were sympathetic to the tomb owners' cause (but one wonders if they were able to leave the names so evident!), or that the damage, even incomplete, was believed to be sufficient to achieve its purpose, and perhaps the intact instances of the names represented further disgrace to their owners and perpetual reminders of their involvement in the crime.

Many suspects

Having analysed the evidence from the fourth east–west street we now summarize the data from the whole cemetery. This will be restricted to tomb owners only as damage to the names and/or figures of their sons and retainers could have been related to subsequent events. The same may also apply to tomb owners buried in marginal locations in the cemetery (Ishfi [21] and Rawer [36]).

Tombs where the figure and name of the owner were erased

	Name	*Location*	*Positions held*
1	Hesi/reused by Seshemnefer [15]	4 E–W	Vizier
2	Mereri/reused by Merynebty [29]	4 E–W	Overseer of weapons
3	Seankhuiptah [37]	4 E–W	Chief physician

Tombs where only the name was erased

1	Semdent [39]	2 E–W	Guard, service of king

Tombs where parts of the owner's body were mutilated

1	Irenakhti [18]	4 E–W	Guard
2	Mereri [28]	3 E–W	Guard, service of king
3	Meru [31]	2 E–W	Guard, service of king
4	Wernu [44]	3 E–W	Guard, service of king

Tombs showing interrupted damage and some repair

	Name	*Location*	*Positions held*
1	Irenakhti [18]	4 E–W	Guard
2	Iries [20]	4 E–W	Judge, king's confidant
3	Kaaper [22]	2 N–S	Administrator

Tombs where decoration was left unfinished, but with no damage to tomb owner

	Name	Location	Positions held
1	Ankh [11]	2 E–W	Guard, service of king
2	Geref [13]	4 E–W	Service of king
3	Ihyemsaf [16]	3 E–W	Guard, service of king
4	Iri [19]	4 E–W	Guard, service of king
5	Mehi [26]	4 E–W	Guard
6	Tjetetu [41]	3 E–W	Guard, administrator
7	Wernu [44]	3 E–W	Guard, service of king
8	Name lost [45]	4 E–W	Judge

Tombs with finished decoration and no damage to tomb owner

	Name	Location	Positions held
1	Ankhmahor [12]	2 N–S	Vizier
2	Hefi [14]	4 E–W	Judge and priest
3	Inumin [17]	1 N–S	Vizier
4	Kagemni [23]	1 N–S	Vizier
5	Khentika [24]	N–E of pyramid	Vizier
6	Khui [25]	3 E–W	Overseer of Upper Egypt, service of king
7	Memi [27]	3 E–W	Service of king
8	Merefnebef [46]	West of Step Pyramid	Vizier
9	Mereruka [30]	1 E–W	Vizier
10	Neferseshemptah [33]	2 N–S	Judge
11	Neferseshemre [34]	2 N–S	Vizier
12	Nedjetempet [32]	1 N–S	Mother of Mereruka
13	Nikauisesi [35]	2 E–W	Overseer of Upper Egypt
14	Sabu [47]	North Saqqara	Overseer of all works, priest
15	Shepsipuptah [38]	2 E–W	Service of king
16	Tetiankh [40]	4 E–W	Administrator
17	Tjetji [42]	4 E–W	Administrator, physician

An examination of the tombs listed above leads to the following important conclusions. Not all the tombs in the Teti cemetery and others from the same reign show evidence of deliberate damage to the figures and/or names of the owners, which indicates that such damage was not due to general vandalism. In support of this deduction is the fact that eight tombs (those of Ankhmahor [12], Kagemni [23], Khentika [24], Mereruka [30], Neferseshemptah [33], Neferseshemre [34], Merefnebef [46] and Sabu [47]) contain erased figures of sons and/or retainers, without any damage to those of the tomb owners themselves. The damage throughout the cemetery appears as punishments inflicted on particular individuals (Figures 2.27, 2.54, 2.55, 2.63, 2.66, 2.68, 2.82, 2.83). No damage is attested for the persons of the royal sons-in-law, Kagemni, Mereruka, Neferseshemptah and Shepsipuptah [38], although the erasure in the first three of these tombs of figures of sons and/or retainers suggests their involvement in a crime, but perhaps at a later date. Also no damage to the tomb owners' figures is evident in tombs of individuals who served early in Teti's reign and who probably died before its end (for example, Ankhmahor, Hefi [14], Kagemni, Mereruka, Neferseshemre, Neferseshemptah, Nedjetempet [32] and Nikauisesi [35]). This may suggest that the crime for which the others were punished occurred towards the end of the reign.

Three officials received the harshest punishment, the erasure of both names and figures from the decoration of their chapels. These are a vizier (Hesi [15]), an overseer of weapons (Mereri [29]) and the chief physician (Seankhuiptah [37]) (Figures 2.32, 2.36, 2.59, 2.60, 2.72–2.75). Such a punishment is not unlikely to have accompanied a death sentence, and in fact the first two of these tombs were given to new owners, which may suggest that the original owners were perhaps somehow destroyed, or at least were deprived of a proper burial. This is clear in the case of Mereri's tomb which was reallocated to a woman, Merynebty, and which mainly contained the remains of a woman. The great majority of the other punished tomb owners were employed as guards and/or in various posts relating to the personal service of the king, while the great majority of individuals who were not punished were employed in other administrative and religious capacities not directly relating to the king, including two women.[341] This fact further confirms that the event which brought about the punishment touched on the person of the king.

The punishments varied from the erasure of the tomb owner's name (Semdent [39]), to the mutilation of parts of the figures (Irenakhti [18], Mereri [28], Meru [31] and Wernu [44]). The former would have probably aimed to achieve perpetual damnation, but the accompanying penalty inflicted in real life on that person is not clear. The mutilation of parts of the figures (eyes, ears, noses, wrists and ankles) may reflect a similar penalty inflicted on the individual in real life. Three tombs show evidence of interrupted damage and some repair (Irenakhti [18], Iries [20] and Kaaper [22]). The significance of this is not clear, but may indicate a pardon, or perhaps that the damage was ordered by the ephemeral Userkare and reversed by Pepy I. The decoration of eight tombs appears to have come to an abrupt halt, but no damage is evident. The owners of these tombs may simply have been sacked for failure in their duties, rather than for involvement in a crime, and accordingly would have been unable, at least financially, to finish the work on their tombs. The variety of the imposed penalties is in total agreement with the Egyptian concept of justice, Maat, where the punishment should fit the crime.

Weighing the evidence

We do not have literary evidence recording a palace conspiracy at the end of Teti's reign as we have for the reigns of Amenemhat I and Rameses III. Yet the archaeological evidence from Teti's time suggests a rough accession to the throne, unusual security precautions throughout the reign and a major crime at its end, for which the closest officials to the king were punished. The very short reign of Userkare, the change of loyalty by some officials and their later punishment, presumably by Pepy I, may well indicate that the end of Teti's reign was not peaceful. Of course it may be argued that even if Userkare were a usurper, he might have simply done so by taking advantage of Pepy I's young age following the natural death of Teti, and that the later punishment of some officials could have been for their support of the usurper. The very nature of the positions held by the people punished would argue against such a scenario; for while the involvement of a vizier would be necessary for the success of any takeover of power, the participation of the chief physician is much more difficult to explain. The involvement of the palace guards and the overseer of weapons surely indicates a premeditated use of force, and a usurper who was prepared to use force and who has gathered the support of those who could provide it, would be unlikely to patiently wait for the natural death of the reigning monarch. If he were to do so, his plot would almost certainly have little chance of success. Circumstantial as it is, the evidence suggests a successful conspiracy which brought about the end of Teti's reign. Manetho perhaps had literary sources, or oral traditions which informed him of the assassination of Teti, but the archaeological evidence, most certainly completely buried in his time, points in the same direction.

Userkare and Pepy I

Userkare succeeded Teti. The fact that he reigned between Teti and Pepy I is conclusive,[342] and he should not be regarded as a stopgap ruler or a regent during the younger years of Teti's son, Pepy I.[343] He is listed in the Abydos King List, and the Turin Papyrus mentioned him as king of Upper and Lower Egypt.[344] Scattered objects bearing Userkare's name were also found, but these are limited in number[345] and do not suggest a long reign. Perhaps one year is all he enjoyed on the throne.[346] Such a short period could hardly justify the unprecedented appointment of a regent with royal titulary. Furthermore, as Pepy I was the child of a political marriage between Iput, daughter of Unis,[347] and Teti, presumably at the time of the latter's accession, and since this king had a reign of not much more than eleven years,[348] Pepy I must have succeeded at a young age; accordingly, if a regent was appointed it would have been for more than one year. We are not sure if Userkare was related to Teti,[349] but he certainly did not belong to the main line of succession, and with the accession of Pepy I very little reminder of his reign seems to have been allowed to remain. His name does not appear in any way in the tombs of officials who served under both Teti and Pepy I (for example, Mehu, Khentika [24] and Inumin [17]),[350] nor in biographies of such officials buried outside the capital (for example Weni of Abydos[351] (Figure 1.1) and Qar of Edfu[352]). In fact those who presumably mentioned his name (for example, Mehi [26]?) had to take extreme measures to dispose of it.

It is uncertain whether Userkare's reign simply represented a challenge to the main line of succession to the throne or an attempt to revert to the former supremacy of the cult of Re and its priesthood, as his name Userkare, 'the ka of Re is powerful', might suggest. How Pepy I regained his father's throne we do not know, but it is unlikely to have been through his own efforts. He must have been still very young, and that is also evident by his relatively long reign. The highest count known from Pepy I's reign was 25, which was taken to indicate a reign of 49 or 50 years. Scholars felt comfortable accepting the biannual count in this case as it almost agrees with the period of 53 years assigned by Manetho to this king. Yet the Turin Papyrus gives him only 20 years. In all probability the figures in both the Turin Papyrus and Manetho are wrong and the 'count' was annual. Recently the 32nd count/year of Pepy I has been identified.[353] Curiously, this brings him very close to Pepy II, whose highest known count is the 33rd,[354] and who is believed to have come to the throne as a child. If Pepy I also acceded at a young age, who supported him? The most powerful men at the time, one would think, were the viziers, who were presumably also able to gather the support of other important officials. Two men, according to our present state of knowledge, remained loyal to Pepy I and may well have played a role in his coming to the throne. These are Mehu, buried in Unis' cemetery, and Khentika [24], in Teti's. Both men served as viziers of Teti and Pepy I. Whether they also served in the same capacity under Userkare, or were excluded and hence possibly reacted, we do not know. Certainly Userkare was never mentioned in their tombs. We are equally in the dark concerning any action which might have been taken in order to put Pepy I on the throne. Secrecy was essential, however, and accordingly the accession appears to have been very smooth, but we do not have to believe that this was necessarily the case.

Pepy I's reign was also troubled by one, or more likely two conspiracies of which we have some information.[355] The first conspiracy, by his wife, is recorded in the well-known biography of Weni (Figure 1.1),[356] who for some reason was the centre of Pepy I's trust and who was repeatedly given responsibilities far ahead of his position and rank. The only justification given by Weni for such seemingly extraordinary treatment was that 'His Majesty trusted me more than any dignitary of his, more than any noble of his, more than any servant of his',[357] and again that 'I was excellent in His Majesty's opinion, I was rooted in His Majesty's opinion, and His Majesty trusted me'.[358] These claims should not be taken as simple bragging, and the element of trust must have been particularly important to Pepy I. This is understandable if his father was assassinated and his own wife conspired against him. As a relatively modest official, judge of Nekhen and superintendent of the palace guards, and later overseer of the palace guards, Weni was responsible for the royal harem and the six great courts, he was in charge of the trial of the queen herself and he led an army of many tens of thousands, five/six times to the lands of the Asiatics. Placing such a huge number of armed men, even if somewhat exaggerated, under Weni's control in itself indicates the unreserved trust of the king, since by doing so he was putting Weni in a tremendously powerful position. However, the king's trust seems well founded as Weni continued to serve even in a higher capacity under his son and successor, Merenre.

The Queen accused

Of particular interest to the present study is Weni's statement about the trial of Pepy I's queen.[359] His biography seems to proceed in a chronological order. Early under Pepy I Weni was a palace official – superintendent of the palace guards, elder of the robing room and in charge of the royal harem. Still presumably early in the reign he was promoted to overseer of the palace guards, and as such he replaced/expelled four other holders of this office. Rather than saying why these overseers of the palace guards were expelled, Weni tells us what he has done in their stead. He provided protection, prepared the king's way and prepared the daises. Immediately after, Weni recounts the secret trial of the queen in the royal harem, which he conducted without any vizier or any dignitary being present. This section of the biography is told in such a way as to hint that Weni's promotion to the position of overseer of the palace guards, the expulsion of four holders of the office and the trial of the queen were interrelated and were connected to the king's security.[360]

Many questions present themselves in regard to this event. Who was this queen and what was the outcome of her trial? Why did she conspire against her husband? Why were the viziers and dignitaries absent from the trial? Who else was involved and what happened to them and to the expelled guards? Although Weni reported the incident, he understandably did not elaborate on the identity of the queen, nor on the outcome of the case, for, as he stated, this was a secret investigation. In fact it is astonishing that he was allowed to mention it at all. Whether the French excavations, currently in progress in Pepy I's cemetery, will uncover evidence of a disgraced queen remains to be seen. The motives behind the conspiracy are also difficult to comprehend. In later plots where women were involved, they were usually royal wives trying to secure the throne for their sons. The multiple marriages practised by the kings must have created an atmosphere conducive to palace intrigues.[361] Yet this is unlikely to have been the purpose behind the plot against Pepy I. Weni seems to place the conspiracy early in the reign. It was after this that he was given the responsibility of raising the large army and of leading it five/six times into western Asia. The devastation to this region described by Weni makes it hardly likely that an annual campaign was necessary,[362] and accordingly the five or six campaigns must have stretched over the greater part of Pepy I's reign. If the queen's plot took place early in the reign and before all the campaigns, then Pepy I was probably still a youth, unlikely to have had numerous sons by a number of wives, which makes a fight in the harem over the succession to the throne less plausible. We know that Pepy I had the name Nefersahor at the beginning of his reign, and that he changed this to Meryre ('beloved of Re') early in the reign.[363] The change certainly represented a deliberate policy, for the overseer of Upper Egypt, Inumin, who became a vizier at approximately this time, took the trouble of chiselling out the name Nefersahor from the inscriptions in his tomb and replacing it, in red paint only, with that of Meryre.[364] Nefersahor was never used later in Pepy I's reign. Whether there is a link between the queen's plot and the king's change of name is not clear from the available evidence, but is also not unlikely.

The absence of any vizier or any dignitary from the queen's trial is very curious. The vizier was also the chief justice and his presence was only to be expected, and so was that of other judiciary officials. Weni's remark on their absence bears witness to this: 'His majesty made me go in to hear it alone. No chief judge and vizier, no dignitary was there, only I alone.'[365] It has been suggested that the need for secrecy was the main reason behind the exclusion of the viziers and dignitaries from hearing the case.[366] Weni was responsible for the royal harem, and might well have already been familiar with the case. In fact it is even conceivable that he played a role in uncovering the plot, and accordingly gained the king's unlimited confidence. As a result, putting him in charge of the trial 'alone with one judge of Nekhen'[367] would have no doubt restricted the number of people gaining intimate knowledge of this court action. On the other hand, one wonders if it were realistically possible to keep the details of such an important event, which must have had far-reaching consequences, hidden even from the viziers! The conclusion that the viziers were excluded is inescapable, and if so they themselves must have been implicated; in fact the support of a vizier would have been necessary for any such plot to proceed. Weni did not state that the viziers were involved, but in a subtle way he appears to imply it; for speaking generally he says that he heard cases in every secret matter whilst alone with the vizier,[368] yet in the trial of the queen he says that the king caused him to hear it alone, and that not any vizier nor any dignitary was present. This appears as a comparison between the usual and unusual; it suggests that at least one vizier should have attended the trial, but that none did. The reason Weni gives for this seemingly unusual situation was the high opinion and trust that the king had in him.[369] There seems to be an indirect comparison between the king's trust in Weni and his lack of trust in the viziers and dignitaries. Such indirect criticism appears elsewhere in Weni's biography. When he mentioned the expulsion of the palace guards for instance, he did not even hint at any failure in their duties, but rather moved directly to his success in their stead. He leaves the comparison to be made by the reader, a style which is particularly effective.

As the intrigue failed, one would expect all the participants, not only the queen, to be punished; and such punishments, as in the case of Teti's officials, would be likely to be manifested in certain damage to their tombs. No known tomb of a vizier who could be dated to the first half of Pepy I's reign[370] shows evidence of intentional erasure to the name or figure of its owner, or mutilation to parts of their figures. Nevertheless, we know that Pepy I's officials were not buried around him, probably a deliberate policy of the king, and that they were 'scattered' in various cemeteries.[371] There is certainly a chance of more tombs of Pepy I's viziers and officials being discovered in the future. An example of this is the recently excavated tomb of the vizier Merefnebef to the west of the Step Pyramid, although the figures of the tomb owner in this case were not attacked [46] (Figure 2.82).[372] On the other hand, other palace officials and guards who served under Pepy I and who were buried in the Teti and Unis cemeteries and elsewhere, received different punishments manifested in some kind of damage or unfinished sections in their tombs. However, as the reign of Pepy I appears to have been plagued by at least one more conspiracy, and as it is almost impossible in most cases to determine whether the punishment was for participation in one plot or the other within the same reign, we will continue examining the events of the reign, then present the suspects collectively.

Pepy's new in-laws

Following the disgrace of his wife, Pepy I married, successively one would assume, two sisters with the same name, Meryreankhnes, daughters of Khui and Nebet of Abydos. By the first sister he had his son Merenre and by the second he had Pepy II. The king appointed his mother-in-law, Nebet, as vizier in the South, the first case of a female vizier, the next case not occurring until the Twenty-sixth Dynasty. This marriage of Pepy I has long been the subject of discussion,[373] and it is not the intention here to reopen the debate. However, certain points are related to the subject of the present study and should be examined. Most scholars believe that Pepy's marriage to the daughters of a noble family from Abydos aimed at strengthening the position of the king in the southern part of the country. This interpretation of the marriage seems to me inconceivable. The monarchy would have been disastrously weak if it needed the support of a provincial family to remain in power, and this family would have had to be tremendously strong if it were able to provide such support. Neither the weakness of the former, nor the strength of the latter is evident in the available records, nor should we assume them. In fact a study of the provincial administration shows that Abydos came to real prominence only after the appointment of Nebet and Khui, and that until the second half of Pepy II's reign the king was in complete control of the administration of the South.[374] Furthermore, as Martin-Pardey argues, if there were political motivations behind this marriage, then the nobles of Abydos would have been the least appropriate, as it was unlikely that in the direct proximity of the overseer of Upper Egypt, the representative of the central government, an opposing power to the throne could have existed. In addition, by such a marriage Pepy I could have addressed only one possible danger to the throne.[375]

It has also been suggested that Nebet's title of vizier was only honorific, and that it was given to her 'to enhance the otherwise commonplace background of a woman who became the grandmother of a king'.[376] There is no reason at all for regarding the title of vizier, the highest administrative responsibility, as being honorific. It has never been so. If the number of viziers in any one reign is embarrassingly large to fit in a succession within a short period, it is because the administration was becoming complex, and accordingly more than one vizier held the office simultaneously, probably with responsibilities in different parts of the country; but that does not make the position honorific. From the end of the Fifth Dynasty onwards there seem to have been two viziers in the capital and a third in Upper Egypt.[377] Moreover, if it were true that in Nebet's case the vizierate was honorific and was granted to her to raise her status as a future grandmother of a king, would it not have been in accordance with the Egyptian tradition to give such an honour to her husband, Khui, who was the grandfather of the future king. The reason for refusing to accept the vizierate as a functional title in Nebet's case would appear to be based only on the fact that Nebet was a woman, and that the Egyptians did not have female viziers. In fact they did not have female honorific viziers either, nor honorific viziers at all, and exactly the same title 'chief justice and vizier' could not have been granted to some individuals in a functional capacity and to others only on an honorific basis. We must also bear in mind that, like the vizierate, kingship was a male prerogative, yet under special circumstances in Egyptian history women occupied the throne.

The appointment of a female vizier in ancient Egypt is certainly perplexing, but the key to understanding such an unprecedented decision by the king probably lies in the identity of the occupant of the office, Nebet. It was she and not her husband whom the king wished to hold the position, no matter how unusual this was. Pepy I's action is paralleled in its oddity by his appointment of Weni, a modest official, to lead the whole army while the highest officials in the country were at the head of one battalion each, and also by his appointment to attend the queen's trial at which the viziers and dignitaries were not allowed to be present. In the case of Weni the appointment was due solely to the king's trust, and it seems more plausible that the choice of Nebet was for the same reason, trust, rather than the need for the support of a provincial family. The presence of a residing vizier in the extended southern part of Egypt, a position first created by Teti not by Pepy I,[378] was necessary for the good administration of the country, but at the same time this placed great power in the hands of one person at a distance from the capital. The central government was probably well aware of the dangers inherent in the system, and accordingly did not allow the position to remain for a long time with the same family or in the same province. Thus the office moved between Edfu, Deir el-Gebrawi, Akhmim, Abydos, Meir and Coptos.[379] For the same reasons, the government would have been particularly unlikely to give the position to a strong family at Abydos, if such a family existed.

The element of trust, which appears to have been of paramount importance to Pepy I, is totally understandable if his father was assassinated and his wife conspired against him. It might not be a mere coincidence that the sudden rise in the fortunes of both Weni and Nebet came at the same time: immediately after, and perhaps as a result of, the queen's conspiracy. Thus Weni tried the queen and led the army, and the king married the daughters of Nebet and later appointed her as a vizier. Without saying that he uncovered the conspiracy, Weni, in his typical subtle style, shortly before mentioning his responsibility for the trial, tells us that he was in charge of the royal harem. One wonders if Nebet was also there and playing a similar role to Weni's! Unfortunately we have no biographical inscriptions of Nebet's which can answer this question. But the biography of her son, Djau, who later became a vizier under Pepy II, refers to Abydos as 'the province in which I was born'.[380] This reference, which could be interpreted to mean that the family originated from Abydos, is in fact more likely to indicate that it did not. Statements like this are usually made deliberately,[381] in Djau's case probably to remind his townspeople that he was born at Abydos, even though perhaps his parents were known to have come from elsewhere. In fact it is reasonable to think that all the early provincial appointments, such as those of Nebet and Khui, originated from the capital.[382] If Nebet was sent to Abydos where she gave birth to Djau, then she must have received the vizierate at a relatively young age, another similarity to Weni who was given important tasks at a young age.

Tracing the origin of Khui and Nebet in the capital is not an easy matter, since once they had moved to Abydos and built their tomb there we are not sure what happened to their earlier tomb in the capital, if one already existed.[383] A connection between Khui and Nebet and some monuments in the Teti cemetery at Saqqara may be made, although it should remain mere conjecture until further evidence confirms or refutes it.[384] The newly discovered tomb of Inumin [17] is well dated to the early part of Pepy I's reign, since a cartouche of Pepy I as Nefersahor was erased and replaced by that of Meryre (Figure 3.1).[385] Inumin was the last official to hold the title overseer of the protection of every house of the king. He was therefore directly involved with the security of the palace and the king. With the change of the king's name to Meryre, which as suggested earlier might have been a consequence of the conspiracy, Inumin was made vizier, presumably late in his career since the decoration of his façade was left unfinished.[386] The date of Inumin and his responsibility for the palace protection means he was the most likely person to play a role in the uncovering of the plot against Pepy I. Inumin's eldest son was named Khui, and a tomb in the near vicinity of Inumin's belongs to an overseer of Upper Egypt and priest of Pepy I's pyramid also called Khui [25].[387] As the office of overseer of Upper Egypt was one of Inumin's main duties, it is likely that the owner of the nearby tomb was his son and successor in the position, and it is possible, although by no means certain, that Khui's familiarity with Upper Egypt encouraged Pepy I to appoint his wife, Nebet, whom he trusted, to the office of the southern vizier, particularly since her husband was to assist her. No wife is depicted in the surviving scenes in the Saqqara tomb of Khui, but a small mud-brick tomb with a limestone false door belonging to a woman named Nebet was found in the vicinity of his tomb.[388] It is evident that this woman was married from the inscriptions of her false door where she is described as being beloved of and honoured by her husband and praised by her children. Independent tombs for women are very rare in this cemetery and the case of Nebet may be compared to that of Nedjetempet [32], also in the vicinity, who was the mother of the vizier Mereruka [30] and the mother-in-law of Teti's daughter. It is possible that the tomb was built for Nebet following a role she played in uncovering the conspiracy, but before Nebet and Khui became the royal in-laws and were posted at Abydos.[389] An examination of Khui's burial chamber shows that this was a miserable place with no stone sarcophagus or even burial pit, which is unusual for a man who was promoted to the office of overseer of Upper Egypt, presumably after he constructed his tomb. One wonders if the chamber was ever used. It is interesting to note that in Khui's tomb at Saqqara and on Khui's stela from Abydos is a son named after the father, Khui, and another son(?) is named Idi.[390] That the names Khui and Nebet became particularly popular after the king married their daughters should not weaken this possible identification, for the individuals considered here were certainly named before this royal marriage. Such identifications are conjectural, but not unlikely.

Further trouble for Pepy I

Later in Pepy I's reign another conspiracy appears to have been organized against the king.[391] This was led by the vizier Rawer [36],[392] whose name has been chiselled out and parts of his figure, mainly the face, hands and feet, have been deliberately damaged in his tomb in the Teti cemetery (Figure 2.71). The eldest son of Shepsipuptah [38], who married Teti's daughter, was called Rawer (Figure 2.76). As this name became very rare in the period, it seems possible that Pepy I appointed his nephew to the vizierate, as he did earlier with Meryteti, son of Mereruka [30] and another daughter of Teti. As the size of Rawer's tomb allows it to be placed in the latter part of Pepy I's reign and a vizier's name has been intentionally erased from the royal decree dated to the 21st count of Pepy I,[393] it is possible to conclude that a second major event occurred at that time that affected the person of the king, since the vizier's name was removed from the royal decree as well as from his own tomb.

The evidence suggests that after this plot Pepy I possibly associated his son Merenre, grandson of Nebet, with him on the throne, thus introducing for the first time, as far as we know, the system of co-regency.[394] If this is correct, it may indicate that the intrigue in which Rawer was involved perhaps aimed at placing a different successor on the throne. To prevent such a possibility Pepy I took the unprecedented step of crowning his son during his own lifetime. We do not hear of further palace intrigues for the remaining part of the Sixth Dynasty, but that of course does not mean that they did not occur. The rapid succession to the throne after the death of Pepy II, the later possible assassination of Amenemhat I of the Twelfth Dynasty, the series of co-regencies of the Middle Kingdom and the attempt on Rameses III's life, show that in spite of the façade of normality which the Egyptian monarchy tried to maintain, the palace, with many wives and children, was a fertile ground for intrigues and sometimes murders.

Many suspects

Having surveyed the possible intrigues against Pepy I, we now examine the archaeological evidence supporting these events. As in the case of the conspirators at the end of Teti's reign, those who plotted against Pepy I are expected to have been punished, particularly since he survived their attempts. The penalties were possibly inflicted on them in life and are expected to be mirrored in the treatment of their figures in their tombs, or even in other tombs of relatives or dignitaries where these were depicted. A study of this problem under Pepy I is more difficult than under Teti for two main reasons. The first is that there was more than one conspiracy against that king and it is almost impossible in most cases with our present knowledge to associate an individual with a particular event within the same reign. For this reason the list of punished people will be given without reference to their involvement in a specific plot. The second difficulty comes from the fact that Pepy I apparently did not wish his officials to be buried near him, perhaps for good reason, and therefore they are not concentrated in one cemetery; accordingly, the list of tombs given below is by no means exhaustive, and is likely to be augmented by examples from various cemeteries.[395] The tombs listed below are those whose owners or their sons served under Pepy I, even if they started under Teti, and were punished under Pepy I. Our examination shows that when a penalty was inflicted on a person, this was not restricted to his own tomb, but also to his figures depicted in his father's tomb or in those of other dignitaries of his time.

Tombs where the figure and name of the owner were erased

	Name	*Location*	*Position held*
1	Ishfi [21]	5 E–W	Guard
2	Neferseshemptah (a chapel in tomb of father, Neferseshemptah) [33]	2 N–S	Guard, service of king, administrator

Tombs where the name of owner was erased and parts of his body mutilated

1	Rawer [36]	S–E of pyramid	Vizier

Tombs where parts of the owner's body were mutilated

1	Meru [31]	2 E–W	Guard, service of king

Tombs where the figure and/or name of son(s) and retainer(s) were erased

1	Ankhmahor [12]	2 N–S	Vizier
2	Iries [20]	4 E–W	Judge, king's confidant
3	Kagemni [23]	1 N–S	Vizier
4	Khentika [24]	N–E of pyramid	Vizier
5	Merefnebef [46]	West of Step Pyramid	Vizier
6	Mereri [28]	3 E–W	Guard, service of king
7	Mereruka [30]	1 E–W	Vizier
8	Neferseshemptah [33]	2 N–S	Judge
9	Neferseshemre [34]	2 N–S	Vizier
10	Sabu [47]	North Saqqara	Overseer of all works, priest
11	Wernu [44]	3 E–W	Guard, service of king

Tombs where the decoration came to a sudden stop

	Name	*Location*	*Position held*
1	Hermeru [2]	Unis	Guard
2	Ishfi (a chapel in tomb of father, Ankhmahor) [12]	2 N–S	Service of king
3	Iy [4]	Unis	Guard
4	Iyenhor [5]	Unis	Guard
5	Niankhkhnum [6]	Unis	Guard
6	Niankhpepy [7]	Unis	Guard
7	Niankhpepy/Hepi [8]	Unis	Guard(?), overseer of the palace
8	Tetiankh (a chapel in tomb of father, Iries) [20]	4 E–W	Guard
9	Tjetu [10]	Unis	Guard

Tombs with finished decoration and no damage

1	Inumin [17]	1 N–S	Vizier
2	Khui [25]	3 E–W	Overseer of Upper Egypt
3	Niankhptah [9]	Unis	Guard
4	Tjetju [43]	1 E–W	Vizier

An examination of the tombs listed above leads to some interesting conclusions. The list includes tombs which show evidence of punishment to the owner or his sons and retainers. The sudden interruption to decoration is taken to represent a form of punishment. A few tombs which show no damage, but which are of similar date and in close proximity to those with erasure or unfinished decoration, are also listed. This demonstrates that the damage is not attested in all tombs from the reign of Pepy I, and the list may be enlarged greatly if tombs of a similar date and from other sites, but with no evidence of punishment, were included. No attempt at this was made here.

Weighing the evidence

With at least two attested conspiracies against Pepy I, it is difficult to associate each individual with a specific plot. However, the two events were separated by a relatively long period, since the queen's trial appears to have taken place early in Pepy I's reign, while the plot in which the vizier Rawer [36] was implicated occurred in, or immediately after, the 21st count of the same king. Individuals who may safely be linked to the queen's conspiracy are the guards buried in the Unis cemetery. No guards of any level would presumably have been able to afford tombs with such beautifully stone-lined and inscribed façades as those in this group after the very beginning of Pepy I's reign. The gradual impoverishment during the reign is evident even in the viziers' tombs.[396] Two tomb owners in this group changed their names from Ptahhetep and Sebekhetep, typical names of the end of the Fifth Dynasty although not exclusively so, to Niankhpepy [7, 8], suggesting that they were granted the right to form new names with the cartouche of Pepy. The former changed his name again to Niankhmeryre, presumably when Pepy adopted this name early in his reign.[397] It is unlikely that any of these guards were still active later in the reign since the decoration of the tombs was left unfinished. It is interesting that none of these tombs shows evidence of any deliberate damage; their decoration was just stopped suddenly. Weni, our only informant on the queen's event, mentioned that he expelled or replaced four overseers of palace guards who were there.[398] Weni did not say that these were implicated or that they were punished, simply that they were expelled, an action which is likely to be the result of their failure in their duties of protection, rather than actively conspiring against the king or supporting a challenger. But their expulsion would have inevitably led to the termination of income and inaccessibility to royal artists, masons and workshops, hence the sudden interruption to the work on their tombs. This is apparent in a group of neighbouring tombs in the Unis cemetery, all dated to the early part of Pepy I's reign, such as those of Hermeru [2], Iy [4], Iyenhor [5], Niankhkhnum [6], Niankhpepy [7], Niankhpepy/Hepi [8] and Tjetu [10], and in the Teti cemetery, in those such as Ishfi (son of Ankhmahor) [21] and Tetiankh (son of Iries [20]). The decoration of these tombs was abruptly stopped, sometimes in the middle of a sentence or scene. While this unusual halt to the preparation is seen in all of the above-mentioned tombs, it is nowhere clearer than in the tomb of Hermeru, where the relief cutting of the inscriptions on his false door, and that of his wife, was interrupted in the middle of words and the spear-fishing scene on the thickness of his entrance doorway is half finished (Figures 2.4–2.6). A likely interpretation is that these men lost their income early in Pepy I's reign, which, considering their occupation, lends support to Weni's statement. However, no further punishment is evident in these tombs and evidence shows that the owners were allowed to be buried in their tombs.

Because Pepy I's officials are not concentrated in his cemetery and instead are scattered in various sites, it is almost impossible with our present knowledge to assess the level of support that the queen's conspiracy, if it was actually a conspiracy, had among his officials. Weni's biography, our only reference to the trial of the queen, does not accuse any of the dignitaries of wrongdoing. On the other hand, Weni's subtle remark that not any vizier nor any dignitary attended the trial with him is, as argued above, very suggestive. It is true that because he was in charge of the royal harem Weni was already familiar with the case, and it is also true that this was a most sensitive case which could affect the dogma of kingship itself and which needed to be handled with absolute secrecy, even though the concept of justice had to be maintained and a trial had to be conducted. Yet this secrecy presumably applied only to the populace and perhaps to the minor officials, and it seems inconceivable that the trial of the queen could have been concealed not only from the viziers but also from the entire administration. The absence of the viziers and dignitaries in this case is very curious; at worst it indicates a widespread involvement in the conspiracy and at best it represents a total lack of trust in, or even a suspicion the king had of, his top administrators. No tombs of viziers or higher officials who may be dated to the earlier part of Pepy I's reign, and whose owners appear to have been punished by erasure of their names and figures, are presently known to us. But the lack of such evidence does not necessarily mean that it does not exist or that it will never be found, perhaps in the least expected site. Until the discovery, in the Unis cemetery, of the tombs of Pepy I's palace guards, whose decoration came to a sudden halt, there was no archaeological data to support Weni's claim that he expelled four overseers of the palace guards. Future excavations in various Old Kingdom sites might well produce new evidence to help document further the event of the queen's trial.

The second group of individuals in the above-mentioned list were mostly sons and retainers of Teti's officials who are likely to have reached the peak of their careers in the latter half of Pepy I's reign, although some of them may have done so earlier. Evidence for this group comes mainly from the Teti cemetery and clearly demonstrates punishment. Harsh penalties seem to have been inflicted on the royal relatives; the vizier Rawer [36] (Figure 2.71) (possibly son of Shepsipuptah [38]), Neferseshemptah (son of Neferseshemptah [33] (Figures 2.66, 2.67)) and Pepyankh (son of Mereruka [30] (Figures 2.62, 2.63) were Pepy I's nephews, or at least the sons of his brothers-in-law by earlier wives, and so was perhaps Ishfi (son of Ankhmahor [12] (Figures 2.26–2.28)) and [21] (Figure 2.52). It now appears that following the queen's 'conspiracy' Pepy I relied heavily on these 'nephews' and other royal relations, appointing them to the most important positions in the administration. His trust appears to have been betrayed late in his reign, around the 21st count/year, and these individuals' tombs demonstrate the consequences. The name of the vizier Rawer was chiselled out and his figures attacked, all inscriptions and figures of Neferseshemptah were damaged, the name and figure of Pepyankh were removed from his father's tomb and possibly from his own tomb,[399] and Ishfi's name and figure were damaged on his false door which was removed from its place and thrown into the shaft. The sons and/or retainers of the other officials of Teti who probably took part in the conspiracy under Pepy I also received severe punishment. This appears, for example, in the tombs of Kagemni [23] (Figure 2.54), Khentika [24] (Figure 2.55) and Mereruka [30] (Figure 2.64). In most cases their names and figures were erased from the tombs of their parents or masters, and wherever private tombs or chapels are known for them it is noticed that the same punishment is also evident in their own tomb. Thus Ishfi was punished in his tomb and in that of his father Ankhmahor, Neferseshemptah was also punished in his chapel and that of his father Neferseshemptah, as is also the case for Tetiankh and his father Iries [20] (Figures 2.49, 2.51).

Of the tombs which do not show indications of punishment, Inumin [17] (regardless of his possible relationship to the king) most probably died before the second conspiracy and was replaced by other viziers; Khui [25] may have been the one sent to Abydos and accordingly was away from the capital; Niankhptah [9] was presumably at the very beginning of Pepy I's reign, even before the queen's plot; and Tjetju [43] was vizier at the end of Pepy I's reign and might have followed Rawer [36].

The archaeological evidence suggests that the reign of Pepy I was plagued by more than one intrigue, but none of these appears to have succeeded. His reign lasted for at least 32 years and the throne passed to his chosen heir, or perhaps co-regent, Merenre.

CONCLUSIONS

The pyramids of Unis, Djoser, Userkaf, Teti and perhaps Menkauhor are aligned into one south-west north-east axis and are very close to each other. It is possible that their owners shared common policies or religious beliefs, or indeed a particular stand *vis-à-vis* the cult or the priesthood of a specific deity, particularly that of Re. Of the sites of the above-mentioned pyramids, that of Teti was the most restricted, with very limited space available for the tombs of his officials and no suitable location within sight for the cemetery of his successor(s). The reason for the choice of this less than appropriate site can only be Teti's desire to associate himself with this particular group of kings, none of whom used Re as an element in his name. A close examination of the evidence from the Old Kingdom suggests that the relationship between the monarchy and the priesthood, particularly that of Re, was not always smooth. It is also noteworthy that personal names formed with those of deities other than Re, for example Ptahhetep, Akhethetep, Sebekhetep, etc., became particularly popular at the end of the Fifth Dynasty, between the reigns of Menkauhor and Unis. We should not, however, think that the above-mentioned group of kings rebelled against the sun cult, for they kept the title Son of Re, and one of the group, Userkaf, was the first to build a sun temple, although at Abusir, far from his pyramid, perhaps indicating a later truce, a compromise, or simply yielding to pressure.

Teti came to the throne by marrying Unis' daughter, Iput, but his succession does not appear to have been peaceful. Akhethetep/Hemi and Ihy were viziers at the end of Unis' reign, one for Upper Egypt and the second for the Delta. Both lost their tombs, which were reallocated to royal children – Akhethetep's was given to prince Nebkauhor/Idu and that of Ihy to princess Seshseshet/Idut. Whether these were the children of Unis or Teti, the tombs were assigned to them and were partly redecorated early under Teti. The reason for the disgrace of the two viziers is unknown, but most probably was by royal order since their tombs were given to royal children. The nature of the transition to Teti's reign may also appear in his Horus-name, Seheteptawy, 'He who pacifies the Two Lands', which hints at problems he may have had to deal with.

Throughout his reign, which did not last much more than eleven years, Teti drastically increased the number of his palace guards, who were also in charge of one or more of the personal services to the king, such as eating, bathing, clothing and adornment. These officials were even granted sites in his very limited cemetery. More importantly perhaps was the introduction of a new title 'overseer of the protection of every house of the king', successively held by the viziers Mereruka, Khentika and Inumin. Inscriptions from Teti's reign suggest that the element of trust was the main criterion for choosing the officials in the service of the king, and it is probably for a similar reason that the king married his daughters to his top officials and placed a great deal of authority in their hands. One of these, Mereruka, was the vizier, the overseer of the protection of every house of the king, the overseer of the house of weapons and the overseer of the king's harem. Even the usually independent position of the High Priest of Re was entrusted to Mereruka. With the death of his in-laws, Teti never again placed all these sensitive responsibilities in the hands of one man.

From the end of Teti's reign evidence shows that a large number of his palace guards were punished by removing their names, or by inflicting damage on certain parts of their figures such as the face or feet, as for instance in the case of Semdent and Mereri. The damage, which most probably was done at the beginning of Pepy I's reign, is consistent and may reflect different punishments to suit the various levels of involvement, probably in the same crime. In addition to the guards, three men with neighbouring tombs received the harshest punishment of erasure of both their names and figures. These were the chief physician, Seankhuiptah, the overseer of weapons, Mereri, and the vizier, Hesi. The tombs of Mereri and Hesi were reallocated to other officials, that of Mereri being given to a female guard. Although the erasure of names and/or figures is found in individual tombs in other cemeteries, it is nowhere as common and systematic as it is in the Teti cemetery. This fact, together with the nature of the positions held by the tomb owners and the likely date of these tombs to the end of Teti's reign, suggests that a drastic event took place at the end of the reign for which these individuals were punished. The historian Manetho wrote that Teti was assassinated by his bodyguards. Perhaps this statement should be taken more seriously.

Teti's successor, Userkare, who used Re in his name and who might have been supported by the priesthood of Re, had a very short reign – perhaps only one year. He should not be regarded as a regent during the minority of Pepy I, son of Teti, for a regent did not hold the full royal titulary, nor was he included in king lists. Even if he was related to Teti, a son by a different wife as some have suggested, he would have still been considered as a usurper who took over the throne from Pepy I, the son by the official queen, Iput, daughter of Unis, who carried the royal blood into the new dynasty. It is important to note that none of the officials who served under Teti and Pepy I, and accordingly also under Userkare, have mentioned this king's name in their inscriptions, and in one case where he was possibly mentioned his name was cut out and replaced by that of Teti as soon as Pepy I regained his father's throne (see the case of Mehi, pp. 93–95). If Userkare was a usurper, which is very likely, this would add weight to Manetho's claim that Teti was murdered.

Pepy I came to the throne with the name Nefersahor, but later changed it to Meryre, 'Beloved of Re', perhaps indicating an agreement reached with the priesthood of Re. This may have followed a conspiracy in the royal harem in which the king's wife was charged. The king curiously did not allow his officials to be buried near his pyramid and placed his trust in a very few, the most important of whom was Weni who tried the queen and was put in charge of protecting the king. He claims to have expelled four overseers of the palace guards, who perhaps failed in their duties, and the archaeological evidence seems to support his statement. The tombs of a number of holders of this office, dated to the earlier part of Pepy I's reign and buried in the Unis cemetery, show that the progress of their decoration came to a sudden halt (see, for example, the case of Hermeru, pp. 27–28). If these officials were sacked they would neither have had the income to pay the artisans to work on their tombs nor had access to the royal workshops. However, there is no evidence of any deliberate damage to their names or figures, nor did Weni say that they were punished, just that they were expelled. As a trusted official Weni was also placed in a most powerful position by being appointed to lead a huge Egyptian army five/six times into the land of the Asiatics. Another trusted person was a woman called Nebet, whose two daughters, both named Meryreankhnes, the king successively married; he appointed her, not her husband Khui, as a vizier at Abydos. The lack of trust that Pepy I apparently had in most people would be totally understandable if his father was assassinated and his own wife conspired against him.

In the 21st count/year of Pepy I another plot seems to have been organized against him, which was equally unsuccessful. The archaeological evidence suggests that a number of men were involved, many of whom were the sons of the trusted officials of his father, Teti. However, although some of these officials were married to Teti's daughters, these sons appear likely to have been by earlier marriages. Examples of these are the sons of Mereruka and Neferseshemptah. The conspiracy was led by the vizier, Rawer, who owned a tomb in the Teti cemetery and who was perhaps the son of Shepsipuptah, another son-in-law of Teti. The punishment of these men was severe, as is evident in their tombs and/or in the damage to their inscriptions and figures in their fathers' tombs. The aim of this plot is not clear, but by that time Pepy I had a number of wives and sons, including perhaps some by the disgraced queen, all presumably aspiring to the throne. Yet despite such a fertile ground for intrigues Pepy I's reign continued at least till his 32nd count/year when he was succeeded by his heir, or perhaps co-regent, Merenre.

NOTES

1 Waddell, *Manetho*, 53.
2 Ryholt, *ZÄS* 127 (2000), 91.
3 von Beckerath, *Chronologie*, 150.
4 *Egypt of the Pharaohs*, 93.
5 *Ancient Egypt*, 81.
6 Waddell, *Manetho*, 53–57.
7 Ibid., 45–49.
8 Herodotus, *The Histories*, 178.
9 See the excellent analysis of this literature in Posener, *Littérature*, *passim*.
10 See Lichtheim, *Literature* 1, 215ff.
11 The same image of King Snefru is found in the Prophesy of Neferti, composed in the Middle Kingdom. For a discussion see Posener, *Littérature*, 21ff.
12 Waddell, *Manetho*, 67–71.
13 For translation of the full text see Lichtheim, *Literature* 1, 145ff. The text was preserved in Papyrus Millingen and parts of the work are on wooden tablets, papyrus fragments and ostraca, all from the New Kingdom.
14 For a detailed analysis of this piece see Posener, *Littérature*, 61ff.
15 For translation see Lichtheim, *Literature* 1, 222ff.; for a study see Posener, *Littérature*, 87ff.
16 *Rank and Title*, 272–73.
17 *Palace Attendants*, 40.
18 *Néferirkarê-Kakaï* 2, 580. For Pepy I's decree see Goedicke, *Königliche Dokumente*, 55ff., fig 5.
19 Borchardt, *Saꜣḥu-Reʿ* 2, 79, 92, 123–24, pl. 17.
20 Porter and Moss, *Bibliography* 3, *passim*; Fischer, *Dendera*, 170–71.
21 *Dendera*, 171.
22 *Néferirkarê-Kakaï* 2, 577ff.
23 *Palace Attendants*, 42.
24 Ibid., 43; Posener-Kriéger, *Néferirkarê-Kakaï* 2, 578; Helck, *Beamtentitel*, 63, 101; Altenmüller, *SAK* 1 (1974), 9.
25 *Néferirkarê-Kakaï* 2, 578 n.5.
26 *MDAIK* 19 (1963), 2 n.4.
27 *Néferirkarê-Kakaï* 2, 578 n.5.
28 See for example Kanawati *et al.*, *Saqqara*, 2 vols; Davies *et al.*, *Saqqâra Tombs* 1; Lloyd *et al.*, *Saqqâra Tombs* 2; Roth, *Palace Attendants*, *passim*.
29 Sethe, *Urk.* 1, 100:9–11; Doret translates these responsibilities as 'in guarding, making the king's way, and in attending' (*Verbal System*, 25–26). For *ʿḥʿw* as 'attendance' see also Fischer, *Varia*, 14. I take *ʿḥʿw* and *stʿḥʿ* to refer to the standing places of the king, perhaps where he gives audience, as against 'the king's way'.

30 Sethe, *Urk.* 1, 105:17–19.
31 *Rev. d'Ég.* 17 (1965), 11.
32 Borchardt, *Sa3ḥu-Reʿ* 2, 79, 92, 123–24, pl. 17.
33 Dunham, *Naga-ed-Dêr*, 59, no. 46.
34 Sethe, *Urk.* 1, 146:10.
35 Ibid., 306:13; Fischer, *Dendera*, 170–71.
36 Fischer, *Dendera*, 171.
37 These titles are *jmj-ḫt pr-ʿ3*, *jmj-r mdw pr-ʿ3*, *jmj-r wpwt pr-ʿ3*, *jmj-r šwj pr-ʿ3* and *ḥrj-pr* respectively (*Palace Attendants*, 42–43).
38 Ibid., 42, 146.
39 For example, Kanawati *et al., Saqqara*, 2 vols, *passim*; Davies *et al., Saqqâra Tombs*, 1 and Lloyd *et al., Saqqâra Tombs* 2, *passim*. For these titles see below under case studies.
40 Kanawati and Abder-Raziq, *Teti Cemetery* 3, 39.
41 Firth and Gunn, *Teti Pyr. Cem.* 1, 136.
42 Ibid., 152.
43 James, *Khentika*, 10, pls 19–22.
44 *Palace Attendants*, 42.
45 Kanawati *et al., Saqqara* 1, 15, 21.
46 Davies *et al., Saqqâra Tombs* 1, 6.
47 Roth, *Palace Attendants*, 166, fig. 206.
48 Badawy, *ʿAnkhmʿahor*, figs 10, 14.
49 Junker, *Gîza* 6, 209ff.
50 Kanawati *et al., Saqqara* 1, 29.
51 Sethe, *Urk.* 1, 101:9ff.
52 Hassan, *Saqqara* 2, 21.
53 See Stadelmann, Bulletin du Centenaire, Supplément au *BIFAO* 18 (1981), 156–57; Roth, *Palace Attendants*, 40.
54 *Palace Attendants*, 43.
55 Simpson, *Western Cemetery* 1, fig. 29.
56 *jmj-r ḫntjw-š pr-ʿ3*.
57 *jmj-r st ḫntjw-š pr-ʿ3*, taking *st* to mean department or office, rather than a rank 'assistant' or the like.
58 *sḥḏ ḫntjw-š pr-ʿ3*.
59 *jmj-ḫt ḫntjw-š pr-ʿ3*.
60 *Palace Attendants*, 40 n.12.
61 Sethe, *Urk.* 1, 100:8.
62 *Néferirkarê-Kakaï* 2, 580–81.
63 Sethe, *Urk.* 1, 98:12.
64 Ibid., 253:18–254:2.
65 *Palace Attendants*, 40.
66 Hassan, *Saqqara* 2, figs 3–5.
67 Unpublished, personal examination.
68 Davies *et al., Saqqâra Tombs* 1, 6–7.
69 His false door is now in the Museum of Fine Arts, Boston – no. 21.3081 (personal examination).
70 Kanawati and Abder-Raziq, *Teti Cemetery* 3, 13–14.
71 Kanawati *et al., Saqqara* 2, 25–26; Kanawati and Hassan, *Teti Cemetery* 2, 14–15.
72 Personal examination.
73 Duell, *Mereruka* 1, pls 7, 44, 88; 2, pl. 158.
74 Kanawati and Abder-Raziq, *Teti Cemetery* 6, *passim*.
75 Roth, *Palace Attendants*, 151, fig. 80.
76 She appears on his false door now in the Museum of Fine Arts, Boston – no. 21.3081 (personal examination).

77 Kanawati and Abder-Raziq, *Teti Cemetery* 7, 33.
78 *Palace Attendants*, 40.
79 Hassan, *Saqqara*, 3 vols, *passim*, and the current epigraphic project by the Australian Centre for Egyptology.
80 Their rather modest conditions were also observed by Posener-Kriéger (*Néferirkarê-Kakaï* 2, 579). For a study of the resources of these officials as reflected in the size of their tombs see Roth, *Palace Attendants*, 49ff.
81 For example Firth and Gunn, *Teti Pyr. Cem.* 2, pl. 73:2; Kanawati *et al., Saqqara* 2, pl. 35 (84:227).
82 Kanawati, *Egyptian Administration*, *passim*; Roth, *Palace Attendants*, 49ff.
83 Kanawati *et al., Saqqara* 2, 10, pl. 3.
84 Hassan, *Saqqara* 1, *passim*.
85 Strudwick argues for a date in the middle of Unis' reign (*Administration*, 56–57 [3]).
86 Hassan, *Saqqara* 1, 5.
87 Ibid., 9, 61.
88 Ibid., 58.
89 For a possible identification of the titles belonging to each individual, see Strudwick, *GM* 56 (1982), 89ff.
90 Hassan, *Saqqara* 3, 69–81, pls 52–57, and personal recording of the tomb.
91 Macramallah, *Idout*, *passim*.
92 Most of the decorated rooms of Unisankh's chapel are now in the Field Museum of Natural History, Chicago.
93 Altenmüller, *Mehu*, *passim*.
94 For a discussion of its date see Harpur, *Decoration*, 38–39.
95 Macramallah, *Idout*, pls 5, 11.
96 Ibid., pl. 7.
97 Unpublished; currently being recorded by the Australian Centre for Egyptology.
98 Hassan, *Saqqara* 3, 59–67, pls 45–51.
99 El-Khouli and Kanawati, *Quseir el-Amarna*, 24.
100 Hassan, *Saqqara* 3, 66.
101 Unpublished; currently being recorded by the Australian Centre for Egyptology.
102 Hassan, *Saqqara* 2, 1–23, pls 1–23, and personal recording of the tomb.
103 For this tradition see Martin-Pardey, *Provinzialverwaltung*, 135.
104 *š* 's' is translated here as 'districts', see argument under 'The Palace Guards', pp. 15–16.
105 Unpublished; currently being recorded by the Australian Centre for Egyptology.
106 Unpublished; currently being recorded by the Australian Centre for Egyptology.
107 Cherpion, *Mastabas et hypogées*, 35.
108 Kanawati and Abder-Raziq, *Teti Cemetery* 6, pl. 48.
109 James, *Khentika*, pls 5–8.
110 Cherpion, *Mastabas et hypogées*, 45ff.
111 Unpublished; currently being recorded by the Australian Centre for Egyptology.
112 For this tomb see Altenmüller, *Mehu*, *passim*.
113 Lloyd *et al., Saqqâra Tombs* 2, 41–42, pls 24–25, 36B.
114 The tomb of Desi is too damaged to contribute to the present study. See Drioton, *ASAE* 43 (1943), 505–06.
115 Kanawati and Hassan, *Teti Cemetery* 2, *passim*.
116 Teti (Cherpion, *Mastabas et hypogées*, 153 and *passim*), mid-Teti (Kanawati, *Egyptian Administration*, 152 [60]), mid to late Teti (Strudwick, *Administration*, 75 [30]), late Teti or early Pepy I (Harpur, *Decoration*, 273 [374]) and Pepy I (Baer, *Rank and Title*, 64 [94]).

117 Compare with the case of Wepemnefert who left a will allocating a section in his tomb for his eldest son Iby (Hassan, *Gîza* 2, 190, fig. 219; Goedicke, *Rechtsinschriften*, 31ff.).
118 Compare with Meryteti, son of Mereruka, who constructed his chapel within the mastaba area of his father, with its access cut through the wall scenes of the north wall of Mereruka's pillared hall (Duell, *Mereruka* 2, pls 164–65, and personal examination).
119 Kanawati, *Chron. d'Ég*. 51 (1976), 235ff.
120 Kanawati and Hassan, *Teti Cemetery* 1, 69–73, pls 35, 65; Kanawati and Abder-Raziq, *Teti Cemetery* 7, 60–61, pl. 53.
121 This moulding, a roll around the door edges with hatching representing the original fibrous binding when the door was made of plants, first appeared in the middle of the Fifth Dynasty.
122 Kanawati and Abder-Raziq, *Teti Cemetery* 7, 45ff., pls 10–11, 49–50.
123 Strudwick, *Administration*, 188.
124 Kanawati and Abder-Raziq, *Teti Cemetery* 3, pl. 58; Mariette, *Mastabas*, 412–13.
125 Cherpion, *Mastabas et hypogées*, 47.
126 Kanawati and Abder-Raziq, *Teti Cemetery* 5, *passim*.
127 Duell, *Mereruka* 2, pls 167–68.
128 Personal examination. The same scene is shown in the tomb of Mehu in the Unis cemetery (Altenmüller, *Mehu*, pl. 32).
129 Kanawati *et al., Saqqara* 1, 21–24, pls 8–10.
130 Lloyd *et al., Saqqâra Tombs* 2, 6.
131 *ASAE* 43 (1943), 453–57, pls 38–46; Drioton, *ASAE* 43 (1943), 487–513, pl. 47.
132 The tomb was discovered by the Australian Centre for Egyptology and is to be published shortly.
133 Kanawati and Abder-Raziq, *Teti Cemetery* 6, 17–23.
134 Kanawati *et al., Saqqara* 1, 43–46, pls 25–27.
135 Ibid., pls 31, 33. See also the tomb of Seankhuiptah (Kanawati and Abder-Raziq, *Teti Cemetery* 3, pls 72, 74).
136 Kanawati *et al., Saqqara* 2, 7–11, pls 2–4.
137 Kanawati and Abder-Raziq, *Teti Cemetery* 5, pls 7, 52.
138 Ibid., 7, pls 8a, 44.
139 Kanawati *et al., Saqqara* 1, 47–58, pls 28–38.
140 For the significance of such references see Kanawati, *Chron. d'Ég*. 51 (1976), 235ff.
141 Kanawati and Abder-Raziq, *Teti Cemetery* 7, 58ff.
142 Lloyd *et al., Saqqâra Tombs* 2, pl. 22. Note that Iries used the back wall of Khui as a common wall in his chapel.
143 Kanawati *et al., Saqqara* 2, 25–29, pls 14–19.
144 Sethe, *Urk*. 1, 105:12, Fischer, *Varia*, pl. 20.
145 Richards, *Archaeology*, May/June 2001, 48–49.
146 Ranke, *Personennamen* 1, 47:6.
147 Kanawati and Hassan, *Teti Cemetery* 2, 12–15. Egyptian officials frequently gave their sons the same name, each followed by a different 'beautiful name'.
148 Personal examination. See also under the case of Neferseshemptah, pp. 108–110.
149 See under the tomb of Mehi, pp. 93–95.
150 Kanawati *et al., Saqqara* 2, 18–19. He probably held the office of overseer of Upper Egypt between Inumin (from the beginning of Pepy I's reign) and Khui (from the middle of Pepy I's reign).
151 Kanawati and Hassan, *Teti Cemetery* 1, 35–51, pls 14–23, 47–55.
152 Ibid., 37–40.
153 von Bissing, *Gem-ni-kai*, 2 vols, *passim*; Firth and Gunn, *Teti Pyr. Cem.* 1, 20–23, 105–30; and personal examination.

154 Sethe, *Urk.* 1, 194ff.
155 Strudwick, *Administration*, 154–55.
156 Publication is in progress by Y. Harpur.
157 James, *Khentika*, *passim.*
158 This is the only case of a decorated burial chamber in the cemetery whose owner was not a vizier.
159 James, *Khentika*, pl. 20.
160 Ibid., 14.
161 Duell, *Mereruka* 1, pl. 46.
162 James, *Khentika*, pl. 20.
163 Lloyd *et al., Saqqâra Tombs* 2, 33–39, pls 19–23, 35–36.
164 Compare with the cases of Meru and Inumin.
165 The tomb of Inumin was recently discovered by the Australian Centre for Egyptology.
166 Kanawati *et al., Saqqara* 2, 12–17, pls 4–9; Edel, *Hieroglyphische Inschriften*, 88ff.; Kanawati, *GM* 83 (1984), 31–38.
167 Altenmüller, *SAK* 1 (1974), 1ff.
168 James, *Khentika*, *passim.*
169 Recently discovered by the Australian Centre for Egyptology.
170 See, for example, the biographies of Weni of Abydos (Sethe, *Urk.* 1, 98:12–15), Qar of Edfu (ibid., 253:18–255:2) and an unnamed official at Saqqara (ibid., 249:18–250:1).
171 Kanawati *et al., Saqqara* 1, 26–28, pls 11–12.
172 Davies *et al., Saqqâra Tombs* 1, 2–20, pls 1–18, 33–35.
173 Ibid., 1.
174 The external false door is well preserved in the case of Kagemni, and its emplacement evident in Neferseshemptah's façade, but could not be verified in the case of Neferseshemre whose façade is partly buried under the remains of a New Kingdom chapel. A comparison may also be made with Hesi, who placed an external false door in the west wall of his portico, i.e., facing east.
175 Kanawati and Abder-Raziq, *Teti Cemetery* 6, 17–23.
176 Ibid., pl. 48; Davies *et al., Saqqâra Tombs* 1, pl. 12.
177 Ibid., 8ff.
178 Kanawati and Abder-Raziq, *Teti Cemetery* 7, 30ff.
179 Duell, *Mereruka*, 2 vols, *passim*; Firth and Gunn, *Teti Pyr. Cem.* 1, 23–27, 131–50.
180 See Strudwick, *Administration*, 100–01.
181 *JAOS* 58 (1938), 638ff.
182 Lloyd *et al., Saqqâra Tombs* 2, 3–20, pls 1–12, 29–31.
183 Lloyd *et al.,* who recorded the tomb, state that 'the face appears never to have been sculpted and was possibly finished in paint' (ibid., 8, pl. 4).
184 Ibid., 15 and *passim.*
185 Kanawati and Hassan, *Teti Cemetery* 1, 11–30, pls 3–11, 36–44.
186 Capart, *Rue de tombeaux* 2, pls 75–101, and personal examination.
187 *JEA* 66 (1980), 2; Strudwick, *Administration*, 111.
188 See Lloyd *et al.*, *Saqqâra Tombs* 3, forthcoming.
189 Strudwick, *Administration*, 111. The same date is given by Baer, *Rank and Title*, 93 [273], and Harpur, *Decoration*, 9, 273 [384].
190 Kanawati and Hassan, *Teti Cemetery* 2, 13–14, pls 22, 31, 62.
191 Daressy, *Mera*, 561ff.
192 James, *Khentika*, pl. 42.
193 Kanawati and Abder-Raziq, *Teti Cemetery* 3, 11–38, pls 3–19, 39–60.
194 Kanawati and Hassan, *Teti Cemetery* 2, 50–54, pls 19–21, 55–60.
195 Kanawati and Abder-Raziq, *Teti Cemetery* 6, *passim.*

196 A second shaft opens into the floor of the offering room, but this is certainly a later one excavated when the mastaba was completely covered with sand and debris and resulted in damaging the scenes on three walls.
197 Sethe, *Urk.* 1, 194:8–12; Firth and Gunn, *Teti Pyr. Cem.* 2, pl. 59.
198 Kanawati and Abder-Raziq, *Teti Cemetery* 5, pl. 59.
199 Strudwick, *GM* 43 (1981), 70.
200 James, *Hieroglyphic Texts* 1, pl. 31; Goedicke, *Königliche Dokumente*, fig. 3.
201 Cherpion, *Mastabas et hypogées*, 60–62, 35 respectively.
202 Kanawati, *GM* 177 (2000), 25ff.
203 El-Fikey, *Re-wer*, *passim*.
204 Kanawati, *Chron. d'Ég.* 56 (1981), 203ff.
205 Kanawati and Abder-Raziq, *Teti Cemetery* 3, 39ff., pls 1–2, 20–38, 61–78.
206 Quibell and Hayter, *Teti*, 20–23; Abder-Raziq, *Mélanges Mokhtar* 2, 219–30, pls 1–4; Kanawati and Abder-Raziq, *Teti Cemetery* 7, 11ff., pls 15, 37, 42.
207 Kanawati *et al.*, *Saqqara* 1, 15–20, pls 3–7; Lloyd *et al.*, *Saqqâra Tombs* 2, 21–31, pls 14–18, 32–33.
208 Kanawati and Abder-Raziq, *Teti Cemetery* 3, 21, pl. 58.
209 Ibid. 5, 19, pl. 63.
210 This includes his own neighbour, Meru.
211 For example, those of Qar and Idu at Giza (Simpson, *Qar and Idu*, figs 32, 40).
212 Lloyd *et al.*, *Saqqâra Tombs* 2, 26.
213 Kanawati *et al.*, *Saqqara* 2, 18–22, pls 10–13.
214 Strudwick, *Administration*, 18.
215 Ibid., 113.
216 Kanawati *et al.*, *Saqqara* 1, 29–36, pls 13–19; Lloyd *et al.*, *Saqqâra Tombs* 2, 47, pl. 27:1.
217 Kanawati *et al.*, *Saqqara* 1, 37–42, pls 20–24.
218 Firth and Gunn, *Teti Pyr. Cem.* 1, 151–56; 2, pls 38, 61.
219 Baer, *Rank and Title*, 295 [576]; Strudwick, *Administration*, 160–61.
220 Davies *et al.*, *Saqqâra Tombs* 1, 21–29, pls 22–33, 36.
221 Ibid., 1.
222 Ibid., 26.
223 Ibid., pl. 25. This appears to be two figures of Wernu, facing each other, each in a separate boat; usually in the one to the left he is fishing, while in that to the right he is fowling.
224 For example Davies, *Ptahhetep* 1, pls 3, 21; Kanawati, *El-Hawawish* 6, fig. 3; 8, fig. 5; 9, fig. 8.
225 Davies *et al.*, *Saqqâra Tombs* 1, pl. 26.
226 Kanawati and Abder-Raziq, *Teti Cemetery* 3, pl. 58; 7, pls 2b, 50.
227 Kanawati, *Chron. d'Ég.* 51 (1976), 235ff.
228 Kanawati and Abder-Raziq, *Teti Cemetery* 7, 41, pls 9b, 46b.
229 Strudwick, *Administration*, 188.
230 Myśliwiec, *Nowe Oblicza Sakkary*, *passim*; idem, *Swiat Nauki* 8 (1999), 28–37: idem, *Archeologia Zywa* 1/6 (1998), 2–8; idem, in *Abusir and Saqqara*, 499–508, pls 72–74.
231 Myśliwiec, *Abusir and Saqqara*, 505.
232 Mariette, *Mastabas*, [E1 and 2], 373ff., and personal examination in the Egyptian Museum, Cairo.
233 Baer, *Rank and Title*, 121 [421]; Strudwick, *Administration*, 130 [116].
234 Firth and Gunn, *Teti Pyr. Cem.* 1, 31.
235 Quibell and Hayter (*Teti*, 16–19) raise the question despite the fact that a wooden cylinder seal of Pepy I was found in the debris filling the chapel of Kaemheset – but at a high level, suggesting a later date than the building.
236 *Rank and Title*, 72 [147].

237 Ibid., 72 [147], 143–44 [527, 528]. His dates are to a certain extent shared by Harpur (*Decoration*, 273 [395], 276 [525]), but not by Strudwick (*Administration*, 149–51 [144]).
238 Recently discovered by Z. Hawass.
239 Two blocks of stone still standing at the southern end of the street appear to have formed the jambs of the entrance to the street and possibly to the whole cemetery.
240 Although the tomb of Ihy, south of that of Kagemni, is well dated to the Middle Kingdom (Firth and Gunn, *Teti Pyr. Cem.* 2, pls 83–85), most of the inscribed objects found in this area seem to belong to the period from the end of Teti to Pepy I (ibid., 67–78). For the dating of the monuments of Rehertep/Iti (ibid., pl. 77) see Kanawati in *L'Art de l'Ancien Empire égyptien*, 287–89.
241 A striking example of this tendency to push monuments into a much later date may be seen in the dating of the tombs of El-Hawawish. Compare Kanawati, *El-Hawawish*, 10 vols and Kanawati and McFarlane, *Akhmim* 1, *passim*, with Brovarski in *Mélanges Mokhtar* 1, 117–53.
242 Lloyd *et al., Saqqâra Tombs* 2, 6–7, 35.
243 Mereri's tomb [28] was totally built of stone (Davies *et al., Saqqâra Tombs* 1, 2–4), but he appears to be earlier than his neighbours (see case study, pp. 95–97) and accordingly constructed the mastaba during a more 'prosperous' period of Teti's reign when tombs of the higher officials were particularly rich (see Kanawati, *Egyptian Administration*, 35–37). The chapels of Irenakhti [18] and Iries [20] have one wall each lined with stone, while the other chapels are only covered with mud plaster and rarely decorated.
244 Kanawati, *GM* 177 (2000), 25ff.
245 James, *Khentika*, 12–14.
246 Duell, *Mereruka* 2, pls 164–65.
247 Hassan, *Gîza* 2, fig. 219; Goedicke, *Rechtsinschriften*, 31ff.
248 Sethe, *Urk.* 1, 146:16–147:6.
249 Firth and Gunn, *Teti Pyr. Cem.* 1, 151–56. The date proposed for Tjetju by Strudwick in the Seventh to Tenth Dynasties (*Administration*, 160–61) is highly unlikely. The T-shaped panel which he uses as evidence of a late date is found not only on his false door, but also on that of Pepydjedi, son of Khentika, as Strudwick himself noticed. His question as to why Tjetju did not site his tomb to the north of the main ones if he was from the reign of Pepy I could now, after the completion of the excavation of the cemetery, be answered by the fact that by that reign this part of the cemetery was fully occupied.
250 El-Fikey, *Re-wer*, *passim*.
251 Kanawati *et al., Saqqara* 2, 10, pl. 3.
252 Ibid., 10, pl. 3 and 15, pl. 6, respectively.
253 The now ruined tomb of Rehertep may have been located in the first east–west street and belong to this category (Firth and Gunn, *Teti Pyr. Cem.* 2, pl. 77; Kanawati, in *L'Art de l'Ancien Empire égyptien*, 287ff.).
254 Baer considers Unis as founder of the Sixth Dynasty, during which time the priesthoods of kings preceding Unis generally had a low rank, whereas those of Unis and his successors were always ranked higher than any other (*Rank and Title*, 267, 297).
255 For example, in the tomb of Mereruka (Firth and Gunn, *Teti Pyr. Cem.* 1, 135–36).
256 Posener, *Littérature*, 11ff.
257 Edwards, *Pyramids*, 175.
258 Firth and Gunn, *Teti Pyr. Cem.* 1, 107, 135, respectively.
259 James, *Khentika*, pl. 16.
260 For the holders of the office in this period see Moursi, *Hohenpriester*, 26–31. The only other possible holder of the title is Isesikhaf.
261 Daressy, *ASAE* 16 (1916), 193ff.; Barsanti, *ASAE* 16 (1916), 213ff.

262 Fragmentary scenes are found with the names formed with Unis in Ankhmahor (Jacquet-Gordon, *Domaines funéraires*, 407) and with Teti in Nikauisesi (Kanawati and Abder-Raziq, *Teti Cemetery* 6, pl. 54).
263 Duell, *Mereruka* 1, pl. 49.
264 Kanawati and Abder-Raziq, *Teti Cemetery* 5, pl. 62.
265 Jacquet-Gordon, *Domaines funéraires*, 271, 294–97, 341, 381–85, 386–95.
266 *Rev. d'Ég.* 31 (1979), 3ff.
267 In *Pharaonic Religion and Society*, 72.
268 Firth and Gunn, *Teti Pyr. Cem.* 2, pl. 59.
269 Kanawati and Abder-Raziq, *Teti Cemetery* 5, pl. 59b.
270 Kanawati, *GM* 177 (2000), 25ff. As a son of Nikauisesi, also named Nikauisesi, later acquired the name Nikauteti, it is possible that this son was also born under Isesi.
271 Nims, *JAOS* 58 (1938), 644ff.; Yoyotte, *BIFAO* 57 (1957), 94ff.; Stadelmann in *Hommages à Jean Leclant*, 328ff.
272 Firth and Gunn, *Teti Pyr. Cem.* 2, pl. 55.
273 Ibid., pl. 57:13; Yoyotte, *BIFAO* 57 (1957), 93.
274 Posener, *Littérature*, 1ff.
275 Ibid., 67–69, 83–85.
276 See, for example, Moussa and Altenmüller, *Nefer*; idem, *Nianchchnum*; Moussa and Junge, *Two Craftsmen*; Altenmüller, *Mehu*; Hassan, *Saqqara*, 3 vols; Munro, *Unas-Friedhof*; McFarlane, *Unis Cemetery* 1. Work is currently in progress by the Australian Centre for Egyptology and by the expeditions of the Louvre Museum and of the universities of Oxford and Liverpool.
277 Kanawati, *Governmental Reforms*, *passim*; Strudwick, *Administration*, 322ff.
278 Kanawati, in *L'Art de l'Ancient Empire égyptien*, 292ff.
279 Macramallah, *Idout*, pl. 7.
280 Strudwick, *GM* 56 (1982), 89ff.
281 The relationship of Queen Seshseshet to Unis is disputed. Altenmüller thinks she was the wife of an official named Shepsipuptah (in *Festschrift Jurgen von Beckerath*, 7ff.). In the tomb of the vizier Mehu, who lived under Unis, Teti and Pepy I, one funerary estate is named after Shepsipuptah and two estates after 'the king's mother, Seshseshet' (Altenmüller, *Mehu*, pls 28–29). Seipel, on the other hand, thinks she was possibly a wife of Unis (*Königinnen*, 229ff.).
282 Macramallah, *Idout*, pls 5, 11.
283 The same deduction was also made by Harpur, *Decoration*, 38.
284 Sethe, *Urk.* 1, 100:13–101:2.
285 Roth, *Palace Attendants*, 40. This is the position of *ḫntj-š* and its hierarchical levels.
286 Duell, *Mereruka* 2, pl. 158.
287 For some examples see Kagemni (Firth and Gunn, *Teti Pyr. Cem.* 1, 107), Mereruka (ibid., 132), Wernu (Davies *et al.*, *Saqqâra Tombs* 1, 23), Iries (Kanawati *et al.*, *Saqqara* 1, 47), Seankhuiptah (Kanawati and Abder-Raziq, *Teti Cemetery* 3, 39), Hesi (ibid. 5, 12), Khentika (James, *Khentika*, 10) and Inumin (to be published).
288 For some examples see Junker, *Gîza* 11, 126, 173. Later examples do exist, see ibid. 8, 70; Hassan, *Saqqara* 3, 26. This title is different from 'confidant (= he who is in the heart) of his lord'.
289 Kanawati and Abder-Raziq, *Teti Cemetery* 5, 37–38, pl. 59b.
290 Duell, *Mereruka* 1, pls 35, 62.
291 James, *Khentika*, pl. 6:C2. The title is partly damaged. James read it as 'overseer of every king's house' (ibid., 39 [9]:2), but noted that it is written without the honorific transposition found in the more regular title *jmj-r pr-nswt* (ibid., 11 n.8, pl. 7). The title is correctly read as '*imy-r {stp-zꜣ} pr-nzwt nb*' by Strudwick, *Administration*, 125.
292 Recently discovered in the Teti cemetery by the Australian Centre for Egyptology.

293 Firth and Gunn, *Teti Pyr. Cem.* 1, 133, 136.
294 Borchardt, *Saꜣḥu-Reʿ* 2, pl. 17. The title is partly damaged.
295 For example Nefer (Strudwick, *Administration*, 109–110 [84] and Mery (ibid., 93–94 [58]).
296 For example Sendjemib was a priest of Neferirkare and Niuserre (Mariette, *Mastabas*, 259), Khainpu is dated by Strudwick to the middle to late Fifth Dynasty (*Administration*, 120–21 [101]), Seshemnefer II is dated to the reign of Niuserre (ibid., 139 [130]), both Seshemnefer III and Sendjemib/Inti were viziers of Djedkare (ibid., 139–40 [131], 132–33 [120], respectively), Sendjemib/Mehi was a vizier of Unis (ibid., 133–34 [121]) and Mereruka was a vizier of Teti (ibid., 100–101 [68]).
297 The exception would be Sabni of Elephantine, if his damaged inscription refers to this title (Sethe, *Urk.* 1, 138:6).
298 Junker, *Gîza* 3, 9, 204–205; Brunner-Traut, *Seschemnofers III*, *passim*.
299 Sethe, *Urk.* 1, 59ff.
300 Firth and Gunn, *Teti Pyr. Cem.* 1, 134. Other holders of this title are, for example, Babaf and Teti; both were viziers (Strudwick, *Administration*, 82 [42], 157–58 [156]).
301 Kanawati and Hassan, *Teti Cemetery* 1, 11ff.
302 She was probably the wife of Meruka of Giza (ibid., 12); Junker, *Gîza* 9, 70–83; Fischer, *MIO* 7 (1950), 310–12.
303 Kanawati and Abder-Raziq, *Teti Cemetery* 7, 30ff.
304 Strudwick, *Administration*, 132 [120].
305 For comments on this office see Junker, *Gîza* 11, 126ff.
306 Sethe, *Urk.* 1, 99:6–8.
307 See Lichtheim, *Literature* 1, 135–39.
308 Kanawati and Abder-Raziq, *Teti Cemetery* 6, 41, pls 1b, 19, 50.
309 Kanawati, *GM* 177 (2000), 25ff.
310 Kanawati, *Governmental Reforms*, 24ff.; Strudwick, *Administration*, 323ff.
311 Kanawati and Hassan, *Teti Cemetery* 1, 31–34, pl. 45.
312 Ibid., 31. Ibi is now believed to have been earlier than originally suggested.
313 Other individuals who almost certainly served under Teti were buried elsewhere, either because of family ties or the shortage of space in the Teti cemetery. Examples of these officials are Sabu/Ibebi [47], buried at North Saqqara (Strudwick, *Administration*, 130 [116], and personal examination in the Egyptian Museum, Cairo), Khnumneti, buried at Giza (ibid., 128 [113]) and Mehu, buried in the Unis cemetery at Saqqara (Altenmüller, *Mehu*, *passim*). It is interesting that in accordance with Teti's apparent desire for protection Sabu/Ibebi boasted of the protection which he provided for His Majesty when he went aboard his bark on ceremonial occasions (Seth, *Urk.* 1, 81ff.; Gardiner, *Egypt of the Pharaohs*, 93).
314 See Grimal, *Ancient Egypt*, 81.
315 Seipel, *Königinnen*, 245ff.; Jánosi, *Pyramidenanlagen*, 43ff.
316 The length of his reign is lost in the Turin King List. If Userkare was the same as Ity who is mentioned in an inscription at Wadi-Hammamat (Sethe, *Urk.* 1, 148:5–10), then the latest date known for his reign is the first count. But this is far from being certain.
317 Goedicke, *ZDMG* 112 (1962), 245; Montet, *Tanis (1929–1932)*, fig. 33, pl. 83.
318 *SAK* 15 (1988), 117, 121.
319 Grimal, *Ancient Egypt*, 275–76.
320 Kanawati and Abder-Raziq, *Teti Cemetery* 7, 66ff.
321 Kanawati *et al.*, *Saqqara* 2, pl. 3.
322 Sethe, *Urk.* 1, 146:16–147:6.
323 Kanawati *et al.*, *Saqqara* 2, pl. 3.
324 Ibid., pl. 6.
325 Kanawati and Abder-Raziq, *Teti Cemetery* 5, pl. 59b.

326 Kanawati *et al.*, *Saqqara* 2, pl. 6.
327 As the inscription on the drum contains only the name Iri it is theoretically possible that this also was originally Tetiseneb, which was completely removed and replaced by Iri, leaving no different levels in the surface for comparison.
328 von Beckerath, *Chronologie*, 188.
329 Iri's shaft had not been excavated.
330 Kanawati and Hassan, *Teti Cemetery* 1, 71–72, pl. 35.
331 Kanawati and Abder-Raziq, *Teti Cemetery* 7, 41ff.
332 Ibid. 5, pls 11, 16.
333 Compare with the tombs of Akhethetep and Ihy in the Unis cemetery (see pp. 25–33, and under case studies).
334 Ibid., pl. 50.
335 For another example of this title held by a woman see Roth, *Palace Attendants*, 151, fig. 80.
336 Lichtheim, *Literature* 3, 159ff.
337 Kanawati and Abder-Raziq, *Teti Cemetery* 3, 27, 30, 33–34, 37–38, 76.
338 Ibid. 5, pl. 34.
339 Ibid. 3, pl. 23.
340 Ibid. 3, pl. 24a.
341 In addition to the tomb of Nedjetempet, the mother of Mereruka, Firth and Gunn found the tomb of a priestess named Satinteti (*Teti Pyr. Cem.* 2, pls 20, 21), who may be dated slightly later than the reign of Teti.
342 Goedicke, *ZDMG* 112 (1962), 245.
343 For example Grimal, *Ancient Egypt*, 81.
344 Gardiner, *Canon of Turin*, pl. 2, V, fr. 59; idem, *Egypt of the Pharaohs*, 436.
345 For example Montet, *Tanis (1929–1932)*, fig. 33, pl. 83; Gardiner, *Egypt of the Pharaohs*, 93; Grimal, *Ancient Egypt*, 81.
346 von Beckerath (*Chronologie*, 188) gives him two years. With the 'count' being possibly annual rather than biannual in the Old Kingdom (Kanawati, *GM* 177 (2000), 25ff.), a reign of one year might be more likely. If he was the same person as Ity, mentioned in an inscription at Wadi Hammamat (Sethe, *Urk.* 1, 148:5–10), which is uncertain (Smith, *CAH*, I:2, 191), the first count would be the highest known of his reign.
347 Yoyotte's suggestion that she may have been the daughter of Teti himself (*BIFAO* 57 (1958), 94, nn.1, 2) seems unlikely.
348 Kanawati, *GM* 177 (2000), 28ff.
349 Stadelmann in *Hommages à Jean Leclant*, 335.
350 See also the inscriptions of a now unnamed official from the Teti cemetery who lists his career under [Teti ?], Pepy I and Merenre (Firth and Gunn, *Teti Pyr. Cem.* 1, 168; 2, pl. 66; Sethe, *Urk.* 1, 249–50).
351 Sethe, *Urk.* 1, 98:12–15.
352 Ibid., 253:18–254:1.
353 Dobrev, 'Builders' inscriptions from the pyramid of King Pepy I, VIth Dynasty', a paper delivered at the ICE 8 in Cairo, 2000, will be published in the Proceedings of the Congress. I am grateful to Dr Vassil Dobrev for this information.
354 Jéquier, *Oudjebten*, 18, fig. 17; Sethe, *Urk.* 1, 274:5.
355 Kanawati, *Chron. d'Ég.* 56 (1981), 203ff.
356 Sethe, *Urk.* 1, 98ff.
357 Ibid., 99:7–8, 101:6–7, 106:1–2.
358 Ibid., 100:2–4, 100:17–101:1, 105:14–16.
359 Ibid., 100:13–16.
360 Helck thinks that perhaps five holders of the office existed in the palace and Weni, as newly appointed, was proud to be placed ahead of them (*Beamtentitel*, 108). However, the text implies a replacement, not being put ahead of others.

361 For example the above-mentioned conspiracies under Amenemhat I and Rameses III.
362 Sethe, *Urk.* 1, 103:7–104:3.
363 *LÄ* 4, 926–27; Sethe, *Urk.* 1, 208–209.
364 The tomb of Inumin was discovered in the Teti cemetery by the Australian Centre for Egyptology and will be published shortly.
365 Sethe, *Urk.* 1, 100:14–16.
366 Polácek, *Chron. d'Ég.* 37 (1962), 23ff.
367 Sethe, *Urk.* 1, 101:2.
368 Ibid., 99:5.
369 Ibid., 100:14–15.
370 For a study of Pepy I's viziers see Kanawati, *Governmental Reforms*, 34–35; idem, *Chron. d'Ég.* 56 (1981), 208ff.; Strudwick, *Administration*, 300ff.
371 All the viziers of Pepy I known to us are found outside his cemetery (Kanawati, *Governmental Reforms*, 34ff.).
372 Myśliwiec, in *Abusir and Saqqara*, 499ff.
373 For example, Pirenne, *Institutions* 3, 181ff.; Stock, *Erste Zwischenzeit*, 6ff.; Goedicke, *JAOS* 74 (1954), 88ff. and 75 (1955), 180ff.; Kees, *Vezirats*, 42; Fischer, *Varia*, 75; Kanawati, *Governmental Reforms*, 30ff.; idem, *Chron. d'Ég.* 56 (1981), 209ff.
374 Kanawati, *Governmental Reforms*, *passim.*
375 Martin-Pardey, *Provinzialverwaltung*, 145–46.
376 Fischer, *Varia*, 75; Strudwick, *Administration*, 303.
377 Kanawati, *Governmental Reforms*, *passim*; Strudwick, *Administration*, 322.
378 The first southern vizier to be appointed was Isi of Edfu in the reign of Teti (Alliot, *Tell Edfou 1933*, 22ff.; Edel, *ZÄS* 79 (1954), 13ff.). It is interesting that like Kagemni [23] and Hesi [15], Isi left a biography in his tomb at Edfu outlining his career under Djedkare, Unis and finally Teti.
379 See Kanawati and McFarlane, *Akhmim* 1, *passim.*
380 Borchardt, *Denkmäler* 1, CG1431; Sethe, *Urk.* 1, 118:14–119:2.
381 A comparison may be made with Ankhtifi of Moalla, whose father was presumably sent from the capital to govern the province, who referred to the people of Hefat, the capital of Moalla, as 'the people with whom I grew up' (Vandier, *Moᶜalla*, 251). Ankhtifi was probably not born in Hefat, but he grew up there.
382 See Kanawati and McFarlane, *Akhmim* 1, *passim.* Many of the early governors refer to themselves as 'honoured before Ptah or Ptah-Sokar', the gods of Memphis.
383 Weni most probably also built a tomb in the capital before he was transferred to Abydos where he constructed another tomb (Kanawati, *Governmental Reforms*, 53–54). No tomb has so far been identified in the cemeteries of the capital as belonging to this official.
384 I am well aware that many scholars prefer to argue cautiously by regarding Nebet and Khui of Abydos and those of Saqqara as two different couples with similar names. While this interpretation is also possible, the similarity in their names and those of their children, Khui's previous interest in Upper Egypt, the promotion of his father, Inumin, to the vizierate, also of Upper Egypt, and Pepy I's general tendency to put his trust in a limited number of people he knew, makes it equally possible that the couple of Abydos originated at Memphis.
385 The tomb is to be published shortly.
386 The title of vizier is inscribed only on the inner walls of the sarcophagus. However, the unfinished representations of the owner seated and invoking on the façade of the tomb is usually characteristic of the vizierate, although sometimes also depicted for non-viziers (Kanawati in *L'Art de l'Ancien Empire égyptien*, 284ff.).
387 Lloyd *et al., Saqqâra Tombs* 2, pls 19–23.

388 Saad, *ASAE* 43 (1943), 454, pl. 40; Drioton, *ASAE* 43 (1943), 495–96.
389 Kanawati *et al., Saqqara* 1, 12.
390 Borchardt, *Denkmäler* 2, CG1578.
391 For a study of this second conspiracy see Kanawati, *Chron. d'Ég*. 56 (1981), 203ff.
392 El-Fikey, *Re-wer*, *passim*.
393 Goedicke, *Königliche Dokumente*, fig. 5.
394 Murnane, *Coregencies*, 111–13. For argument against the presence of co-regencies, see Uphill, *Discussions in Egyptology* 49 (2001), 81–94.
395 Tombs from the reign of Pepy I have, to my knowledge, recently been discovered, for example, by the Czech expedition at Abusir, but no details are available to me.
396 Kanawati, *Chron. d'Ég*. 56 (1981), 206ff.
397 Compare with Meru [31] who adopted the names Tetiseneb, Pepyseneb and Meryreseneb successively.
398 Sethe, *Urk*. 1, 100:7–8.
399 Although the location of his tomb has not yet been found, many blocks from it were discovered in the Teti cemetery and indicate deliberate damage to the name and figure.

BIBLIOGRAPHY

(Bold type indicates the form of presentation in the Notes section.)

Abusir and Saqqara: Barta, M. and Krejci, J., eds, *Abusir and Saqqara in the Year 2000* (*Archivorientalni*, Supplementa IX: Prague, 2000).

Alliot, *Tell Edfou 1933*: Alliot, M., *Rapport sur les fouilles de Tell Edfou 1933* (*FIFAO* X.2: Cairo, 1935).

Altenmüller, *Mehu*: Altenmüller, H., *Die Wanddarstellungen im Grab des Mehu in Saqqara* (Mainz, 1998).

Archaeology: *Discovering Archaeology*.

Archeologia Zywa.

ASAE: *Annales du Service des Antiquités de l'Égypte*.

Badawy, *ʿAnkhmʿahor*: Badawy, A., *The Tomb of Nyhetep-Ptah at Giza and the Tomb of ʿAnkhmʿahor at Saqqara* (Berkeley, 1978).

Baer, *Rank and Title*: Baer, K., *Rank and Title in the Old Kingdom: The Structure of the Egyptian Administration in the Fifth and Sixth Dynasties* (Chicago, 1960).

von Beckerath, *Chronologie*: Beckerath, J. von, *Chronologie des pharaonischen Ägypten: Die Zeitbestimmung der ägyptischen Geschichte von der Vorzeit bis 332 v. Chr.* (Mainz/Rhein, 1997).

BIFAO: *Bulletin de l'Institut Français d'Archéologie Orientale du Caire*.

von Bissing, *Gem-ni-kai*: Bissing, F. W. von, *Die Mastaba des Gem-ni-kai*, 2 vols (Berlin, 1905, 1911).

Borchardt, *Saꜣḥu-Reʿ*: Borchardt, L., *Das Grabdenkmal des Königs Saꜣḥu-Reʿ*, 2 vols (Leipzig, 1910, 1913; repr. Osnabrück, 1981–82).

Borchardt, *Denkmäler*: Borchardt, L., *Denkmäler des Alten Reiches* (Cat. gén. du Musée du Caire), 2 vols (Cairo, 1937, 1964).

Brunner-Traut, *Seschemnofers III*: Brunner-Traut, E., *Die altägyptische Grabkammer Seschemnofers III aus Gîza* (Mainz/Rhein, 1977).

CAH: *The Cambridge Ancient History*, 9 vols (Cambridge, 1970–75).

Capart, *Rue de tombeaux*: Capart, J., *Une rue de tombeaux à Saqqarah*, 2 vols (Brussels, 1907).

Cherpion, *Mastabas et hypogées*: Cherpion, N., *Mastabas et hypogées d'Ancien Empire: le problème de la datation* (Brussels, 1989).

Chron. d'Ég.: *Chronique d'Égypte*.

Daressy, *Mera*: Daressy, G., *Le Mastaba de Mera, MIE* 3 (1898).

Davies, *Ptahhetep*: Davies, N. de G., *The Mastaba of Ptahhetep and Akhethetep at Saqqarah*, 2 vols (London, 1900–1901).

Davies *et al.*, *Saqqâra Tombs* 1: Davies, W. V., El-Khouli, A., Lloyd, A. B. and Spencer, A. J., *Saqqâra Tombs I: The Mastabas of Mereri and Wernu* (London, 1984).

Doret, *Verbal System*: Doret, É., *The Narrative Verbal System of Old and Middle Egyptian* (Geneva, 1986).

Duell, *Mereruka*: Duell, P., *The Mastaba of Mereruka*, 2 vols (Chicago, 1938).

Dunham, *Naga-ed-Dêr*: Dunham, D., *Naga-ed-Dêr Stelae of the First Intermediate Period* (London, 1937).

Edel, *Hieroglyphische Inschriften*: Edel, E., *Hieroglyphische Inschriften des Alten Reiches* (Göttingen, 1981).

Edwards, *Pyramids*: Edwards, I. E. S., *The Pyramids of Egypt* (Harmondsworth, 1972).

El-Fikey, *Re-wer*: El-Fikey, S. A., *The Tomb of the Vizier Re-wer* (Warminster, 1980).

Festschrift Jürgen von Beckerath: *Festschrift Jurgen von Beckerath: zum 70. Geburtstag am 19. Februar 1990* (Hildesheim, 1990).

Firth and Gunn, *Teti Pyr. Cem.*: Firth, C. M. and Gunn, B., *Teti Pyramid Cemeteries*, 2 vols (Cairo, 1926).

Fischer, *Dendera*: Fischer, H. G., *Dendera in the Third Millennium B.C. Down to the Theban Domination of Upper Egypt* (New York, 1968).

Fischer, *Varia*: Fischer, H. G., *Egyptian Studies I: Varia* (New York, 1976).

Gardiner, *Canon of Turin*: Gardiner, A. H., *The Royal Canon of Turin* (Oxford, 1959).

Gardiner, *Egypt of the Pharaohs*: Gardiner, A. H., *Egypt of the Pharaohs* (Oxford, 1964).

GM: *Göttinger Miszellen: Beiträge zur ägyptologischen Diskussion.*

Goedicke, *Königliche Dokumente*: Goedicke, H., *Königliche Dokumente aus dem Alten Reich* (Wiesbaden, 1967).

Goedicke, *Rechtsinschriften*: Goedicke, H., *Die privaten Rechtsinschriften aus dem Alten Reich* (Vienna, 1970).

Grimal, *Ancient Egypt*: Grimal, N.-C., *A History of Ancient Egypt,* trans. I. Shaw (Oxford, 1994).

Harpur, *Decoration*: Harpur, Y., *Decoration in Egyptian Tombs of the Old Kingdom: Studies in Orientation and Scene Content* (London, 1987).

Hassan, *Gîza*: Hassan, S., *Excavations at Gîza*, 10 vols (Oxford/Cairo, 1929–60).

Hassan, *Saqqara*: Hassan, S., *Excavations at Saqqara*, 3 vols, ed. Z. Iskander (Cairo, 1975).

Helck, *Beamtentitel*: Helck, W., *Untersuchungen zu den Beamtentiteln des ägyptischen Alten Reiches* (Glückstadt, 1954).

Herodotus, *The Histories*, trans. A. de Sélincourt, rev. A. R. Burn (Harmondsworth, 1972).

Hommages à Jean Leclant: Berger, C., Clerc, G. and Grimal, N., eds, *Hommages à Jean Leclant*, vol. 1, *Études Pharaoniques* (Cairo, 1994).

ICE: *International Congress of Egyptologists.*

Jacquet-Gordon, *Domaines funéraires*: Jacquet-Gordon, H., *Les noms des domaines funéraires sous l'Ancien Empire égyptien* (Cairo, 1962).

James, *Khentika*: James, T. G. H., *The Mastaba of Khentika Called Ikhekhi* (London, 1953).

James, *Hieroglyphic Texts*: James, T. G. H., *Hieroglyphic Texts from Egyptian Stelae, etc., in the British Museum*, vol. 1 (London, 1961).

Jánosi, *Pyramidenanlagen*: Jánosi, P., *Die Pyramidenanlagen der Koniginnen {Untersuchungen der Zweigstelle Kairo des Österreichischen Archäologischen Institutes, 13}* (Vienna, 1996).

JAOS: *Journal of the American Oriental Society.*

JEA: *Journal of Egyptian Archaeology.*

Jéquier, *Oudjebten*: Jéquier, G., *La pyramide d'Oudjebten* (Cairo, 1928).

Jéquier, *Particuliers*: Jéquier, G., *Tombeaux de particuliers contemporains de Pepi II* (Cairo, 1929).

Junker, *Gîza*: Junker, H., *Grabungen auf dem Friedhof des Alten Reiches bei den Pyramiden von Gîza*, 12 vols (Vienna, 1929–55).

Kanawati, *Egyptian Administration*: Kanawati, N., *The Egyptian Administration in the Old Kingdom: Evidence on its Economic Decline* (Warminster, 1977).

Kanawati, *Governmental Reforms*: Kanawati, N., *Governmental Reforms in Old Kingdom Egypt* (Warminster, 1980).

Kanawati, *El-Hawawish*: Kanawati, N., *The Rock Tombs of El-Hawawish: The Cemetery of Akhmim*, 10 vols (Sydney, 1980–92).

Kanawati, *El-Hagarsa*: Kanawati, N., *The Tombs of El-Hagarsa*, 3 vols (Sydney, 1993–95).

Kanawati and Abder-Raziq, *Teti Cemetery*: Kanawati, N. and Abder-Raziq, M., *The Teti Cemetery at Saqqara*, vols 3, 5–7 (Warminster, 1998–2001).

Kanawati and Hassan, *Teti Cemetery*: Kanawati, N. and Hassan, A., *The Teti Cemetery at Saqqara*, 2 vols (Sydney/Warminster, 1996–97).

Kanawati and McFarlane, *Akhmim* 1: Kanawati, N. and McFarlane, A., *Akhmim in the Old Kingdom: I Chronology and Administration* (Sydney, 1992).

Kanawati *et al.*, *Saqqara*: Kanawati, N., El-Khouli, A., McFarlane, A. and Maksoud, N. V., *Excavations at Saqqara: North-West of Teti's Pyramid*, 2 vols (Sydney, 1984–88).

Kees, *Vezirats*: Kees, H., 'Beiträge zur Geschichte des Vezirats im Alten Reich', *Nachrichten von der Gesellschaft der Wissenschaften zu Göttingen, N.F.,* IV, No. 2 (1940), 39–54.

El-Khouli and Kanawati, *Quseir el-Amarna*: El-Khouli, A. and Kanawati, N., *Quseir el-Amarna: The Tombs of Pepy-ankh and Khewen-wekh* (Sydney, 1989).

LÄ: Helck, W., Otto, E. and Westendorf, W., eds, *Lexikon der Ägyptologie* (Wiesbaden, 1975–86).

L'Art de l'Ancien Empire égyptien: *L'Art de l'Ancien Empire égyptien*, C. Ziegler, ed. (Paris, 1999).

Lichtheim, *Literature*: Lichtheim, M., *Ancient Egyptian Literature: A Book of Readings*, 3 vols (Berkeley, 1975–76).

Lloyd *et al.*, *Saqqâra Tombs* 2: Lloyd, A. B., Spencer, A. J. and El-Khouli, A., *Saqqâra Tombs II: The Mastabas of Meru, Semdenti, Khui and Others* (London, 1990).

Macramallah, *Idout*: Macramallah, R., *Le mastaba d'Idout* (Cairo, 1935).

Mariette, *Mastabas*: Mariette, A., *Les mastabas de l'Ancien Empire* (Paris, 1889).

Martin-Pardey, *Provinzialverwaltung*: Martin-Pardey, E., *Untersuchungen zur ägyptischen Provinzialverwaltung bis zum Ende des Alten Reiches* (Hildesheim, 1976).

McFarlane, *Unis Cemetery* 1: McFarlane, A., *The Unis Cemetery at Saqqara*, vol. 1 (Warminster, 2000).

MDAIK: *Mitteilungen des Deutschen Archäologischen Instituts Abteilung Kairo.*

Mélanges Mokhtar: *Mélanges Gamal Eddin Mokhtar*, 2 vols (Cairo, 1985).

MIO: *Mitteilungen des Instituts für Orientforschung.*

Montet, *Tanis (1929–1932)*: Montet, P., *Les nouvelles fouilles de Tanis: (1929–1932)* (Paris, 1933).

Moursi, *Hohenpriester*: Moursi, M., *Die Hohenpriester des Sonnengottes von der Frühzeit Ägyptens bis zum Ende des Neuen Reiches* (Berlin, 1972).

Moussa and Altenmüller, *Nefer*: Moussa, A. and Altenmüller, H., *The Tomb of Nefer and Ka-hay* (Mainz/Rhein, 1971).

Moussa and Altenmüller, *Nianchchnum*: Moussa, A. and Altenmüller, H., *Das Grab des Nianchchnum und Chnumhotep* (Mainz/Rhein, 1977).

Moussa and Junge, *Two Craftsmen*: Moussa, A. and Junge, F., *Two Tombs of Craftsmen* (Mainz/Rhein, 1975).

Munro, *Unas-Friedhof*: Munro, P., *Der Unas-Friedhof Nord-west* (Mainz, 1993).

Murnane, *Coregencies*: Murnane, W. J., *Ancient Egyptian Coregencies* (Chicago, 1977).

Myśliwiec, *Nowe Oblicza Sakkary*: Myśliwiec, K., *Nowe Oblicza Sakkary* (Warsaw, 1999).

Pharaonic Religion and Society: Lloyd, A., ed., *Studies in Pharaonic Religion and Society: in Honour of J. Gwyn Griffiths* (London, 1992).

Pirenne, *Institutions*: Pirenne, J., *Histoire des institutions et du droit privé de l'ancienne Égypte*, 3 vols (Brussels, 1932–35).

Porter and Moss, *Bibliography*: Porter, B. and Moss, R., *Topographical Bibliography of Ancient Egyptian Hieroglyphic Texts, Reliefs and Paintings*, 7 vols (Oxford, 1927–52; 2nd edn J. Málek, 1960–).

Posener, *Littérature*: Posener, G., *Littérature et politique dans l'Égypte de la XIIe dynastie* (Paris, 1956).

Posener-Kriéger, *Néferirkarê-Kakaï*: Posener-Kriéger, P., *Les archives du temple funéraire de Néferirkarê-Kakaï, les papyrus d'Abousir*, 2 vols (Cairo, 1976).

Quibell and Hayter, *Teti*: Quibell, J. E. and Hayter, A. G. K., *Teti Pyramid, North Side* (Cairo, 1927).

Ranke, *Personennamen*: Ranke, H., *Die altägyptischen Personennamen*, 3 vols (Glückstadt, 1935–77).

Rev. d'Ég.: *Revue d'Égyptologie.*

Roth, *Palace Attendants*: Roth, A. M., *A Cemetery of Palace Attendants, including G 2084–2099 G 2230 + 2231 and G 2240* (Boston, 1995).

SAK: *Studien zur Altägyptischen Kultur.*

Scipel, *Königinnen*: Seipel, W., *Untersuchungen zu den ägyptischen Königinnen der Frühzeit und das Alten Reich* (Hamburg, 1978).

Sethe, *Urk.*: Sethe, K., *Urkunden des Alten Reiches*, vol. 1 (Leipzig, 1933).

Simpson, *Qar and Idu*: Simpson, W. K., *The Mastabas of Qar and Idu: G7101 and 7102* (Boston, 1976).

Simpson, *Western Cemetery*: Simpson, W. K., *Mastabas of the Western Cemetery: Part I* (Boston, 1980).

Stock, *Erste Zwischenzeit*: Stock, H., *Die Erste Zwischenzeit Ägyptens* (Rome, 1949).

Strudwick, *Administration*: Strudwick, N., *The Administration of Egypt in the Old Kingdom* (London, 1985).

Swiat Nauki: *Swiat Nauki – Scientific American.*

Vandier, *Mo^c^alla*: Vandier, J., *Mo^c^alla: La tombe d'Ankhtifi et la tombe de Sébekhotep* (Cairo, 1950).

Waddell, *Manetho*: Waddell, W. G., trans., *Manetho* (London, 1980).

ZÄS: *Zeitschrift für ägyptische Sprache und Altertumskunde.*

ZDMG: *Zeitschrift der Deutschen Morgenländischen Gesellschaft.*

INDEX

Deities

Kings

Personal names

Titles

Places

General